EMOTION AND PERSONALITY

VOLUME I   Psychological Aspects

Emotion and Personality

VOLUME I PSYCHOLOGICAL

ASPECTS

By Magda B. Arnold

 New York

COLUMBIA UNIVERSITY PRESS

First printing 1960
Third printing 1969

Published in the British Commonwealth and Empire
by Cassell and Company, Ltd.

Library of Congress Catalog Card Number: 60-7481

SBN 231-08939-2

Printed in the United States of America

PREFACE

This work, which has been divided into two volumes for the sake of greater convenience to the reader, represents an attempt to survey the area of emotion and bring some order into a long neglected field. There is no adequate theory of emotion today, that is, no theory that can integrate the psychological, neurological, and physiological aspects of affective phenomena and place emotion in its proper perspective as a factor in personality organization. To formulate such a theory, it is necessary to review and evaluate the explanations given thus far, and to see what can be accepted in the light of recent research.

Thus far, theories of emotion that have taken account of neurological or physiological findings have started from some particular piece of evidence from these fields and have attempted to work out the psychological implications (for instance, Cannon's emergency theory and thalamic theory, Papez's theory based on the hippocampal circuit, Hebb's theory based on reverberating circuits in the brain). In contrast, it will be demonstrated in these two volumes that a phenomenological analysis of emotional experience can guide us in identifying the brain structures and pathways that mediate feelings and emotions. The resulting theory of brain function is not a speculative "model" that has only the most tenuous connections with experimental evidence. Rather, the brain circuits mediating various psychological activities have been worked out link by link from a vast array of research studies culled from many fields until a well-articulated structure could be discerned. It is true that some neural connections are not fully documented and some details are missing that may turn out to be crucial. But there is a hope that such an effort at integrating a vast and chaotic field, though it may be deemed premature, may prove its value by giving direction to at least some research that otherwise might have been haphazard. Psychologists no less than other scientists feel the urge to know the how and why of things; they may distrust what seems a deceptively simple answer but they cannot be content to have the answer delayed indefinitely. The theory here sketched may not be in accord with currently fashionable ways of looking at things, but it does integrate psychological, neurological, and physiological data in a consistent way.

The psychological aspects of emotion and personality organization are stressed in the present volume. They include a historical review of theories of feeling and emotion, a phenomenological analysis, and a theory of emotion that seems to be supported by research and experience. Part I gives a critical review of theories of feeling, distinguishing feeling from emotion (Chs. 1–3), and attempts to sketch a theory of feeling (Ch. 4). Part II presents a similar historical review of theories of emotion (Chs. 5–8), while Part III contains a phenomenological analysis of what goes on in emotion (Ch. 9) and a theory of emotion that answers the questions left unsolved by other theorists (Ch. 10). In Chapter 11, the relation between emotion and motivation is discussed, while Chapter 12 treats the more important theoretical and experimental studies of those emotions that have been of particular interest to psychologists (fear, anxiety, anger, aggression). Parts II and III together do for emotion what Part I has done for feeling.

In the second volume, the available neurophysiological and physiological evidence will be reviewed and integrated into a connected theory of brain function. Emotion will then be shown to be a factor in personality organization.

This work has been made possible by two fellowships that have given me the necessary leisure to begin it and, some years later, to complete it. My grateful thanks are due to Radcliffe College for awarding me the Helen Putnam Fellowship for Advanced Research, which gave me two happy and productive years at Harvard; and to the Guggenheim Foundation for a Guggenheim Fellowship, which made it possible to take a year's leave of absence when it was most useful.

During the arduous years of preparing the manuscript, there have been many who have given unstintingly of their time and interest. While I was in Cambridge, Professor Gordon W. Allport, Dr. J. G. Beebe-Center, Dr. Stanley Cobb, and Dr. J. C. Laidlaw, all of Harvard University, were my main advisers. Later, in Chicago, Dr. Percival Bailey and Dr. Frederick A. Gibbs, of Illinois University Medical School, were good enough to read the relevant chapters in the manuscript; Dr. Wendell J. S. Krieg and Dr. Ray S. Snider, of Northwestern University Medical School, gave me the opportunity to discuss with them some problems in their own fields. Dr. W. R. Hess, of Zurich, Switzerland, read several chapters and expansively discussed some of the points that were raised during two memorable visits, one to his country house and another to his town house. Dr. Paul D. MacLean, of the National Institute of Mental Health, at Bethesda, Maryland, read an earlier version of the first several chapters in the second volume and kindly drew my attention to recent work in his field with which I had not been previously acquainted. To all of them I am more grateful than I can say. Most of all, I owe a debt of gratitude to a colleague and helper in a former work, the Reverend J. A. Gasson, S.J., of Spring Hill College, Mobile, Alabama. He graciously and patiently read each chapter as it was written, criticized it, and encouraged me, often drew my attention to problems I had glossed over, and was always willing to discuss a difficult point until a feasible solution was reached. Without his steadfast encouragement I might have given up trying long before such consistency as I have achieved was possible.

I want also to thank the Widener Library and the Library of the Medical School at Harvard University for granting me staff privileges during my stay in Cambridge, as well as the Dean of the Northwestern University Medical School for his generous permission to use the library facilities there. Finally, I am grateful to the head of my department, the Reverend V. V. Herr, S.J., at Loyola University in Chicago, for his unfailing consideration during the years spent in preparing this work.

MAGDA B. ARNOLD

Chicago
Winter, 1959

ACKNOWLEDGMENTS

Grateful acknowledgment is made to the following for permission to quote from the works indicated:

Addison-Wesley Publishing Co., Inc., for "Cognitive Theory," by M. Scheerer, in *The Handbook of Social Psychology,* ed. by Gardner Lindzey, 1954; and *The Nature of Prejudice,* by G. W. Allport, 1954; American Book Co., for *Feeling and Emotion,* by H. N. Gardiner, R. C. Metcalf, and J. G. Beebe-Center, 1937; *American Journal of Orthopsychiatry,* for "The Trend in Motivational Theory," by G. W. Allport, in Vol. 23, 1953; *American Journal of Psychology,* for "An Experimental Study of the Affective Qualities," by J. P. Nafe, in Vol. 35, 1924, "The Psychology of Felt Experience," by J. P. Nafe, in Vol. 39, 1927, "Studies in Affective Psychology," by P. T. Young, in Vol. 38, 1927, "Sensation and System," by E. B. Titchener, in Vol. 26, 1915, "The Meaning of Pleasantness and Unpleasantness," by W. A. Hunt, in Vol. 45, 1933, "An Experimental Study of Fear," by V. Conklin and F. L. Dimmick, in Vol. 36, 1925, and "Emotional Effects Produced by the Injection of Adrenalin," by H. Cantril and W. A. Hunt, in Vol. 44, 1932; American Psychological Association, Inc., for "The Judgmental Theory of Pleasantness and Unpleasantness," by H. N. Peters, in *Psychological Review,* Vol. 42, 1935, "The Concept of Energy Mobilization," by E. Duffy, in *Psychological Review,* Vol. 58, 1951, "A Motivational Theory of Emotion to Replace 'Emotion as Disorganized Response,'" by R. W. Leeper, in *Psychological Review,* Vol. 55, 1948, and "Emotion as Disorganized Response—a Reply to Professor Leeper," by P. T. Young, in *Psychological Review,* Vol. 56, 1949; Appleton-Century-Crofts, Inc., for *Purposive Behavior in Animals and Men,* by Edward Chace Tolman, copyright 1932, The Century Co.;

K. M. B. Bridges and Routledge & Kegan Paul Ltd, for *The Social and Emotional Development of the Pre-School Child,* 1931; Francke Verlag

Bern, for *Wesen und Formen der Sympathie,* by Max Scheler, 2d ed., 1923; Henry Holt and Company, for *Personality: A Psychological Interpretation,* by G. W. Allport, 1937; G. Humphrey and the British Psychological Society, for "There Is No Problem of Meaning," by G. Humphrey, in the *British Journal of Psychology,* Vol. 42, 1951; Bruce Humphries Inc., for *An Introduction to Social Psychology,* by W. McDougall, rev. ed., 1926; S. Karger A. G., for "Angst und Zwang," by V. E. Frankl, in *Acta Psychotherapeutica,* Vol. 1, 1953; J. B. Lippincott Co., for *Psychology from the Standpoint of a Behaviorist,* by J. B. Watson, 3d ed., 1929; McGraw-Hill Book Company, Inc., for *Feeling and Emotions,* ed. by M. L. Reymert, 1950, and *Frustration—the Study of Behavior without a Goal,* by N. R. F. Maier, 1949; W. W. Norton & Company, Inc., for *The Psychoanalytic Theory of Neurosis,* by O. Fenichel, 1945, *New Introductory Lectures on Psychoanalysis,* by S. Freud, 1933, *An Outline of Psychoanalysis,* by S. Freud, 1949, and *The Problem of Anxiety,* by S. Freud, 1936; Oxford University Press, Inc., for *The Study of Instinct,* by N. Tinbergen, 1951: Philosophical Library, Inc., for *The Emotions: Outline of a Theory,* by J.-P. Sartre, 1948; Presses Universitaires de France, for *Nouveau Traité de Psychologie,* by G. Dumas, Vol. II, 1932;

Quelle & Meyer, for *Experimentelle Untersuchungen über die elementaren Gefühlsqualitäten,* by B. Koch, 1913; The Ronald Press Company, for *The Meaning of Anxiety,* by Rollo May, 1950; Charles Scribner's Sons, for *The Outline of Psychology,* by W. McDougall, 1923, and *The Energies of Man,* by W. McDougall, 1933; Smith Ely Jelliffe Trust, for *The Attitude Theory of Emotion,* by Nina Bull (Nervous & Mental Disease Monograph No. 81), 1951; Estate of E. B. Titchener, for *Lectures on the Elementary Psychology of Feeling and Attention,* by E. B. Titchener, 1908, and *Primer of Psychology,* by E. B. Titchener, rev. ed., 1925; D. Van Nostrand Company, Inc., for *The Psychology of Pleasantness and Unpleasantness,* by J. D. Beebe-Center, 1932, and *Theoretical Foundations of Psychology,* ed. by H. Helson, 1951; John Wiley & Sons, Inc., for *Cerebral Mechanisms in Behavior,* ed. by L. A. Jeffress, 1951; The Williams and Wilkins Company, for "Orienting Concepts in the Study of Affective States," by A. Gemelli, in the *Journal of Nervous and Mental Disease,* Vol. 110, 1949.

CONTENTS

PART II. THE NATURE OF EMOTION IN HISTORICAL PERSPECTIVE

PART III. THE PSYCHOLOGY OF EMOTION

INTRODUCTION

SCIENCE AND COMMON SENSE

There was a time when common sense was acknowledged by scientists as being something like rudimentary science. As Thomas Huxley put it, science was organized common sense. But gradually this notion went out of fashion, and psychology, the latecomer among the sciences, was the first to recant.

Men's loves and hates, their trials and tribulations, their successes and failures are all highly complex phenomena that somehow must be analyzed into manageable components. To control these variables and to vary them one at a time, the scientist has to narrow his field. Narrowing the field means concentrating on one particular factor that may never be found in isolation outside the laboratory. There is no doubt that this highly purified variable will yield precise results that can be quantified and generalized. The generalization, however, is restricted to the level of complexity which was chosen for investigation. In the first flush of victory psychologists were slow to realize this limitation.

THE SEARCH FOR SIMPLICITY

Ebbinghaus, for instance, wanted to investigate pure memory, uncontaminated by experience, in the form of nonsense syllables learned by heart. The laws of memory he discovered are precise and can be graphed and quantified, but they are valid only for the learning of nonsense syllables. Yet it has long been assumed on the basis of his findings that distributed practice is better than massed practice; that short practice periods are better than long ones; that frequency, recency, and repetition favor the acquisition of knowledge—all this despite the personal experience of countless scholars who have found that they can achieve more when they have a whole day rather than half a day at their disposal, when they are trying to understand the material instead of repeating it by rote, when they have worked through a problem until it is solved, instead of toying with it in periods regularly distributed; and who also know that once understood a problem is mastered for good.

Thus the scientist's laudable attempt to narrow his field, to select his variables, to simplify the response and control it by means of instructions and instruments, has given him exact results from which it could be tempting to generalize. Though he was aware of the danger of undue generalization, he forgot to take into account that his selective process might affect his own thinking. Common experience had to be abandoned for purposes of study because it was too unwieldy. But the beautifully controlled, polished, and antiseptic variables he selected from it began to develop a subtle attraction for him. He began to think that they alone could give a scientific explanation of everyday experience. The system of variables he had selected because he found them convenient developed into a system that claimed to explain the common human experience from which it was derived.

Psychologists with a flair for systematizing developed rival systems that claimed to give a better account of human experience than common sense could: if common experience contradicted this account, common sense must give way. Titchener, one of the first systematizers, derided common sense and insisted that all our psychological processes could be reduced to sensation and therefore explained by it. Association psychologists and their twentieth-century successors, the behaviorists, insisted on explaining all human activity as a connection of either ideas or reflexes. Gestalt psychology explains psychological processes as configurational tendencies that are active in all nature including the human being. Psychoanalysis explains human activity as a dynamic pattern of cathexes and countercathexes, an "odyssey of the libido." Each one of these systems is based upon a different set of abstractions from everyday life and experience, yet every system claims to be a valid scientific explanation and refuses to recognize its rival systems or their rival abstractions. With an air of scientific tolerance, some systematizers hold that theories cannot be either true or false, that they fulfill their function if they provide testable hypotheses or demonstrate an acceptable way of thinking about the subject matter.

We may be more sophisticated than were our predecessors, but that sophistication is shown mainly in the construction of bolder (though not always better) theories, fashioned ever more closely after physical, rather than psychological, reality. Physicalism has become not only a fashion but a virtue, yet the reality of the physicist is only another set of abstractions, another step away from the world in which we live and move.

COMMON EXPERIENCE AS A GUIDE

Sartre has shown convincingly that these rival explanations of reality will break it up more and more but will never coalesce and form one science out of ever more numerous and ever smaller rival groups. The remedy cannot be a new set of abstractions but must be the awareness that our common human experience is the matrix of every system. If we use such common experience as a guide when we try to see how various facts fit together, we shall be able to give an intelligible explanation of the world we live in and the way in which we deal with it. Unless we do so, we may find ourselves building a modern Tower of Babel: every smallest group will try to develop its own jargon to convey the subtle shades of meaning emphasized by its particular system in which the common meaning is all but forgotten.

Instead of mocking the poor layman with his notion of a little manni-kin in his head who is pulling the strings, Titchener might have tried to see just why that notion was so hard to combat. The conviction that one's self lives, experiences, acts in a real world is so secure in all of us that we destroy the basis of our thinking if we try to remove it.

Titchener tried his best to disregard the object by concentrating on "immediate experience," and to disregard the subject by insisting on the observation of nothing but sensations—and did it with the praiseworthy intention of constructing the best possible scientific method for psychological observation. What he observed, or rather what he concluded from his severely restricted observations, was so far removed from the living, breathing reality and so obviously artificial, that his results have been shelved and his very method has fallen into disuse. In fact, so suspicious have we become of the whole method of introspection (not just

the use Titchener made of it) that we do not even want to use it for
problems that obviously require it. Titchener's fate, I believe, will be that
of anyone who ignores common experience and sets up a system in de-
fiance of it, for such experience is the only common ground for theorists
of every persuasion. It is the only guarantee that a scientist's observations will outlast the fashion of the day. When the connection between
any system and common experience snaps, that system (and not common
sense) is doomed. At best, it will maintain itself in a forgotten eddy in
the stream of scientific endeavor without contributing to scientific advance.

COMMON SENSE AS THE MOTHER OF SCIENCE

Common experience or common sense must not be understood as the
common sense *explanation* of various facts. Titchener rightly saw that
such popular opinions are the philosophy of past ages. Obviously, such
opinions are not common sense but would-be sophistication and have no
claim to special consideration. But the *direct experience* of human beings is the basis of all science and all speculation. If we see someone
throw a stone and follow the stone's course until it hits a window, we
are sure that the stone moved (even though our retina has recorded
only stills), and we are also sure that the man threw the stone and is
responsible for breaking the window. We may make mistakes in as-
signing legal or ethical responsibility—the thrower may be a minor or
an imbecile. But we are sure of the causal connections of throwing and
breaking.

If we see a red brick, that experience is our primary datum. Scientific instruments may convince us that light of a wave length of 7000
Ångstroms has impinged upon our retina, but we do not see a wave
length, we see a red brick. When we move, we move among red and
brown and green things, not among wave lengths, however accurately
measured. For our orientation in space, what counts is our experience
of colored objects, not pointer readings. Scientific observation and theory
themselves rely on veridical sense experience. Unless we assume that our
senses give us correct information, we can never be sure that our logical
or mathematical reasoning is reliable, because our only check is verifica-
tion by sensory experience. Either we trust our senses to give us valid information of the world outside us, or we deny their trustworthiness

and reconcile ourselves to the total impossibility of reaching truth of any kind. Just as the accuracy of our statistical results can never be greater than the accuracy of our data, so our theories can be no more reliable than the facts upon which they are based, the sense data from which they derive. Unless we trust our senses, science itself becomes impossible because every hypothesis, every theory, every law is the free creation of a mind eternally barred from verifying it.

THE OBJECTS OF SCIENCE

It is often said that the objects of science are not the objects of common experience, that the physicist does not see what common sense sees. That is true in the sense that the common man looks for the function of a thing in the world of everyday experience, while the physicist is interested in a specific aspect that cannot be found in simple sense perception but requires high order abstractions and judgments. The physicist's water is the same kind of water we use for the baby's bath, but the physicist is interested in it not because it washes off dirt, but because it has a certain density, specific gravity, coefficient of friction, and the like. The physicist isolates these variables, measures them by varying experimental conditions one at a time and finds uniformities that can be expressed mathematically and further developed. To verify even the most abstruse equation, the physicist must go back to the objects of common experience. If he does not, the most elegant mathematical formula will remain a quaint conceit that has no link with the real world.

Thus all science is based upon common experience, though it has nothing to do with popular interpretations. From this common matrix, the scientist selects his objects and the ways in which he wants to deal with them. Obviously, he must not be restricted in this selection of variables by common sense categories, even though he must perforce start from them. Physics has treatises on "heat" and "light," even though the physicist has found that light as well as heat can be expressed as a wave length and that there is a continuum from the short wave lengths of cosmic rays and X rays through the visible spectrum to heat waves, to the still longer waves of radar, television, and finally radio. The physicist refines common sense categories and orders them within a continuum when the differences between them are merely quantitative.

In psychology, also, the scientist may choose the variables he finds useful for the clearer understanding of his subject matter. To coin new terms for these variables is legitimate if common terms provide only crude distinctions and the scientist needs a sharper focus. But to discard common terms that imply a qualitative difference for new terms that obliterate it is another matter. The terms "tension-reduction" or "drive-reduction," for instance, are used to describe the experience of satisfaction when a goal is reached. Such a term completely obliterates a distinction we find in experience. We know that rest after heavy work is a different experience from the satiation of hunger; the joy of lovers reunited after long separation is a different experience from the enjoyment of a meal or the relief of a runner who has broken through the tape at the end of the course. These differences are not only quantitative but qualitative. Yet the term "tension-reduction" implies that all states of tension are similar and that one kind of satisfaction could be substituted for another.

Such terms merely give the impression of being scientific because they are borrowed from physics. Actually, they are figures of speech, metaphors used in such a way that human activities are made to correspond to the movement of bodies in physics. In the course of our discussion it will become clear that the scientist often follows the logic of the metaphor rather than the logic of actual observation and so is misled by his terms. Whether the metaphor is taken from physics or economics, borrowed from the latest developments in cybernetics or communications theory, it is no more than a makeshift adopted arbitrarily because as yet no explanation can be given that would describe the functional relationships. If it is taken seriously, it may delay progress. To speak, for instance, about "maximizing probabilities for action" is to imply that certain conditions like motives, rewards, or organismic states will increase the probability of action to practical certainty. But such a metaphor disregards the fact that no condition can increase the probability of action unless it is *perceived and appraised* as favorable for action.

Obviously, scientific terms are indispensable in every area that cannot be known by direct experience. Hence terms that indicate the various structures of the brain had to be newly coined in neurology. As long as the terms used are established and are not taken as descriptions of function, they are entirely legitimate. (The Autonomic Nervous System, for instance, is a label, not an indication that this system is independent of the Central Nervous System.)

How far we have departed from common sense can best be judged by the fate of various common terms in psychological literature. In most traditional psychological categories the terms have changed together with the psychologist's changing assumptions, and every change has led further away from common usage.

Under the influence of behavioristic principles, "thinking" turned into "subvocal speech" or into "problem-solving," depending on whether the writer's emphasis was on observable behavior or on its adaptive character. Today psychologists prefer to speak of "symbolic behavior," because by so doing they can avoid using a so-called mentalistic term or a purposive reference and can emphasize that what is meant is the manipulation of an object substitute. The term "will" or "volition," so prominent in early studies, has been similarly dropped from our vocabulary and replaced by various terms, from "self-determination" (which is close to the historical and experiential meaning) to "need" or "want." At present, the concept of will seems to have all but disappeared because of the current conviction that all behavior is determined by motivating causes that do not include voluntary decision.

Similar changes of terminology have occurred in the field of emotion. The older writers used the term "passion" because they meant to indicate something which the person *suffered*. This usage is still preserved in our common use of the term, for passion is something that possesses a man and controls him. The "grande passion" of the novelists leaves him little sovereignty over his actions. Later, the emphasis was put not on *suffering* an emotional compulsion, but on *being moved* to some action, hence the term "passion" was supplanted in scientific terminology by the term "emotion." The term "affect," however, was still used to indicate a man's reaction to anything that affects him emotionally; this includes pleasure and pain as well as love, fear, anger, and other emotions. Still later, when emotion was considered little more than a bodily upset, it seemed more important to emphasize the conditions that led to it. "Drives" were postulated as forcing men to action; "conflict" was considered an obstacle to single-minded action, which therefore arouses bodily upset felt as emotion.

PRESENT STATUS OF EMOTION

At present, we seem to have gone one step further by eliminating the term "emotion" almost completely from our professional vocabulary. In the *Annual Review of Psychology* for the years 1950 through 1958 there is no such topic as emotion under this or any other term. Nor is emotion treated under such topics as Personality or Personality Dynamics, though MacKinnon, for instance (1951), reviews under the latter heading studies on perception, values, frustration tolerance, aggression, and the like.

To make up for this eclipse of theoretical interest in emotion, an amazing concern with practical emotional problems has arisen. Anxiety and frustration are topics that have been treated in many recent monographs by clinicians as well as philosophers, topics that are of the greatest interest to professional and layman alike. In fact, our intellectual climate has become so anxiety- and frustration-conscious that we seriously question whether our educational practice and our social institutions do not arouse more anxiety and frustration than the human being can safely handle.

Now anxiety and frustration certainly have to do with emotion—why, then, do psychologists refuse to investigate and reevaluate the whole area systematically? Not, surely, because it is one of the most difficult and confused fields in the whole of psychology. Difficulties have never yet daunted the brave. Nor would the topic be avoided today because it is "mentalistic" in flavor. The enormous growth of psychological clinical practice has taught us that we cannot safely avoid human experience and concentrate on behavior. Even for the behavioristically inclined, there is more external activity to be observed during an emotional episode than, for instance, during perception—yet "new look" studies are popular and there is a decided revival of interest in streamlined theories of perception.

True, there is a variety of topics in general psychology that seem to admit emotional factors: drive, attitude, motivation, frustration, level of aspiration, psychosomatic phenomena. But in each one the emotional quality is either disguised or subordinated to motor and "symbolic" activity. It almost seems as if the belated realization that human activity is never purely emotional or purely intellectual had resulted in a refusal, as frantic as it is futile, to admit the existence of qualitatively different

aspects in total human activity. Surely there is a happy medium between the determination to look for static elements of sensation and
feeling, and the no less abortive attempt to deal with total behavior
without any kind of analysis at all. To say, for instance, that the concept
of "attitude" comprises emotional and conceptual factors but has also a
motor component, requires an explanation of how these factors are combined. To look for the precise *proportion* of each component would lead
us to the old atomistic analysis. But to refuse to investigate the *way* in
which they combine is to pretend to a knowledge of the complex that we
do not really possess.

So we see that the changing emphasis in psychology has not only
influenced the selection of scientific concepts but has at last brought us
to an impasse: the theory of emotion has come to a standstill because
qualitative differences within emotion do not fit our scientific precon-
ceptions; and on the other hand, the concern with particular emotions
(anxiety, aggression, and the like) has resulted in a considerable amount
of research and clinical speculation that cannot be integrated into an
over-all view of the phenomenon.

THE FACTS OF EMOTIONAL EXPERIENCE

To take our bearings, let us return to the common human experience of emotion that is as accessible to the psychologist as it is to the
layman and is described by both in the same terms in their daily lives.
We know passion as a persistent and overwhelming urge, and emotion
as an experience that not only disturbs but also arouses to action. When
a man is profoundly moved, he does not lose control over his actions,
but he is completely engrossed, almost lost in the thing he loves or hates;
he is shaken to his depths, committed body and soul.

We also know from experience that there are many emotions. There
is the grief of a mother whose child has died, the joy of reunion felt
by lovers, the fear of a driver before an imminent collision, a child's
anger when another has taken his toy, the longing for home experienced
by exiles, the remorse felt after an injury done to a friend, the exhilara-
tion of a hand-to-hand fight, the worry over the threatened loss of a job,
a mother's love expressed in cuddling her babe. These are experiences
felt or observed by all of us, easily distinguished one from the other. On
further reflection we also find that we can distinguish clearly between

something we do out of compulsion or necessity and something we do from choice and preference. The difference, we know, is emotional in nature. Finally, we know that some emotions are pleasant and some unpleasant, and that feelings of pleasantness or unpleasantness may accompany other experiences as well; there is no doubt in our mind that these feelings also have an emotional quality.

Hence any discussion of emotion must include an account of the different types of emotion that we as human beings experience. There should be some attempt to distinguish emotional from nonemotional activity, however doubtful we may be that such boundaries could be established in practice or that we could ever prove the existence of a completely emotionless experience. Any theory of emotion relevant to human life would also have to account for the apparent blending or fusion of emotions or the transition from one emotion to another: fear seemingly can turn into anger, love into hate; love may be accompanied either by tenderness or by aggression; jealousy seems to include both love and hate. The very appearance or nonappearance of emotion must be explained; frustration may produce aggression but does not always do so; in some cases it is followed by fear and withdrawal, in others by highly constructive action.

Throughout this discussion I am going to talk about emotion as a human experience, a human activity, and shall not apologize for taking as fact what you, the reader, and I, the writer, experience first hand and can identify without scientific terminology. This does not mean, of course, that we can do without such evidence as professional workers have collected, but it does mean that we cannot let them dictate to us their particular definition of emotion or their particular explanation, without any regard to our experience. If such definition and explanation accords with human experience, well and good. If it provides additional information, so much the better. But we must insist that in this field we as human beings have the advantage of the scientist. If I experience joy, no measurement of muscular tension or of patterns of autonomic excitation can give a more valid account of this particular experience. If a theorist should insist that this pattern *is* the experience of joy, we cannot follow him: we are not aware of a pattern of excitation but of a quality of experience that is *sui generis,* whatever may be the sensations and other excitations included in it. If another theorist insists that the emotion I experience here and now can be completely explained as the remnant of earlier actions (whether ontogenetic or phylogenetic), I cannot rest content with his statement, because I feel the emotion right now and know what has aroused it. This is not to say that the physiological aspects of emotion or its historical development should be neglected. But the subjective experience must be acknowledged as primary and cannot be reduced to something for which there is no evidence in my experience.

It is often claimed that subjective experience is unreliable and cannot be used as scientific evidence. But such an objection overlooks the fact that each person's experience is analogous to, though not identical with, that of another person. No two people will describe the same happening in exactly the same way, nor will they describe it accurately, unless specially trained for a particular kind of reporting. But neither will their descriptions be so different that we cannot recognize the same event in their reporting. If they do contradict each other seriously (for instance, in the report of an accident), we usually assume either that they were influenced by emotion or that they are deliberately trying to mislead us. There is a communality of experience that accounts for the agreement among normal people as to what things are like, in spite of individual differences in perception.

In an analysis of experience such as is proposed here, it is this common factor of analogous subjective experience that is investigated. We grant individual differences and provide for these in our account, but we want to isolate the common features. Our phenomenological analysis is not meant to give an accurate description of one person's experience which will be used as the literal equivalent of everyone else's experience. Rather, we take the differences in analogous experience for granted and discuss the conditions under which every human being will have a similar but not identical emotional experience. Men may differ widely in the degree of their emotion or the kind of action they will take in consequence; if two men find themselves confronted by mortal danger, they will be afraid. But though one may be paralyzed by fear, the other may act courageously. If one of them does not realize the danger, he will not be afraid, whatever his overt reaction.

To discover the nature of emotion, I will try to isolate this common factor in emotional experience and discuss the conditions that bring it about. This phenomenological analysis of emotion will provide the basis for an inquiry into the neural connections that mediate this process and the physiological changes which accompany it. The usual procedure of theorists has been to start with neurological findings and speculate as to what these findings could mean. Such an approach overlooks the fact that we must know the exact sequence of psychological processes before we can identify the structures that mediate it. As long as we limit ourselves to sensation or movement, we are never in doubt what process we are investigating and have no difficulty identifying the structures responsible for it. But when we try to discover the circuits serving emotion, we must first clarify what goes on in experience before we can know what to look for in the brain. Scheerer has advocated this approach and has even predicted its results when he says:

Writers on this subject nearly all see an inherent connection between striving, feeling and knowing. . . . Yet the problem of how to conceptualize this unity and how to demonstrate it is still unresolved. The most promising avenue of solution seems to come from a phenomenological analysis of emotions which is followed up by an empirical search for the underlying intraorganismic processes. Emotions may well turn out to be the unique expressions of the unity of cognitive and conative functioning. (Scheerer, 1954, p. 122)

In Part III of this volume the phenomenological analysis of emotions sets the stage for the discovery in Part I of the following volume of the circuits in the brain that are active during perception, emotion, and action. Part II of that volume is a critical survey of recent physiological research which provides evidence for the extent of somatic effects of emotion.

In the course of our inquiry into feelings and emotions, it is obviously advisable to go into the explanations that have been given throughout history. This will be done in Parts I and II of this volume. The purpose will not be to refute theories, whether ancient or modern. Rather, these theories will be examined point by point to separate what has been or can be proved from unconfirmed guesses. It is sometimes said that modern science need not disprove older explanations but should merely substitute new conceptions for old. Underlying this view is the idea that theories are neither true nor false, they are merely more adequate or less adequate for the purpose of the moment. But science is not only a method but also a body of knowledge. Our respect for genuine human endeavor surely requires that we accept only what can be proved and discard what has been disproved or is incapable of proof. What is *true* in scientific theories is never disproved by later theories. Newtonian geometry is not superseded or invalidated by Einsteinian relativity theory; it is recognized as a special case of the general theory and is still applicable and applied in its own sphere. In our own science, it is not a sign of maturity to abandon older views without a thought. Dead theories may have a grain of truth that might be a needed corrective for modern scientific fashions; or views stemming from a theory which has been discarded because it was obviously inadequate may still be widely held, preventing further progress.

If we take the adventure of ideas seriously, we are duty bound to screen the wheat from the chaff, even if that screening is a thankless task and takes time that could be devoted to original work. For the sake of our scientific integrity and for the sake of our obligation to those who look to the expert to give them reliable information, we must make the effort to weigh the evidence; we must follow the implications of a theory, even though they may be disappointing, to see what we can reasonably hold and what we must discard, albeit regretfully. It is exhilarating to propound new theories, and stimulating to follow the theorist's brilliant flight. But unless we take stock now and then and see where we stand, the science of psychology may easily exhaust itself in brilliant speculations instead of gathering the rich harvest which is the reward of honest labor.

Part I. THE NATURE
OF FEELING

I. FEELING AS MENTAL ELEMENT

It is a curious fact that there is no intransitive verb in English to express any and all emotions except *feel*. So it is not surprising that in common usage feelings properly so called and emotions in the strict sense are put in the same category. But even in common usage a difference between the two is recognized.

DEFINITION OF FEELING

When we attempt to define feeling from direct experience, to distinguish it from emotion, we find first that most feelings are experiences of mild intensity while emotions imply that we are strongly moved. We might suspect that there is merely a distinction of degree and not of kind. But on closer examination we find that there is a qualitative difference also.

Emotions vary in kind: there is fear, anger, joy, love, or hate. Feelings are positive or negative, pleasant or unpleasant. Emotions themselves can be either pleasant or unpleasant, without losing their distinctive emotional quality. Both fear and anger may be unpleasant, but however much they are reduced in intensity, fear will still be fear and anger will remain anger. They will never blend into one diffuse feeling of unpleasantness. But if the feeling of unpleasantness is increased in intensity, it will eventually become pain (a piercing sound, a bright light, increasing pressure). If pleasantness is increased, it will become pleasure (a warm bath may be a real pleasure for a man who is cold and tired). Accordingly, the extremes of pleasant feelings may be called pleasure, those of unpleasant feelings, pain.

Increased unpleasant feelings are never felt as fear or anger or hate.

Emotions may be like feelings in that both indicate that something is agreeable or attractive, and something else disagreeable and unattractive. But they are unlike feelings in that emotions are going out to some object while feelings merely indicate our reactions to a particular aspect of an object or a situation. Feelings can vary while the emotion remains the same: anger expressed without any fear of retaliation may be rather pleasant; anger unexpressed is extremely unpleasant. Requited love is pleasant, love unrequited, most disagreeable. If we agree that feelings include pleasantness and unpleasantness, then we must conclude that they are distinct from emotions.

To define this distinction, let us examine the usage of the term *feeling*. Our common usage indicates not so much an arbitrary convention as an agreement on common experience. We say: I feel cold, warm, tired, rushed; I feel happy, sad, fearful; I feel joy, anger, fear, hope; I feel that I am right; I feel that I understand; I feel confident, certain; I feel I am paying attention; I feel I am making an effort; I feel pleasantly warm; this sound, fragrance, color, is (felt as) pleasant.

In every case we say something about our own state of being, something we know by direct experience, which we therefore need not or cannot prove. When we say, "I feel cold," we report upon direct sense experience that affects us as a whole. When we say, "I feel happy," we report upon direct emotional experience. The statement "I feel that I am right" indicates that some decision has been reached which I personally know is the right one though I may not be able to formulate the steps that led to it. "I feel I am making an effort" merely indicates our direct experience of making an effort, asserted against someone who doubts it. Finally, when we say, "I feel *pleasantly* warm," we report not only that we are experiencing a particular bodily state but also that it is agreeable.

This, then, is the connection between the term "feeling" and pleasantness or unpleasantness. If feeling is used to indicate awareness of some bodily or psychological state which I experience directly, that state itself can be felt as either pleasant or unpleasant. If it is neither, it will be reported as indifferent. In every case pleasantness and unpleasantness refer to the way in which this state is felt: how it feels to have a sensation or an emotion, to make a deliberate effort, or to engage in psychological or physical activity. Eventually, what produces a pleasant or unpleasant state of mind is itself called pleasant or unpleasant. Following common usage, we can use the term "feeling" to indicate a state of mind.

Emotions can now be distinguished from feelings. While an emotion indicates my attitude to an object (I want a thing or fear it), feelings merely refer to one of its aspects. When I say, "The taste of wine is pleasant," I mean that I like the taste, though I do not necessarily want or take wine. But when I say that I like wine, it means that I will take it when it is offered. If I say that quinine is unpleasant, I mean that I dislike its taste though I may willingly take it as a remedy for malaria. When I find something pleasant, I regard a particular feature or quality of the object. When I like something, I usually react to the whole object. Emotion always focuses on the object, while feeling reveals my momentary state of mind. Thus we say, "I love my wife (or husband)" but "Love is pleasant." In the first phrase, we indicate that we are occupied with another person; in the second, that we are occupied with our own feeling state.

This common sense analysis of emotion and feeling will, of course, have to be tested by comparing it with the available evidence. Down the ages, psychologists have tried to explain these experiences and have collected and systematized the facts they observed. We shall briefly examine their theories and see whether they complement or contradict common experience and later research. Historically, the first theories in this field were theories of feeling. Hoping to complement common sense by scientific evidence, we shall follow this historical precedent and examine first theories of feeling and later theories of emotion.

PSYCHOLOGICAL FORMULATION OF THE PROBLEM OF FEELING

When psychology became a science, the first problem that occupied the psychologist's attention was the quest for ultimate units of experience. Physics had found that atoms were the last indivisible units; chemistry had isolated the ultimate elements into which all kinds of compounds could be analyzed. What wonder that psychology also was concerned to find units that could be considered the ultimates for psychological analysis.

For psychologists in the early days of the science, the subject matter was unquestionably subjective *experience*. Hence it was important to decide what were the irreducible elements of experience. Nobody had any doubt that sensations were among the building blocks from which mental life was built; but there was great doubt whether feeling also could be called a mental element or whether it was reducible to sensation.

Both Wundt and Titchener, the two giants in the new science of experimental psychology, maintained that there is a qualitative difference between sensation and affection, and that the one could not be reduced to the other. But although they agreed as to the elementary character of affection, Wundt and Titchener soon separated in their account of the nature of affection.

Wundt started out from the assumption that emotions are complex processes that must be reducible to simpler elements, and then cast about for the elements that could make up an emotion. He saw that emotions cannot be explained simply as various degrees of pleasantness or unpleasantness. Anger is more than a combination of pleasantness or unpleasantness and various sensations (of strain, effort, and the like). Sensations are the result of physiological changes; before there can be a sensation of strain, there must be actual muscular contractions induced by some emotional state. Trying to isolate the distinctive quality of the complex experience of emotion, Wundt was forced to add to the elements of pleasantness and unpleasantness such other mental factors as would induce muscular contractions, increase or decrease muscular activity.

Since emotions were for him combinations of elementary feelings, he insisted that the fundamental types of emotion must be preformed (*vorgebildet*) in *affective elements,* rather than compounded of feelings and sensations. In his *Tridimensional Theory of Feeling* he suggested that these feeling elements are pleasantness/unpleasantness, tension/relaxation, and excitement/quiescence.

Titchener, on the other hand, confessed himself unable to discover any other affective elements than pleasantness/unpleasantness. His objections to Wundt's tridimensional manifold stem fundamentally from his conviction that the only elements clearly accessible to introspection are sensations. Therefore he granted only one real distinction between sensation and affection; the one possesses clearness, the other does not. He says:

Attention to a sensation means always that the sensation becomes clear; attention to an affection is impossible. If it is attempted, the pleasantness or unpleasantness at once eludes us and disappears, and we find ourselves attending to some obtrusive sensation or idea that we had not the slightest desire to observe. (1908, p. 69)

What Titchener really wanted was to observe the affection apart from the sensation, and since that is not possible, he found himself observing not the affective reaction but its occasion. He saw that every emotional state is either pleasant or unpleasant, in which case feeling is part of the content of consciousness. Therefore feeling is conceded to be an element apart from sensation. But the other two of Wundt's three pairs of elements, strain/relaxation, excitement/quiescence, are accessible for him only as sensations. Wundt reported that he discovered *feelings* (not sensations) of strain/relaxation, excitement/quiescence, and that the former correspond to the intensity, the latter to the duration of affection, while pleasantness/unpleasantness is its qualitative aspect. To this Titchener retorted that for him introspection does not yield such results.

Both Titchener and Wundt found what they were looking for. Neither of them, I hasten to add, found figments of his own imagination. They both reported actual experience. But Wundt started from emotional experience, which he believed to be a complex of simple heterogenous feeling elements, and tried to isolate the elements. Titchener, on the other hand, tried to isolate mental elements, starting from the simplest experiences of pleasantness/unpleasantness, and paid only scant attention to the way in which these elements are composed. He says:

I believe that simple feelings—our experiences when we "feel hungry," "feel dizzy," "feel tired," "feel comfortable," "feel poorly," "feel first-rate"—represent a stage or level from which we ascend to the emotions; and that the emotions, again, represent a stage or level from which we descend to secondary feelings: our anger weakens and simplifies to a feeling of chagrin or annoyance, our joy to a feeling of pleased contentment, our grief to a feeling of depression. I believe that we are here in presence of a general law or uniformity of mental occurrences; that all conscious formations show like phenomena of rise and fall, increase and decrease in complexity, expansion and reduction. (1908, p. 34)

It seems as if Titchener were overlooking qualitative differences in favor of differences in intensity. More precisely, for him an increase in complexity seems to mean merely an increase in the number of affective elements, all of which are *homogeneous*. Wundt assumed that emotion consists of *heterogeneous* affective elements, because he discovered as the content of an emotional experience strain, excitement, and pleasantness, and was logically compelled to look for the feelings that induced them. Thus he identified as elements what he could distinguish in the complex.

And Titchener assumed that a complex affective experience must be composed of sensations and simple homogeneous elements of feeling; therefore he concentrated on isolating the elements by a description of simple sensations and feelings, and was content to let the composition take care of itself.

From our present perspective both formulations are unacceptable. Though we can distinguish an emotion as pleasant or unpleasant, involving strain or relaxation, excitement or quiescence, we are not convinced that an emotion is either logically or genetically *compounded* of these experiences. We have seen that feeling varies independently of the emotion, that one and the same emotion can be either pleasant or unpleasant. The same can be said of the other two pairs identified by Wundt. In joy there may be varying degrees of strain or relaxation; in worry there may be not only varying degrees of strain but varying degrees of excitement. Thus a given emotion cannot with any certainty be located on Wundt's tridimensional manifold. It may remain qualitatively the same (joy remaining joy, worry remaining worry), yet vary in each of these dimensions. Rather than supposing these three pairs to be irreducible elements of an emotion, we could consider them factors that accompany an emotion but do not constitute it. Feelings of great pleasantness, considerable excitement, and some strain still do not add up to the emotion of joy. Nor is it conceivable that a mere substitution of unpleasantness for pleasantness will turn the combination into sorrow.

FEELING OR ORGANIC SENSATION?

In 1907, Alechsieff tried to determine the nature of Wundt's six elements of feeling. He found them distinctly different from sensations because they were nonlocalizable, nonobjectifiable, independent of specific sense organs, dependent upon the condition of consciousness, and nondescribable. Neither Alechsieff nor other experimenters reached any agreement that elements other than pleasantness/unpleasantness existed. In particular, the observers could not agree whether tension/relaxation, excitement/quiescence are sensations or affective elements.

In a later study (1913) Koch argued that the observer must be given reliable criteria before he can decide whether a given "content of consciousness" is a sensation or a feeling. He collected eleven criteria that had been listed by earlier theorists and asked his observers (some trained psychologists like Meumann, some naive subjects) to bear these criteria in mind when reporting about their experiences. From his results Koch concluded that there is a reliable distinction between feelings and *external* sensations; but there is no such distinction between feelings and *organic* sensations (visceral, kinesthetic, pressure, and pain sensations). Hence Koch concluded that feelings are *diffuse organic sensations.*

Since Koch's experiment is carefully reported and typical for introspective experiments on feeling, it seems advisable to discuss his results in some detail, particularly since they have been accepted without question as supporting the view that feelings are a combination of organic sensations.

The eleven criteria Koch used to judge whether feeling and sensation can be distinguished were suggested by various psychologists:

1. Feelings are independent of specific sense organs (proposed by Jodl).
2. Feelings are relatively independent of outside stimuli (Jodl, Külpe).
3. Feelings, unlike sensations, depend upon the total state and the constellation of stimuli (Jodl, Lipps, Külpe).
4. Feelings are aroused by sensations, concepts, images; hence feelings always occur later in time (Jodl).
5. Feelings cannot persist after their intellectual content has disappeared (Lehmann).
6. Feelings, unlike sensations, cannot remain unnoticed; they always arouse attention (Titchener).
7. Feelings are weakened by attention, while sensations are intensified (Külpe).
8. Feelings are perceived not as qualities of the object but as states of the subject (Jodl, Lehmann, Külpe); they do not increase knowledge (Kant).
9. Feelings, unlike sensations, cannot be reproduced. When we attempt to do so, we reproduce the sensation, or we remember that we had a feeling, or we let the feeling occur anew (Külpe).
10. Pleasantness and unpleasantness are mutually exclusive; but all states of pleasantness (or unpleasantness) are qualitatively alike (Külpe).
11. Feelings are not localizable but are perceived as total states of the subject (Lipps).

These criteria, according to Koch, do not distinguish feeling from organic sensation. Let us see on what reasoning his conclusion is based.

1. Feelings independent of specific sense organs. According to Koch, this criterion does not distinguish feeling from sensation. True, the same feeling can be aroused via different sensory avenues, and the loss of one or even two senses does not prevent the normal development of feelings. However, feelings are always accompanied by organic sensations; when organic and cutaneous sensitivity is reduced, feelings are noticeably impoverished. Hence Koch implies that the receptors of organic sense impressions are also the organs of feeling.

We shall see later (in Ch. 4) that somatic sensations are essential for feeling physical discomfort or pain. Organic sensations are essential for the general feeling of well-being or malaise. But feelings may depend on sensations because they are a reaction to them, not because they are identical with them. In common experience, pleasantness and unpleasantness, pleasure and pain, are experiences *sui generis,* different from the sensations on which they depend, and different even from the sensations that can be noticed at the same time. When organic sensations are reported together with feelings, it is always noted that special attention must be directed to them before they are noticed. Even so, they disappear again as soon as the observer becomes practiced in making judgments of pleasantness and unpleasantness; yet these feelings continue to be reported without difficulty (Yokoyama, 1921).

As Koch says, there is no doubt that feelings are accompanied by physiological changes. But it is quite another matter to equate them with these changes. Two things may always occur together, yet they need not be identical. It seems arbitrary, to say the least, to reduce the more noticeable (feelings) to the less noticeable (organic sensations) among the "contents of consciousness." There is the additional fact that organic sensations may sometimes be felt as pleasant, sometimes as unpleasant. The muscular tension felt while playing a game is pleasant; but the same tension felt during work may be indifferent or even unpleasant. Since feelings vary independently of organic sensations, they must be independent of the specific sense organs for these sensations; hence the criterion for distinguishing feelings from sensations does apply.

2. Feelings relatively independent of outside stimuli. Koch points out that feelings share this characteristic with organic sensations: eating with loathing arouses different feelings as well as different organic sensations than does eating with appetite; dislike and worry are accompanied by markedly different organic sensations from the sensations felt during joy and enthusiasm.

Here Koch is begging the question. Assuredly, emotions as well as feelings are accompanied by organic changes, and all these experiences are relatively independent of immediate stimuli. But do feelings and organic sensations vary together because they are identical or because, perhaps, one arouses the other? Without establishing the fact, Koch assumes them to be identical. I hope to show (in Chapter 4 of this volume and in Chapter 7 of the following volume) that, while feelings are reactions to sensations, they also produce physiological changes that can be sensed in turn. Both feelings and organic sensations are relatively independent of outside stimuli, and therefore this criterion cannot distinguish them; but this does not mean that they are identical.

3. Feelings dependent upon the total state. According to Koch, both feelings and organic sensations depend on the total state of the person and on the constellation of stimuli; hence this criterion will not distinguish between them. He says:

The function of the inner organs itself is influenced by the total state of consciousness. Fear produces a decrease of secretions, spasmodic contraction of blood vessels, tremor; deep sorrow often results in loss of appetite; disgust causes antiperistaltic motions of the oesophagus. . . . Like feelings, organic sensations depend on the total state of consciousness and on the constellation of stimuli. (1913, p. 84) *

Here, as in his discussion of the second criterion, Koch assumes the identity of feeling and organic sensations instead of proving it. Organic sensations do not *necessarily* depend on the state of consciousness. Though emotions produce bodily changes, so does an upset stomach or a head cold. All these bodily changes may be sensed; they may also be found pleasant or unpleasant. There is no a priori reason why organic sensations should behave differently from other sensations, all of which are experienced and are found pleasant, unpleasant, or indifferent.

Most of Koch's subjects seem to be clearly aware that feelings and organic sensations are two different types of experience, even though this particular criterion may not clearly distinguish the two. Often they are also aware that the feeling may produce an organic sensation, as the following example will show:

25. (Stimulus: color combination.) *Pleasant.* [Visual] sensation is primary. I don't notice any organic sensations connected with the feeling of pleasantness and possibly localized. Now I localize the feeling of pleasantness on top of the head a little in front of the crown. The feeling of pleasantness is in-

* All quotations from Koch have been translated by me.

dependent of the organic sensation and does not occur later than that. *It almost seems* as if the organic sensations were produced by the feeling of pleasantness. As a result of these organic sensations there is a *new feeling*, perhaps that of fusion of both contents, expressed as harmony. New feeling of pleasantness. It is, however, qualitatively like the first. The feeling has not changed during this close observation, not in intensity either. (1913, p. 15; Koch's italics)

Incidentally, reports of the most varied states seem to be accompanied by the same organic sensations. Remorse, regret, pleasantness, and also unpleasantness are evidently accompanied by organic sensations in the upper forehead. If the various affective states were nothing but organic sensations, they could never be distinguished from one another. It is much more likely that the reported sensations are of muscular tensions produced by the very effort to localize sensations. That they are results of attention is actually stated in one of the reports.

4. *Feelings aroused by sensations, etc.* Koch claimed that feelings may occur earlier than sensations or images; he referred particularly to Experiment 94, in which the subject was asked to imagine the emotion of hate. This is the reply: "I am clearly aware that here the feeling comes before the image.—Yet contained in the feeling there is a striving, a tendency. I cannot say more about it" (1913, p. 47). This is another example showing that Koch makes no distinction between feelings and emotions. In this report there is a striving for something to hate. We can assume that this is a reinstatement of a state well known to the subject, accompanied in his experience by all kinds of expressive movements. Whether he reinstates the psychological tendency or the expressive movements that accompany it, the emotion tends toward *something*, expresses *something*. It may be reproduced either by concentrating on the object, or by concentrating on the habitual expressive movements.

In another case the subject was asked to feel as unpleasant a triangle which before he had called pleasant. He reported:

107. The attempt to feel unpleasantness on seeing the pleasant stimulus has this result: I try to perceive the picture as unclear as possible, *to inhibit the psychological process,* to press my eyes together tightly, and to act physically in such a way as corresponds with the state of unpleasantness, particularly by inhibiting breathing.—Involuntarily the visual picture of the unpleasant stimulus appeared. But even before that there had been unpleasantness. (1913, p. 54; italics added)

Here the person deliberately inhibited the processes of seeing, breathing etc., to produce sensations that arouse unpleasantness.

In every case where Koch speaks of a "direct production" of feeling, the feeling (or emotion) occurred as a result either of an imagined objective situation, of concentrating on the remembered expressive action, or of a deliberate interference with a perceptual process that aroused unpleasantness. Whenever a feeling occurred, it was a reaction to perceiving, thinking, remembering; hence feelings do depend on sensations or other activities and can thus be distinguished from sensations.

5. *Disappearance of feelings with disappearance of content.* Koch's observers reported that feelings sometimes persisted after the sensations or images that had aroused them had disappeared. There is no reason to doubt that this criterion is invalid and cannot distinguish feelings from sensations.

6. *Attention aroused by feelings.* Koch points out that many of his observers noticed feelings only when asked about them, and were astonished that they had not noticed them before. Koch rightly concludes that this criterion also is invalid.

7. *Feelings weakened by attention.* Some of Koch's subjects reported that feelings are intensified with attention, others that they are weakened. Now the question is really what kind of attention is meant: attention to the feeling completely apart from the stimulus, attention to the organic sensations to be noticed while pleasantness is felt, or attention to the way in which the stimulus affects the observer's state of being? Koch's subjects, as well as many observers in later experiments, reported that feeling increases when they "let the stimulus or image affect them strongly." When the organic sensations are in the center of attention, the feeling weakens.

We can agree with Wohlgemuth (1925) who maintains that the feeling becomes clearer and increases if it is attended to as part of an objective situation; but if the object is excluded from attention altogether, feeling is destroyed. And we see why Titchener, who insisted that introspection must abstract from the object, and had his subjects attend exclusively to the feeling, denied clearness to feelings and claimed that they disappear on attention.

Koch himself claimed that feelings are not weakened by attention because "in cases in which feeling seems weakened under the influence of attention, organic sensations come clearly into awareness" (1913, p. 87).

If it were certain that organic sensations are identical with feelings, this observation could be offered as proof that feelings do not weaken with attention. Since observers report that feelings decrease, while sensations increase, they cannot be identical. But we can conclude that feelings are not weakened by attention if it is directed to the object *as it is pleasant or unpleasant;* hence this criterion will not distinguish feelings from sensations.

8. *Subjectivity of feelings.* According to Koch, both feelings and sensations are subjective states, psychologically speaking. We have merely learned to attribute a measure of objectivity to external sensations and to expect from them information about the outside world, about the objects we have inferred. Organic sensations, like feelings, reveal properties of the subject, increase our knowledge of subjective states. Since both sensation and feeling are subjective and yet increase our knowledge (one of objects, the other of the subject), Koch held that this criterion cannot distinguish between them.

The contention that we experience sensations and infer objects depends upon a particular epistemological standpoint which we will discuss later. Whether the contention is justified or not, there is no doubt that common experience finds objects and not sensations; in common experience, we infer sensations, not objects. In the same way, in common experience there is always some *thing* which we find pleasant or unpleasant. For common sense, neither feelings nor sensations exist abstracted from the object, the situation, or the state that aroused them; hence they both have an objective reference.

Organic sensations also give us information, increase our knowledge. They inform us whether the body is functioning normally or whether there is some interference with normal functioning. These sensations are subjective because they do not give us information about the outside world but about our own body. Sensations of nausea or feverish chills inform us that all is not well with our bodily processes. Intestinal colic is a sign that there is a pronounced interference with the process of digestion. Thus organic sensations provide information about our body; they are subjective. External sensations provide information about the outside world; they are objective.

Feelings and emotions, however, do not provide information in this sense. They indicate rather how the external world affects us: emotions, how it affects us as persons; feelings, how it affects us via one particular sense modality. Because of this insistent self-reference inherent in feeling, it is perceived as a state of the subject. Such a self-reference is explicit in feeling, only implicit in sense knowledge. We say, "This is an apple," and assume that the apple exists without necessary reference to us. We have to direct our attention deliberately to our own activity before we say, "*I see* this apple." But we say, "I like apples, or comfort, or a good meal." Here the self-reference is explicit. Even in saying,"This color is pleasant, the taste of wine is pleasant, quinine is unpleasant," we mean primarily that it is pleasant or unpleasant *for us.*

There is a genuine difference between feelings and sensations. Sensations simply inform us what is there, while feelings *assess* what is there, including our own mental and bodily state. Of course, organic sensations have a self-reference as well because they inform us of our bodily state. We say, "I feel restless, tired, sleepy." Lest it be supposed that to be tired or sleepy is not a sensation because there are no specific receptors to mediate it, let us remember that organic sensations as a rule inform us of our total bodily state rather than of the state of single organs. There is an integration of bodily sensations that produces our "body sense," just as there is an integration of external sensations that gives us the object. Only when a particular organic sensation becomes unpleasant or painful do we attend to it separately. Thus we experience intestinal colic but not the smooth working of the digestive system. Organic sensations are not always felt as pleasant or unpleasant. Tiredness is sometimes pleasant, sometimes not. Sleepiness is usually indifferent, but may be sometimes pleasant, sometimes unpleasant. If that is so, there must be some difference between organic states and feeling.

To sum up: organic sensations as well as external sensations provide information about things (including our body), while feelings indicate how things affect us. The criterion therefore provides a valid distinction between feelings and sensations.

9. Impossibility of reproducing feelings. Koch admitted that feelings are usually not reproduced directly, as sensations or images are, but they share this difficulty with organic sensations. When feelings are reproduced directly, according to Koch, the organic sensations are reproduced and are then joined by the feeling.

However, organic sensations cannot be reproduced directly. A sensation of nausea or the aches and pains of muscular fatigue cannot be reinstated. We merely remember that we had them. What Koch's observers did was to reproduce the postural set, a change in breathing, a tensing or relaxing of muscles, which either enhanced or impeded functioning, and aroused either pleasure or unpleasure. Hence feelings were not reproduced directly, nor were organic sensations; feelings and organic sensations were produced anew as the result of such deliberate movements.

We might note, however, that feelings and sensations cannot be distinguished on this basis because sensations also cannot be reproduced directly, apart from the object that aroused them. We cannot reproduce a *sensation red;* we have to remember or imagine *something red,* or the *word red.* We cannot reproduce a touch sensation; we can only remember something touching us. It is impossible to reproduce an organic sensation precisely because there is no reference to anything that produced it. We remember that we had a stomach-ache, but we cannot reproduce it imaginatively. In reproducing a "sensation," we remember *the object as we perceived it;* in reproducing a feeling, we remember *the object as it affects us,* as it enhances or impedes functioning. If such change in functioning is produced deliberately by reinstating expressive action, feelings will come even without imagining the object that first aroused this action.

10. Pleasantness and unpleasantness mutually exclusive. This criterion holds that pleasantness and unpleasantness will not mix, and cannot be experienced at the same time. According to Koch, pleasantness and unpleasantness did occur simultaneously in several of his experiments; but when we examine the reports we find that opposite feelings never refer *to the same aspect at the same time:* "63. (First a melancholy, then a sprightly musical selection.) The first piece was intensely moving, the second was pleasant because of the harmonious and rhythmic tonal pattern. At the same time it aroused unpleasantness because the resulting feelings contradicted the preceding mood" (1913, p. 36).

Later research (Beebe-Center, 1932) seems to have confirmed that it is possible to have opposite feelings in regard to different things, or in regard to different aspects of the same thing. If these opposite feelings occur at the same time, one is in the center of attention, while the other forms the background.

Koch also reported that there are qualitative differences within pleasantness and unpleasantness. From the introspective accounts it appears that pleasantness differs not only in the reaction to different emotions, but also in the reaction to a taste, a smell, a tone, or a chord. No doubt there seem to be qualitative differences in both pleasantness and unpleasantness comparable to the qualitative differences between various shades of red or green. These differences could be accounted for by the difference in the functions by which we experience the object and through which the object affects us. However, Koch does not explain these differences. He merely mentions that such differences exist within feeling as well as within sensation. We agree that in this respect the two cannot be distinguished; but the main criterion holds, that pleasantness and unpleasantness are mutually exclusive, that they cannot both be felt for one and the same aspect at the same time.

11. Feelings not localizable. According to Koch, some observers were clearly able to localize feelings, though such localization is difficult with feelings as well as with organic sensations. The observers described the pleasantness or unpleasantness of simple sounds, tastes, and colors, as "more physical" and easily localizable, as compared to that of pictures, musical selections or emotions. Here are two examples:

96. (1 cc. sodium bicarb. on tongue; after a second, sensation is eliminated by washing of mouth.) As soon as the sensation was clearly perceived I had a strong feeling of unpleasantness which was quickly removed by washing it out. No mood remains from this unpleasant feeling. I even feel comfortable now. Whether there was something strictly psychological in the feeling I cannot say with certainty. There was a noticeable *contraction in the pharynx* as of a beginning swallowing reflex. I am inclined to localize the unpleasant feeling on the tongue and it is difficult to separate it from the unpleasant sensation. This separation is doubtful, both are interwoven. (1913, p. 48; Koch's italics)

And the feeling connected with a complex experience:

46. (Viewing the landscape through a blue transparency for three seconds, then viewing it directly.) Here the character of the unpleasant feeling is depressive; then it clearly becomes lively and there is a vivid feeling of pleasantness. With this change in feeling there is connected a change in organic sensations which I cannot localize definitely. The landscape seems objectively gay because this dour character is gone, and curiously enough it seems distinctly brighter. (1913, p. 24)

It seems that it is difficult to distinguish feeling and sensation when the sensation is clearly localized and quite prominent, or when it is a simple sensation that is felt as pleasant or unpleasant. But there is no exact correspondence between the strength of the feeling and the intensity or localizability of the sensations. Sometimes it is possible to distinguish organic sensations that are connected with particular aspects of the stimulus, as, for instance, in this report:

60. (Stimuli: first a chord on the piano, which breaks off suddenly. After 2 seconds pause, a dissonance.) Clear feeling of pleasantness, strong organic sensations in neck and upper back. Then a jar (on breaking off the chord) which is also noticeable in the larynx. This unpleasant feeling is probably identical with organic sensations. Afterwards when the dissonance begins, new unpleasantness, after organic sensations had appeared. I would call this new feeling a hammering. It waxes and wanes quickly; it is almost a vibrating. The first unpleasant feeling was like an inner emptiness and protest. There was no waxing and waning. (1913, p. 35)

Here we see first sense-bound unpleasantness (in the larynx), then an unpleasant emptiness and protest against the breaking-off of the chord, then the vibrating unpleasantness of the dissonance.

When specific localization near the affected sense organ is not possible, the sensation is described as general: in pleasantness, there is a general expansion, a lifting of the chest, and an easing up of the whole posture; in unpleasantness, a shrinking, a contraction, a malaise. There seems to be a difference between these two types of sensation: the first is noticed with simple stimuli, close to the sense organ to which they are applied and usually occurs before the feeling; the second is observed only with complex stimuli and comes together with the feeling or immediately afterwards. These diffuse sensations seem to occur only when the experience is fairly intense or prolonged.

All observers distinguished easily between feelings and sensations, even though some suggested that the two are "essentially" one. Since every subject made this distinction, it cannot be assumed that they really localized *feelings;* rather, they seem to have localized the sensations that accompany feelings. Koch's conclusion that feelings can be localized is hardly justified.

CONCLUSION

In short, most of the criteria validly distinguish between feelings and sensations. Even those that do not (nos. 5, 6, 7, 9) establish no proof that the two phenomena are identical. The very existence of the problem proves that the distinction between a given feeling and a given organic sensation may not always be easy. But the facts that all subjects distinguish between feeling and organic sensation in their descriptions and that doubt exists among theorists proves that there must be some difference in experience, for identity would admit of neither doubt nor distinction. Feelings and organic sensations become difficult to distinguish when the observer tries to report on his feelings and at the same time to observe organic sensations. It is as if he were trying to observe hearing a tone and also to observe various muscle sensations in or around the ear, in shoulders, neck, or chest. The observer himself will always distinguish between the tone he hears and the muscle sensations he feels; but a theorist could form the notion that hearing really is the combination of muscular sensations that were observed while hearing the tone.

The notion that feeling is identical with organic sensation not only contradicts the evidence but also leads to outright theoretical inconsistencies. Pleasantness and unpleasantness can easily be distinguished in experience, but cannot be distinguished as organic sensations. In many experiments, "sensations" of pleasantness *and* unpleasantness were localized in the same area. Moreover, Koch admits that future research will have to decide whether there are functional differences in physiological processes that give rise to pleasantness, indifference, or unpleasantness, or whether the difference between pleasantness and unpleasantness is the result of different psychological processes—in which case the same psychological factor (feeling), which he was at such pains to eliminate before, is reintroduced.

2. IS FEELING AN EXPERIENCE OR A CONSTRUCT?

Psychologists after Koch continued to follow his point of view, though in a more sophisticated vein. They reduced feeling, not to organic sensation, it is true, but to vague "felt experience," or to an abstraction, a mental or scientific "construct." As a result, there is no clear distinction between feeling and emotion in the extensive literature that is the fruit of their research. Nevertheless, the distinction between emotion as a tendency toward or away from some object and feeling as the direct awareness of one's state of functioning (see Ch. 1, pp. 1ff.) is not only implicitly recognized by the same investigators but is unwittingly established by their own experiments.

NAFE'S INVESTIGATIONS

Nafe's first experiments in 1924 were an attempt to find a new approach to the psychology of affectivity. He started from the assumption that affective qualities must be "palpable," and open to observation. In his view the diversity of opinion regarding feeling was produced by the mistaken approach of earlier investigators: they had overwhelmed their subjects with stimuli and made them "feelers" rather than observers of feeling. Nafe decided to use stimuli of merely medium intensity and to tell his subjects so, thereby preventing any fear or apprehension.

Ruckmick (1936) later objected to Nafe's criticism of earlier work and pointed out that well-trained observers have little difficulty in observing carefully even in a highly emotional situation. This is probably quite true, and we might even believe Titchener who claimed, according to Ruckmick, that he would be able to introspect even if he were in imminent danger of death. But Nafe's contention has a point that was not considered by later critics: when observers are transformed into "feelers," what happens is that they experience emotions instead of states of pleasantness or unpleasantness. This may not interfere with their self-observation, but the organic sensations that go with the emotion will confuse the issue hopelessly.

This failure to distinguish between emotion and feeling has been quite general in the field. Beebe-Center (1932), in his exhaustive survey, never makes a clear distinction, nor does Ruckmick; both imply that emotions are more complex forms of feeling. As long as feelings were considered mental elements that may become emotions by combining with other elements, it was reasonable enough to make such an assumption. But although the theory that feelings are elements had long been abandoned, emotion was still considered to be merely a more complex feeling. Such confusion is bound to lead to serious misconceptions. As an example, Koch identified feelings with organic sensations because both are independent of external stimuli—and gave as proof the organic sensations admittedly produced by emotion.

At least, Nafe's investigations leave no doubt that he really dealt with feelings of pleasantness or unpleasantness, not with emotions. He instructed his subjects to direct their attention as much as possible to the affective side of the experience and to describe the feeling as accurately as possible. Later, he cautioned them: "Continue the effort to get affection palpable under observation for itself. Look for concomitant organic sensations with a view to determining whether affection is simply a meaning laid over these organics" (1924, p. 510).

Nafe used mostly simple sensory stimuli: one whiff of various solutions or oils of some kind (sweet orange, rose geranium, asafetida, etc.); a chord and the sound of a rattling screw-fork; sweet chocolate, vinegar, salt solution. Touch stimuli were varied; hot and cold steel; a warm egg rolled in the palm; fur drawn across the neck; glass, sandpaper, and a felt eraser, all of them moved across the finger tips; a needle prick; wool cloth between the teeth; string moved across the lips. Visual stimuli were: a rainbow-colored strip; a flicker; a dog fetus in alcohol; an opal, a cut citron. The results were most interesting. Nafe summed them up as follows:

The observers agree that the affective experience comes as a unit, and that only when the pressure described as bright etc. is present can such an experience be described as pleasant, and only when the pressure described as dull etc. is present can an experience be characterized as unpleasant. Experience may be neither P nor U: but if it is either, the experience as a whole is different. The pressures add themselves to the sensory core and, observationally, the primary experience becomes more vague, less sharply defined, less clear. (1924, p. 511)

The terms "bright-pressure" and "dull-pressure" evidently were introduced by Titchener about 1919 and were generally used in the Cornell laboratory. Bright-pressure is on Titchener's touch pyramid between strain and tickle, dull-pressure between strain and neutral pressure. As this usage differs from the common meaning of the terms, I will give Nafe's report of Titchener's definition verbatim:

Bright-pressure. A diffuse bodily feel, bright, buoyant; an experience that goes with a general feeling of well-being. It is not described as containing an element of pressure, pressure being in this instance a general term. The experience could as well have been called a "felt-brightness" and it does not necessarily occur so diffused as to include the whole body.

Dull-pressure. Dull-pressure is a diffuse bodily feel also, but duller, heavier, more as one feels the day before one comes down with influenza, yet not strong like drag. (Nafe, 1927, p. 370)

Now let us look at the experimental reports and see whether we can form some notion of the kind of pressure that was experienced. (The type of stimulus, number of sittings, and kind of feeling are given in brackets.)

1. *Pleasantness* (P)
   Observer B.
   (Vanillin 21) I don't think it's possible to break the experience apart into an odor component as such, and into a sort of pressure-expansiveness. That massive experience is a good deal like an orange in respect to red and yellow. One of them is an odor, in this case flowery, and the other is something related to pressure. (Nafe, 1924, p. 515)
   (Jasmin 7) It's like expansiveness of the body. (Same, 9) The P is like an expansiveness somehow. It is linked up with a bodily state of a pressure sort. (p. 518)
   (Pyridine 16) It was light like a light pressure, and I think I didn't have P except when that spread was present. . . . (Caryophylline 17) This body reference is a good deal like pressure, very much the same character that the growing pressure of chilly gooseflesh has. The swell is much the same sort

of thing in both cases. I'm not ready to say that the P swells; the experience swells and that swelling is attended by, or is, the P. (p. 519)

Observer N.

(Jasmin 11) All the time it was active it was P, and all the time it was dead it was U. (Rose geranium 12) Luminous, active and light as if a light pressure. . . . (Chord 14) The P is light, mild, smooth, but a very thin experience. Still it is exceedingly active, active within itself. It's a bright, lively, slight pressure. . . . (Chord 15) Mild and soft, and while it lasted I felt live, soft pressure sort of envelop me. There is a brilliance about it, sparkliness. (Vanillin 15) A mild experience, quick, active, bright pressure. (p. 520)

The observers here commented that pleasantness is like bodily expansion, a light, smooth, soft activity, living, bright and pressure-like. It would be easy to see it as pleasantly accelerated vital functioning, though Nafe, of course, did not use that term.

2. *Unpleasantness* (U)

Observer B.

(Rose geranium 20) A big, massive pressure experience. These pressures come in the general setting of this big spread; that is, pressure-like, but not identifiable with any particular pressure I've experienced so far. I've been puzzled for a difference between the spread I call P and that I call U. In U there is a hardness or rigidity; I might say it is more tense. There is a hint of dullness or darkness about it. (Glue 25) This accruing mass of near-pressure seemed to be heavy and dull, rigid; insistent, somehow: sort of leaden, heavy, dead. I want to give the notion of somber character, inertness and hardness, not hard like ice, but hard and tough like lead. Just an impression of that kind of pressure. I think it was harder, duller, heavier than those for P. They are bright, lively, vaporous, instead of leaden. (p. 521)

Observer M.

(Asafoetida 2 U) The U itself seemed shorter, more compact, as compared with the P of the former experiment; that is, there wasn't this general, widespread feeling. . . . (Needle 3 U) It was different from the P in that my feel was limited. (Eraser 3 U) It was a restricted field of consciousness. (p. 526)

Here the comments suggest that unpleasantness is leaden, dead, tensive, inert, constrictive. Again it seems that they describe an experience that could be called dulled, slowed, deadened vital functioning. Nafe, however, used Titchener's terms of bright pressure for pleasantness and dull pressure for unpleasantness. In a later comment he reported that bright pressure is vaguely localized in the upper part of the body while dull pressure is localized in the abdomen or lower part of the body.

Nafe's own conclusion from his experiments, systematically formulated in 1929, is that feelings as well as emotions are fundamentally similar to sensory experience; and that all felt experiences are, qualitatively regarded, patterns of brightness and dullness. This conclusion, however, must be understood in its context. Nafe was investigating "mental elements," as were his predecessors and colleagues in the Cornell laboratory. If the experience of sensation or feeling is elementary, it would be impossible to analyze it further. Nafe shows that it can be so analyzed; hence neither sensations nor feelings are "elements" in Titchener's sense.

But now let us see just what happens in such analysis. Pain, which to common-sense judgment surely is an experience in its own right, different from other experiences, also dissolves on analysis into brightness and pressure. The pain of a dentist's drill is "a hard, sharp, shooting brightness," extremely attention-demanding; the pain experiences are also reported to be very dense, hard, and fine. "Like a live wire but dense like glass." "Very fine and extremely dense." These introspective descriptions are Nafe's justification for considering pain a pattern of bright pressure. There is a similar basis for his characterization of *ache*. When an observer's hand is plunged into ice and salt water at about −10° C, he says:

At first it is just cold. The ache comes quickly and is a pressure that surrounds fingers and hands. It is light and pressing, a pressure all over. That is the ache. It also pricks all over; but that is not the ache. The ache was at first in my hand, but became big and bright and went clear up to my shoulder. Attention-demanding but not diffuse. (Nafe, 1927, p. 374)

Now we may readily grant that the pain from a dentist's drill can be compared to a live wire, or a hard, sharp, shooting brightness, but let us not forget that these are metaphors used by the observer to describe a special quality that has no other name than pain. The descriptive words are used to distinguish differences between one pain and another, to distinguish, for instance, the pain of a dentist's drill from the ache brought on by ice water.

What makes it pain and not pressure is not that it is shooting or tensive or tearing. We can have a sharp, shooting *pain* or a tensive constrictive *pain;* but we can have also a sharp, shooting *sensation* and a *sensation* of tension and constriction. What makes the one experience pain and the other merely a sensation is not its aspect of brightness or pressure. True, increased intensity of the experience may turn it into pain; but that intensity may be comparatively slight for a sense experience from one part of the body to be experienced as pain, while it must be much greater to be so experienced when it comes from other parts. According to the location, the same degree of pressure will be felt either as indifferent or as extremely painful; in the first case the pressure has not appreciably interfered with physiological function, in the second it threatens to injure a delicate mechanism (for instance, pressure on the arm as compared with pressure on the eyeball).

The same holds good for ache. Not every "light pressing pressure" is an ache. What makes it an ache instead of a sensation of pressure is the fact that this light pressing pressure (experienced when the hand is immersed in ice water) is produced by a contraction of the blood vessels that interferes with the blood supply. It is beside the point to say that the ache is *like* light pressure. What matters and what distinguishes the one from the other is the degree to which this particular pressure menaces vital functioning or leaves it undisturbed. This is indicated by the feeling of unpleasantness, and later by its extreme of pain. Hence feeling indicates how the stimulus (in this case ice water), in contracting bloodvessels and therefore giving the sensation of pressure, affects the functioning of the organism.

Nafe hoped that in reducing all felt experience to patterned bright or dull pressure he had restored the common-sense meaning to the term "feeling," which includes the whole gamut of experience, from touch to kinesthetic and organic sensations, as well as affective experience. But common sense has never given up the qualitative distinctions between these experiences. True, we *feel* touch, movement, hunger, pleasantness, and joy, but that does not mean that these experiences are all qualitatively alike. Nor do we make the distinction between various kinds of "felt experience" *after* we have come to know the various patterns of bright and dull pressure. The distinction between pleasantness and unpleasantness, touch and pain, hunger and love as different kinds of experience is primary; they are felt directly and need no intermediary knowledge of pressure patterns. We distinguish them by their experienced differences, and never by their similarity to pressure.

Significantly enough, Nafe's solution has consequences not only for a theory of feeling but also for a theory of emotion. He said:

If these affective experiences are patterns of sensory experience, then the function of the affection to form a core for emotional experiences has disappeared, and if these experiences are not "simple," in a Titchenerian sense, by what criterion shall we distinguish an affective experience from an emotional one? There appears to be none. Psychologically an emotion and an affection must be defined alike and both are complexes of sensory experiences. The terms "emotion" and "affection" may still be useful words to express degrees of complexity, particular types of pattern, methods of arousal, or to differentiate one type of felt experience from another. The older distinctions had their being, from the very first, only for systematic purposes. There never existed any considerable evidence for them. (1927, p. 387)

There is no real distinction between emotion and affection, nor between one type of felt experience and another, so we had better use the old words to pretend to such a distinction for practical purposes—is that what Nafe means? But surely the distinction between pleasantness/unpleasantness and emotions (or passions) existed long before scientific psychology developed the theory of simple and complex feelings. Actually, Nafe has shown that his theory allows of no distinction, but not that there is no difference. We cannot tell emotions from feelings on the basis of their complexity; but that does not mean that there is no valid distinction, though such a distinction could not be made on the basis of an elementaristic system.

Nafe's real contribution is to have shown that feelings are not elements of consciousness in the sense that a particular feeling experience could be dissected into simple sensory and feeling constituents. He pointed out that feelings are somehow like *patterns* of bright and dull pressure. Whether pleasantness/unpleasantness itself can be "analyzed" into pressure patterns or whether these pressure patterns merely accompany feeling, in either case the content of consciousness in Nafe's hands becomes a *pattern,* rather than an aggregate of simple elements. But it does not follow that nothing but sensory patterns can be observed. The reports of Nafe's observers are sufficiently similar to Koch's experimental reports so that our objections to Koch's conclusions will hold also for Nafe's. Nafe's subjects, like Koch's, always distinguish between the feeling and the pressure pattern; hence the two cannot be identical.

Nafe further showed that there are definite differences in the localization of pressure experiences during pleasantness and unpleasantness. Koch's subjects, as well as those of various previous investigators, reported similar differences in diffuse organic sensations for pleasantness and unpleasantness, but it was left for Nafe to note their consistency. Later experimenters all confirmed his observations, though they took issue with his interpretation.

YOUNG'S RESULTS

Young, for instance, had obtained results very similar to Nafe's in an investigation he undertook in 1918. Like Nafe, he found that pleasantness was reported as a bright pressure vaguely localized in the chest region, while unpleasantness was a dull pressure, vaguely localized in the abdominal region. In a later study (1927), undertaken to verify Nafe's conclusions, in which he obtained the same results, he felt that the reports might conceivably reflect the attitudes and convictions of his observers, just as his earlier work reflected his own attitude while at Cornell where the experiments were conducted. To check on this conclusion, Young selected three observers for a repetition of the experiment, and used Nafe's instructions. One of the observers was a psychologist from the Cornell laboratory (Observer M.), formerly one of the subjects in Nafe's experiments; the second was a behavioristically oriented psychologist (Observer E.); and the third was a naive but intelligent student. The first observer reported, as did Nafe's subjects throughout, that pleasantness is like a bright pressure and unpleasantness like a dull pressure, so confirming Nafe's results. The behaviorist, however, gave entirely different reports. Here are some of them:

(40A) * When I say "pleasant" it doesn't stand for anything more than "I would smell it more if I could." I am not able to discriminate anything beside that in most cases. (Young, 1927, p. 180)

(48A) * I find this difficulty. The instruction asks me to watch for organic sensations. *That means* that I have a tendency to respond to various conditions in the abdomen which are present all the time but to which I don't ordinarily respond. When I read the instructions I begin responding to them. I have difficulty in knowing whether I am reporting something as from the stimulus or from other conditions after stimulation. An utter blankness as to what to report. Usually there is nothing except the stimulus is so-and-so or suggests so-and-so. (52-colored band) Well, I identified it as a spectrum and perhaps found some pleasure in inspecting the colors although *I don't know what that means when I make use of that expression except that it is the verbal equivalent* for continuing to look. . . . (63-anethole) A suggestion first of

* A chord was struck on tuning fork A.

an association with some sort of medicine. Perhaps a slight nausea of the sickly sweet type again, although I am not at all certain of that. At the present instant I can discriminate nausea. *I think the sequence is a verbalism* "sickly sweet" that reminds me of the instruction about organic sensation, and that leads me to make abdominal discriminations which are likely to be of the order of nausea. It happens that my digestive processes are not perhaps what they should be to-day. (p. 181; italics added)

The observer remarked later that he found it difficult to follow instructions:

The part about "organic sensation" annoyed me very much. I seemed to be doing business with the upper part of my body and I had to identify and this took most of the time. There wasn't time for other types of discrimination such as organic. I was also disturbed by paying attention to the abdominal region rather than to the stimulus. When I was discriminating what was going on in the abdomen I wasn't responding to the stimulus. (p. 182)

Young claims that the reports of both observers were exactly what could be expected from their psychological training and convictions, neither was better than the other; neither could be called more accurate than the other. He says in effect: if Observer E. failed in his reports, then Observer M. failed, too. Lest we suspect lack of practice in E.'s introspections, Young points out that more practice would not have changed E.'s reports, which were as accurate as he could make them, given his particular convictions.

The answer is that what Observer E. needed was not more practice but more instruction. He obviously tried to translate the instructions into his own terminology and did not succeed too well. He had not learned to discriminate between different organic sensations, was puzzled by the instructions, and tried as best he could to respond to the stimulus continuously with the whole of his attention. He also *interpreted* his experiences instead of merely describing them (see italicised phrases). In spite of these difficulties, however, he did report feelings as such, even though he afterwards called them "verbalisms." But he insisted that pleasantness meant continuing (or wanting to continue) to smell, hear, taste; his sensory functioning at the time must have been affected favorably.

The same inability to distinguish between different organic sensations, or rather the same lack of realization where to look for them, can be seen also in the reports of N., the naive subject:

(56A Chord.) There is some organic reaction with the U. Odors make you pull your head aside or shudder. Mild stimulations don't seem to give the organic reactions that the strong ones do, or if there is any organic reaction it is so slight that I didn't notice it. (Young, 1927, p. 184)

(48A Chord.) I haven't yet found U as organic except in one or two instances—in a smell and in one taste there were organics. I did get organic sensations in drawing my hand away in the pain. I drew away from the sound a few days ago. (p. 184)

These reports (the other reports of this observer are all similar) show clearly that she did not know where to look for "organic sensations," but assumed they must be connected with the sense organ mediating the impression and with movements toward or away from the stimulus object. We are well aware from other studies that it takes time before the diffuse organic sensations in the body are noticed. After all, introspective observation is no different from other observation in this respect: any student who for the first time looks at a paramecium under a microscope will only notice the vaguest outline, if he sees anything at all, while the expert can make the most detailed drawing and description. And whoever would expect an untrained observer to look at an X ray of the lungs and distinguish the lighter and darker areas correctly?

This difficulty of observation does not, however, justify Young's conclusion that every observer will see what he wants to see or what he is trained to see (see Young, 1927, 1930). If we compare the reports of Koch's and of Nafe's observers (and many more could be quoted from other studies), we see a degree of agreement that could not have been reached if the observers had reported fancies rather than facts. An attitude such as Young's would reduce psychology to a game of make-believe in which any genuine scientific progress is impossible. What one generation of psychologists is looking for (and therefore producing) would be not only superseded but discredited by the next generation's preoccupation with something else, and the phenomena on which so much observation and effort had been spent would disappear with the changing scientific fashion. No doubt this attitude has contributed much to the present contempt for careful introspective observation. Today we trust any college freshman answering questionnaires to be more reliable in self-observation than the most carefully trained introspective observer of a generation ago. But surely we must trust the scientific integrity of other psychologists, even those with whose views we do not agree. We cannot assume that their scientific naïveté was such that they would consistently mistake fancy for fact.

It was bad enough when it was assumed out of hand, with the advent of scientific psychology, that previous philosophical psychologists could not have been reliable in their self-observation, no matter how carefully they might have trained themselves. But when we begin to dismiss the introspective findings of psychological scientists as well, only because their interests are different from ours, we might seriously ask ourselves whether psychology is as yet a science at all. It has been well said that the science of one age is the superstition of the next. But that applies to theories, not to observations. Because the *conclusions* of such men as Wundt, Titchener, Koch, Nafe, all differ they cannot all be right; but that does not mean that therefore we can dismiss just as easily the careful introspective *observations* on which these conclusions were based.

EXPERIENCE VERSUS CONSTRUCT

Now Young's implication actually is that training can produce any kind of experience because experiential facts are completely dependent upon the observer's systematic convictions. He says:

The present situation can be cleared up only by the frank recognition of the complete relativity of so-called fact to the logical system which is the product of training. It is important to find common ground which is independent of training. In the search for data which are independent of training I see hope; not in further training of trick observers. (1927, p. 189)

When Young comes to enumerate such independent data, he finds them in reflex reactions (vomiting, groaning with pain, eating when hungry, specific sex responses). Surely there is little hope for psychology if it is to be restricted to reflex behavior. Behaviorists at least admit *conditioned* reflexes; but for Young these would be similarly taboo because dependent on training.

The reason for Young's pessimism lies in the conviction he shares with many psychologists that what used to be called "immediate or direct experience" is really nothing but an inference—and inferences, of course, depend on their logical premises. He says, for instance, in the article outlining the assumptions required for a psychologist: "When once we realize that the real object is an inference and seek to understand it through logical analysis we are left with a bare object of perception and a point of view taken up towards the object. We are reduced to datum and logical system" (1927, p. 190, footnote). Once we consider the real object as an inference, we are left with subjective states which we call either sensation or affection, depending on whether we refer these experiences either outside or inside our body. But since, as Koch and Nafe have seen, the inside reference is the same for organic sensations and for affections, the two come to be identified and all experience becomes sensation. When we investigate this ubiquitous sensation (which for Nafe is fundamentally pressure), we discover that sensation itself is not a fact, is not real experience (for no one has ever seen or touched or handled a sensation), but a logical construction. So Beebe-Center says: "Today it is generally accepted that the term sensation refers not to a constituent of experience, to a datum, but to a conceptual entity constructed from experience" (1932, p. 106). And he agrees with Young that these constructs depend upon the general systematic background. But that brings us to the strange conclusion that we infer objects from sensations that are not data, that is, from sensations we do not experience. Thus we experience neither sensation nor object, for the sensation is a construct, the object an inference. Then what do we experience, what is the material out of which we build these constructs, from which we draw these inferences?

Sensation a datum. In our quest for the *what* of experience, we might see what would be required to make sensation a datum rather than a logical construct. Titchener, who at first considered sensation an immediate experience but later conceded that it was an abstraction or construct, has this to say about it: "It would be a great simplification of psychology if a sensation, tota, teres, atque rotunda, would stand before us under a single comprehensive determination and allow us adequately to observe it as a whole" (1915, p. 262). Sensation, then, would be a datum if it were a *thing*. But a tree, a girl, the earth itself does stand before us tota, teres, atque rotunda! When we see, we do not see a sensation (or light waves) but a *thing*. When we touch, we do not touch a feeling but some *thing*. When we hear, we do not hear sound waves or an auditory sensation, we hear some *thing* sounding. Gestalt psychology has for many years insisted that we see wholes first and then distinguish their pattern. Recent investigations (cf. Gibson, 1951) have shown, moreover, that we see *primarily* objects, that is, a world of solids, before we see them two-dimensionally, in a visual plane. True enough, vision itself, as a sense function, can give us only impressions of color, not those of objectness. Every sense function apprises us of objects only according to their sense qualities. Therefore, touch can give us only impressions of smoothness, not those of a smooth object; the kinesthetic sense can give us an awareness of increased resistance, but not of a heavy object. Yet in actual fact we do experience *objects,* not color, touch, or kinesthetic *sensations.* We also experience our body as a body, not as isolated sensations. The "local sign" controversy bears eloquent witness to the importance of this problem. When the furor subsided, the problem was shelved, not solved.

The experience of objects (not isolated sensations) must be primary because infants and animals react to objects *as objects.* Even animals reared in darkness react to the sight of an object as to an object, not as to a patch of color. On the contrary, they react to patches of color *as if they were objects* (Lashley, 1938; Hebb, 1949). If the single sense functions do not integrate the various sensations so as to construct the object for us, and if we know that such integration does not come about by any act of deliberation or logical inference, the only alternative we have is to suppose that there is some *sensory* integrative function which we know only in its effects, not in its working. In so doing, we would only postulate an intervening variable that we can infer from its effects. The alternative, that we only know sensations, not objects, contradicts our common-sense experience and forces us into paradoxes from which there is no escape: we know only sensations, but sensations cannot be directly known because they are constructs; and we infer the object from sensations, but sensations are themselves inferred.

If a datum would have to be a solid body to be a datum at all, as Titchener implies, then our data must be *the things we experience* in our commerce with the world outside us. Then sensation becomes the psychological *function* by means of which we experience objects, rather than an elementary *content* of consciousness. Actually, even in the most rigorous introspective accounts of sensory experience, the object is always there as a reference point. When the matching of color mixtures is described introspectively, the reference is always to the object, the color on the color wheel. The subject describes the colors seen, not his visual sensations apart from the color wheel. He experiences the color as part of an object. No matter how hard he tries, the color will always remain "out there"; it never becomes a property of the subject. If he could really get rid of the object reference, the color would disappear with the object and nothing would remain but the awareness that he did see but now does not.

Attributes of sensation. The very "attributes" of sensation in Titchener's formulation refer not to sensation but to something else. Close reading of what Titchener says indicates that he is talking really of the quality, intensity, clearness, and duration of a *content*—the object in sensation— and not of the *process* of sensation. The process has attributes, which may be called by these names; but they are not what Titchener describes, as the following passages will show. In talking about intensity, Titchener says, for instance:

Intensity is the attribute to which we refer when we say that a given sensation is brighter or duller, louder or fainter, heavier or lighter, stronger or weaker, than another sensation. In making such comparisons, we think of the sensations as possessing the same quality: both are blue, both are b^b, both are pressure, both are cold or salt or asafoetida. (1925, p. 53)

His example "both are salt or asafoetida" inclines us to think that "cold, blue, salt," must be in the same category—but salt and asafoetida refer to objects, not to sensations. One could as easily call "nylon" a sensation.

Clearness, in Titchener's view, belongs to sensation. But actually the contents are clear only to the extent that attention or reflection makes them so. He says, for instance:

If . . . we are listening to tones in order to decide whether or not they all alike possess the attribute of volume, the sensations are clear; if we are absorbed in work of a different kind, and someone is experimenting with tones in the next room, we still have the tonal sensations, but they are obscure. (1925, p. 53)

Here clearness is the result of turning one's attention toward the object, unclearness the result of turning one's attention away from it. Clearness is not an attribute of the process of sensing.

As for extension, Titchener says:

Sensations of color are spread out areally into length and breadth; they appear as spatial extents. . . . So with pressures: set the point of a stiff horse hair lightly down upon the skin, and the sensation is extended, diffused over a mental area. (1925, p. 54)

Clearly, Titchener confuses a "mental area" either with the extension of the stimulus object or the skin area stimulated. For him,

psychological extension is the aspect of sensation that we attend to when
we are called upon to answer the questions (perhaps with reference to an
after image, perhaps with reference to a cutaneous sensation): How large
is it? What shape has it? Is it regular or irregular? large or small? continuous
or patchy? uniform or broken? (1908, p. 23)

This "it" surely cannot refer to sensation apart from the object; it refers
to the object itself. It is the object (or its impact on the body) that is large
or small, regular or irregular, continuous or patchy, uniform or broken.
A sensation does not exist apart from the object sensed, nor do we experience it directly. If we experience it at all it is by reflection, and that is not
sensory experience.

Experience as the experience of an object. If the only direct experiences
we have are experiences of some *thing,* this must mean that the object is
not inferred but is directly given. Then sensing or sensory knowledge
would be the direct experience of some object by means of sensory functions. The introspective report would be: *this thing is there.* And feeling
would be the direct *experience* of some object *as it affects me via some
sense modality.* The introspective report would be: *This is pleasant or
unpleasant.* An emotion would be the direct experience of an object *as it
attracts or repels me,* and the introspective report: I want it, fear it, etc.

In sensory knowledge the object reference is explicit, the subject reference implicit. It requires an *abstraction from the object* to experience the
activity of the subject, which I make when I say: I see (this thing). If that
abstraction is complete, the only report (and the only experience) possible
is *that* I see, yet I don't see any *thing.* In other words, the strictly subjective, psychological aspect of the sense experience is without content; it
cannot be inspected at all. Whenever there is a content that can be
inspected, it is given, directly experienced; but this content is the *object*
of sensation and not itself a sensation.

In feeling and emotion, the subject reference as well as the object reference is explicit: *I* want *this thing.* In feeling the subject reference is always
implied in the adjective: *This is pleasant* always means *This is pleasant
for me.* Because there is this subject reference in feeling and emotion, it
has seemed possible to inspect the feeling of pleasantness/unpleasantness,
or the emotion of fear, anger, etc., apart from its object. But when I am
asked to say how I feel or what I feel when I feel pleasantness or love or
fear, there is the same difficulty of abstraction. All I can say is *that* I feel
fear or anger or love; but their import can only be understood when I

refer to the object. Now as in Titchener's time, whenever we attempt to attend to feelings apart from their objects, they promptly evaporate. But whenever the observer focuses on the object or one of its aspects *as it affects him,* the feelings and emotions aroused by it can be described and reported. The only reason why sensations do not similarly disappear on introspection is the fact that no observer manages to abstract from the object. It is always there but disguised as "sensation."

When Titchener says that "the psychological element has no part or lot in knowledge, has no reference or meaning or object or cognitive content of any sort" (1908, p. 37), he is reflecting the widespread confusion that comes from making experience (sensations, ideas, feelings, reflexes, etc.) the direct object of awareness. What we live through ("experience") is *our response* to the impact of the environment on us. What we do as a response is our experience (we see or feel or understand); and only in so far as we know we do something, whether implicitly or reflectively, do we *experience.* We have no experience of brain waves or pupillary contractions or basilar membrane displacements and the like. What we experience directly is not the living through but the environment that impinges upon us. We do not experience our vision or hearing: our experience is that we see a tree or hear a noise. We experience our *experiences* only when we reflect on them and direct our attention to the "psychological element" in them. But in that case we make the original experience the "cognitive content" of another experience.

Experience is important not because it is a "living through" but because we experience something specific. Seeing is an experience. But it is *seeing* because we have responded to the impact of an object radiating or reflecting a wave length within the visual spectrum. *What* we experience is more important than *that* we experience or *how* we experience; and what we experience is specified by the object. Ignoring this fact has confused "content psychologists"; failing to distinguish between direct and reflex awareness has confounded them.

Titchener, having made conscious contents and process coextensive, neglected to study what processes might be in addition to conscious contents. His method of introspection is a kind of reflection on the contents of imagination (memory). Attention is concentrated on images. In presuming that these images were the processes he wished to investigate, Titchener fell into a "stimulus error" of his own.

While Wundt's and Titchener's elementalistic psychology has long been

superseded, the conviction lingers on that the process of sensation provides us with images rather than the experience of objects. Titchener derived this notion from the philosophical views of his time and set up his
experiments in accordance with it. He and his school made rigorously accurate observations but they were not observations of "immediate experience." Immediate experience is the sensory experience of objects or the
emotional experience of their impact on us, not our reflection on the
memory images or kinesthetic sensations that are the result of experience.

3. FEELING AS MEANING, ATTITUDE, JUDGMENT, AND AS SUCCESS OR FAILURE

While Titchener was convinced that feeling was an element of consciousness (at least in his formulation of 1908), later psychologists inclined more and more to the view that feeling is not directly experienced but is a "meaning" that is gradually built up.

FEELING AS MEANING

Carr (1925), for instance, thought that pleasantness and unpleasantness are names given to two distinct meanings. Pleasantness means the habitual approach response to the stimulus, unpleasantness the habitual withdrawal response. In this way, he equated feeling with wanting or not wanting as tendencies to approach and withdrawal. This is difficult to reconcile with some experiential facts. For instance, anger is an approach reaction, yet it may be unpleasant; fear is a withdrawal reaction, yet it may be pleasant, as in the thrill of riding a roller coaster. We hope to discuss the view of feeling as approach or withdrawal later. At present it is the meaning aspect that interests us.

Hunt (1939) agreed with Carr that feeling "means" habitual reaction tendencies, but for him it also "means" bright and dull pressure. Hunt came to this conclusion from his own experimental findings which confirmed Nafe's results and are not open to Young's objections (see Nafe's Investigations, in Ch. 2). In one of his experiments he gave stimuli found consistently pleasant or unpleasant, and asked his observers to report any organic pressures they could detect. They located organic pressure in the upper trunk that correlated extremely highly with the "bright pressure" as felt and reported in another experiment during pleasantness. They also reported organic pressure in the lower trunk that correlated very highly with "dull pressure" as felt during unpleasantness. Hunt refused to identify feeling and organic pressures, as did Nafe. He suggested instead that feeling "means" these pressures but is not limited to them, since "sensory experience may or may not be present when a report of pleasantness or unpleasantness is given" (1933, p. 347). For Hunt, these organic pressures are the result of the readiness for action that is experienced as emotion.

How pleasantness and unpleasantness can be reported when these sensory pressures are not felt is explained as the result of conditioning:

Originally the verbal response of "pleasantness" or "unpleasantness" may have been attached to the sensory experience that we call a bright or a dull pressure: but by conditioning it then may have become directly attached to the stimulus arousing this pressure. This "short-circuiting" might even result in the stimulus-object calling forth the verbal response before the appearance of the sensory content which originally gave rise to it. Thus the taste of sugar might call forth the response "pleasantness" without any necessary intervention of a bright pressure experience. (1933, p. 347)

Here the object that arouses the feeling is the unconditioned stimulus (for example, sugar), the bright pressure pattern in the upper trunk the unconditioned response, and the term "pleasant" the conditioned response. Considering that bright and dull pressures are noticed only "under a sensory attitude of report," but that ordinarily, when pleasantness is felt and reported, these pressures are not experienced at all, such an explanation seems to miss the point. Unless we want to assume that pleasantness is not *experienced* when reported, the subject's assurances to the contrary, there must be some experience in the child or naive subject before his attention is drawn to these pressures. How could the term "pleasantness" become conditioned to pressures that are neither experienced nor reported? Training is needed for a subject to become *aware* of organic pressures, but not for him to *experience* pleasantness or unpleasantness. This particular hypothesis was intended by Hunt to explain cases of reported pleasantness and unpleasantness without experienced pressures. Instead of doing so, it complicates the issue. Still, for our purposes, whether feeling "means" habitual reaction tendencies, as it does for Carr, or whether it "means" these action tendencies as they are experienced in organic pressures, as postulated by Hunt, we are concerned here with the term "meaning" and to what it refers. If feeling is a meaning, just what are we to understand by that? According to Beebe-Center, considering feeling and emotion as meanings is to admit that they are constructs. He says:

We have seen that the terms pleasantness and unpleasantness, as used by observers, represent meanings. Such meanings are the concepts built up by the layman to interpret his world. The psychologist, seeking to interpret his facts, does essentially the same but does so wittingly and, in so far as possible, according to strict logical procedures. Such concepts he calls constructs. (1951, p. 260)

And later: "The introspective work of Conklin and Dimmick (1925) can be interpreted as a demonstration that emotion, in its common-sense usage, is a reification—a common-sense construct" (1951, p. 282). Carr and Hunt, as well as Conklin and Dimmick, use "meaning" in Titchener's sense, and so does Beebe-Center. Before we examine Titchener's context theory of meaning, however, let us see what Conklin and Dimmick actually found. Once we know the facts from which it was deduced that emotion is a meaning or a construct, we may be better able to follow the reasoning involved.

Conklin and Dimmick set out to arouse an emotion by having the subject sit with closed eyes, his back to the experimenter, who would unexpectedly place something on his hand (cold metal, a rubber glove filled with water, soaked macaroni, a wet rubber snake), make a sudden sound (whistle, file on tin, bang), or show him an object (a preserved frog, a preserved brain, pictures of snakes). Not all stimuli produced emotion; but some emotions were quite intense. These are typical reports:

(Loud noise) "That always scares me, and is unpleasant, I think of a huge hammer striking near me and I don't want to be struck."

(Cold metal) "A cold wet pressure at first; then I got to thinking that it was that frog and it became very unpleasant and repulsive, and I wished you would take it away."

(Wet macaroni placed on hand—eyes closed) "That was horrible—very unpleasant. It was a wet slimy feeling. It made me feel creepy all over and sort of sinking inside. It felt like a lot of wet angle-worms." (1925, p. 98)

For one observer, the sudden touch of the rubber glove while his eyes were closed had always aroused violent fear. Afterwards, he was told to open his eyes and grasp the glove. Now the experience was unpleasant but did not arouse an emotion. When his eyes were closed again, he was told, "This is the rubber glove," and then the glove was placed on his hand. This sometimes aroused an emotion and sometimes did not. It did not whenever the subject identified the touch as that of the rubber glove he had seen before, whether or not organic sensations were present. Here are illustrative reports:

(Glove *seen* and *touched*) "That felt cold and clammy and nasty, and my stomach felt contracted; but I was not frightened as I used to be."

(Glove touched, with knowledge, *eyes closed*) "That was rather unpleasant and made my stomach start to feel queer; but when I realized that it was the rubber glove, it stopped, and that was all. I was not frightened."

(Eyes closed, glove touched *without knowledge*.) "That frightened me." (O screamed.) "I feel completely out of breath and my stomach caught inside. I couldn't help but yell. Shivers went over me. I didn't think it was the glove. As soon as I did realize that it was the glove, I was no longer frightened, though I still feel queer inside and am out of breath." (1925, p. 99)

In ordinary language we would say that the observer experienced fear whenever the object (for instance, a rubber glove) appeared to him as something unknown and threatening. Once it was recognized as harmless, fear as a psychological experience disappeared, though the organic changes connected with fear might persist. Therefore fear is a psychological reaction to an object thought harmful, and includes a felt tendency to flee or withdraw.

Conklin and Dimmick concluded from their experiment that emotion consists of a "core," namely, the sense perception of the object; and of a "context" consisting of images (wet angleworms), organic sensations (feeling out of breath, stomach feeling queer), or both. The affective element (fear, unpleasantness) adheres to both core and context and carries the "meaning" of withdrawing from the object. For Conklin and Dimmick, the feeling or emotion "depends not upon any particular group of processes such as organic sensations, but rather upon some perceptual meaning of the object for the observer which is carried by the particular sensations, images or both" (1925, p. 100).

It is difficult to see how the affective element could adhere to visual images and organic sense perceptions or how it could develop from a "meaning" that includes both the objects and the contemplated action.

Perhaps it is for this reason that Beebe-Center calls feeling and emotion "common-sense constructs."

But when we look at both feeling and emotion as we experience them, can we call either of them a reification or a construct? The observers in Conklin and Dimmick's study surely experienced not only an emotion called fear, but fear aroused by a particular thing. This is direct experience, an experience that is immediate, unanalyzed, almost automatic in character: given a threat of harm, fear is sure to follow. Just as surely, this fear is unpleasant. Clearly, the fear and unpleasantness experienced by the observer are not common-sense constructs; they are direct experience if anything is. What is a construct is the "meaning" character of feeling and emotion. This will become clear from an examination of Titchener's concept of meaning.

For Titchener, meaning is always context; and context consists of the sensations and images that occur during the perceptual experience from habit. The sensations and images aroused by an object produce a bodily attitude that gives rise to kinesthetic and organic sensations. These are the "meaning" of visual images. Thus one mental process is the "meaning" of another, and never do we get to the object, the process, or ourselves acting and dealing with the object. As soon as sensations and feelings turned out to be constructs (see Experience versus Construct, in Ch. 2), meanings, of course, had to become constructs also.*

When Beebe-Center says that emotion in its common-sense usage is a reification, he seems to mean that emotion (a common-sense construct) is only assumed to be real—at least it is so assumed by Tom, Dick, and Harry, even by Tom the psychologist outside his laboratory. But what Tom, Dick, and Harry feel is an actual experience; and only an abstraction can be reified. If we do not grant the objective reality of what we

---

* Humphrey points out that such an approach to direct experience is bound to reduce it to a set of abstractions: "as soon as we forget that *to perceive* is a transitive verb, and thus separate it from the *environment perceived*, we find ourselves in the world of primary sensations, presentations, ideas, the 'two worlds', and so on, from which we can never escape except by a pre-established harmony, an act of 'reference,' by the assumption of 'intentional inexistence' or other postulated mechanism. Or we have to speak in terms of symbols, which have the outside world as their 'meaning.' The 'problem of meaning' in perception is an artificial one made necessary by putting a tertium quid between the process of perceiving and the environment perceived, and made even more difficult by the invention of the word 'percept.'" (1951, p. 240; Humphrey's italics)

sense and feel, we have to say that there cannot be any direct experience at all, except perhaps the experience of our abstractions. Without direct experience of something concrete, we have no basis for inferring an external world or for making constructs. Science becomes illusory and theories irrelevant.

The only alternative to such solipsism is to admit explicitly that sensing and feeling are real experiences, and that we can experience real objects. In common experience, the person feeling pleasure and the pleasant object are complementary, just as the person seeing and the thing seen. In direct experience, a man wants some *thing,* he feels some *thing* as pleasant. When emotion and feeling become constructs, feeling and wanting are isolated from the thing felt or wanted and become elusive and unobservable because the connection with their source has snapped. If feeling is a "conscious element," emotion is a combination of such elements, and the process that produced them has to be inferred; or if feeling and emotion are "meanings," they are both abstract, inert constructs. But if feeling and emotion are the lively going out of a living being to an object, then feelings and emotions are real, as real as the dog that chases us or the sip of wine we savor.

FEELING AS ATTITUDE

If we ask how an object acquires the meanings "pleasant" and "unpleasant," Carr and Hunt would answer that we do so "in virtue of our normal reaction tendency toward it" (Carr, 1925, p. 290). They seem to imply that pleasantness and unpleasantness are attitudes. Now if feeling is linked with approach and avoidance, there is the possibility that we approach something because it is pleasant and avoid something because it is unpleasant. Or we may approach something and in approaching experience pleasure, and avoid something and in withdrawing experience unpleasantness. In the first case, approach or avoidance would be consequences of feeling pleasure or pain; hence they would have no part in the origin of these feelings. In the second case, approach and avoidance would somehow produce feelings of pleasure and pain and would have to be investigated to discover the nature and origin of these feelings. Since Carr and Hunt chose the latter alternative, let us see whether there is experimental evidence to support it.

Münsterberg (1892), reporting on an early experiment, mentioned that the extension and contraction of voluntary muscles were different in pleasure and pain. When an individual reported pleasure, extension movements were larger and flexion movements smaller than normal. During unpleasantness, extension movements were smaller, and flexion movements larger than normal. This agrees with the consistent introspective reports from other studies that pleasantness is accompanied by a kind of bodily expansion, unpleasantness by a kind of internal constriction. Münsterberg's study shows that such expansion and contraction are not confined to involuntary muscles but extend to voluntary movements as well.

Remmers and Thompson, Jr. (1925) reported similar findings. They asked their subjects to draw freehand lines, twenty while thinking of pleasant things, twenty while thinking of unpleasant incidents. The lines drawn during pleasant thoughts were found to be significantly longer than those drawn during unpleasant thoughts. Whether we agree with the authors' conclusion that pleasure increases and unpleasantness decreases muscular activity, or with Beebe-Center's (1932) comment that movements of extension (used in drawing lines) are increased during pleasure and decreased during unpleasantness, both Münsterberg's and Remmers and Thompson's studies show that such changes are the *result* of affective experiences. The subjects had to imagine or experience something pleasant before their movements became expansive.

If expansion and increased activity are the result of pleasurable experiences, it is possible that approach to something pleasant is also the result of the experienced pleasure and not its cause. The available experiments are somewhat ambiguous because they were not designed to settle this point. Young, for instance, found in 1921 that pleasantness was accompanied by relaxation. Seeking movements also occurred, but were deliberate and meant to maintain stimulation. Unpleasantness, on the other hand, was accompanied by voluntary or involuntary movements of avoidance, by startle or strain. For Young, these have the biological meaning of avoidance, defense, or resistance (1922, p. 523).

Corwin (1921) repeated Young's experiment (cf. Young, 1922); but instead of instructing her subjects to remain passive and let themselves experience the effect of the various stimuli, as did Young, she had them sitting in a chair that was not too comfortable, and had the stimuli gradually moving away from them. In this situation the subjects showed decided tendencies to move after the receding stimulus during pleasantness.

Corwin, like Young, regularly found avoidance movements with unpleasant stimuli and concluded that the most natural response to unpleasantness is withdrawal, and to pleasantness, relaxation or pursuit.

Young duplicated Corwin's experiment in an attempt to check her
conclusions and found that, under her conditions, seeking and avoiding
movements could be found regularly. But seeking movements also occurred with an indifferent stimulus (a ticking watch), when it was
gradually moved away from the subject. Young concluded that the seeking movements seen by Corwin were not necessarily associated with
pleasantness but rather with the person's attempt to continue observing.
However that may be, movements of pursuit or avoidance seem to be
the result of pleasurable or unpleasurable experiences and not their cause.
Pursuit seems to occur only when the pleasant object is withdrawn. As
far as the available evidence goes, there are no grounds for suggesting
that pleasantness is the result of approach, and unpleasantness the result
of avoidance reactions.

That any shift from pleasantness to unpleasantness or vice versa is not
the result of a change in attitude from approach to avoidance has been
shown experimentally by Pan (quoted by Flügel, 1939). From the
subjects' reports it appeared that such a change needs a *change in regard*
in such a way that pleasant elements of the stimulus are brought out and
attended to, while unpleasant elements are neglected. In two cases where
the subject was unable to bring about this change, he merely changed
his general attitude so that now he tolerated pain while before he had
resisted it. As a result, the unpleasant feeling remained, though he experienced an improvement in general mood.

Pan's findings completely agree with the introspective reports given by
Koch. Two examples from Koch will illustrate this point:

108. (Unpleasant stimulus, triangle 4:2.5:2.5 cm.) "Attempting to feel pleasantness, I try to see the picture as unclearly as possible. Involuntarily I breathe
deeply, let the neck musculature relax and seek to inhibit the tension of the
eye muscles. As a result, the whole thing seems much brighter and gayer."
(Koch, 1913, p. 54)

To see an unpleasant figure in an indistinct way or to relax the neck
muscles could hardly be called approach behavior. The other report is
even clearer:

109. (Triangle 4:6:6 cm., instruction to feel first pleasantness, then unpleasantness.) "I try to feel pleasantness on looking at the drawing. My face

is becoming smooth and I feel pleasantness. This is directly connected with the agreeable balance of the black lines and the proportion of the white areas. There is no effort, but calmness. It is quite different when I now try deliberately to feel unpleasantness. I try to see the drawing as blurred as possible, I squeeze my eyes together. The black lines seem bent. Now I have a dull sensation in my head." (Koch, 1913, p. 55)

Here is the same attempt to see the lines blurred as in the first example; yet the result is unpleasantness instead of the pleasantness experienced in 108. Then, the triangle originally had unpleasant proportions; in trying to see it as pleasant, the observer does not regard it in the same way he did before. He tries to let the unpleasant shape affect him less, by seeing it as blurred as possible; in addition, he relaxes. Thus he himself creates conditions that affect him favorably, and feels pleasantness. When he shifts from pleasantness to unpleasantness in observing the triangle with pleasing proportions (109), he refuses to let himself be affected favorably but lets the lines blur and tries to see it indistinctly. In addition, he makes seeing difficult by squeezing his eyes together. Thus he produces conditions that affect him adversely and feels unpleasantness.

We may conclude that it is not the change in attitude from acceptance to rejection that produces the shift from pleasantness to unpleasantness, nor is it the opposite shift that produces pleasantness. Rather, it is the fact that the individual succeeds in creating conditions which affect him favorably that produces pleasantness, and the fact that he has created conditions that affect him adversely which produces unpleasantness. The experimental evidence does not show that feeling is the *result* of a movement toward or away from something; hence feeling cannot be an attitude. The evidence does show that pleasantness is experienced when something affects us favorably, unpleasantness when something affects us adversely.

FEELING AS JUDGMENT

Interpreting Carr's and Hunt's theories, Peters (1935) suggested that the awareness of our normal or usual action tendency toward something is in fact a judgment that this is to be approached, that to be avoided. Hence he claimed that feelings are judgments that depend on approach-avoidance reactions but have no special conscious content. For Peters the normal reaction is the reaction that would be made if no other motive intervened. Thus a man may say opium smoking is pleasant, though he has never done it. The knowledge that he would do it if no other motive conflicted with it is all there is to his experience of pleasure. For this reason, Peters insisted that feeling is to be found only "in organisms which can give a verbal or other form of symbolic report."

Peters cited experiments in support of his theory (1938, 1939). In two of them he presented ten words tachistoscopically and asked his subjects to pronounce five words and give no response to the other five. The choice of words to be pronounced he left up to the subject. All ten words were then ranked according to pleasantness as reported by the subjects. When they were asked afterward what in their opinion influenced their judgment of pleasantness or unpleasantness, they gave these reasons:

	Experiment 2	Experiment 3	Total Subjects
For Pleasantness			
Increased familiarity	6	3	9
Pronouncing the words	3	10	13
Awareness of impulse to pronounce	1	1	2
For Unpleasantness			
Words to which reaction was difficult to learn	19	30	49
Words difficult to pronounce	0	2	2

While it is true that thirteen people reported pleasantness when pronouncing the words, it is not certain that the increase in pleasantness was the result of approach (pronouncing). If the subjects' explanations can be trusted, familiarity also produced pleasantness, and pronouncing the words may have increased such familiarity.*

Moreover, the vast majority insisted that they felt unpleasantness when

* That familiarity is a better explanation than positive reactions for the observed increase of pleasantness is suggested also by Maslow's (1937) experiments on familiarity. In this study there were some objects (pictures hung on the wall, the click of a metronome) to which no positive response was required or given; yet increasing familiarity produced or increased felt pleasantness. Familiarity, of course, will have this effect only when there is a possibility to come to know the object better. With simple stimuli such as odors, where nothing more can be learned, pleasantness is not increased. Quite on the contrary, the more often the odor is noticed, the more easily may it produce satiation.

the reaction was difficult to learn or a word was difficult to pronounce. It seems that unpleasantness was connected with doing something difficult rather than with avoiding the response, for there is no indication that it was more difficult to avoid responding than to pronounce the word. Hence this experiment provides evidence for the view that unpleasantness is felt when something is difficult to learn or difficult to do, in contrast to Peters's view that it goes with an avoidance reaction.

As further evidence for his theory Peters mentioned that judgments of pleasantness and unpleasantness show the same law of contrast as psychophysical judgments (see Beebe-Center, 1932). But the similarity lies in the fact that in both cases objects are judged on the basis of immediate experience. A man notes how heavy one weight feels and how heavy the other; he notes how pleasant one object is and how pleasant another: then he gives his judgment. Both are judgments of immediate experience and hence both are existential judgments. In psychophysical judgments, the experience is sensory; in feeling judgments it ought to be affective. Nobody would suggest that the *experience* of heaviness is "judgmental," or, in other words, reflective and not sensory. But Peters suggests that the *experience* of pleasantness and unpleasantness is not affective but judgmental; that it is a judgment based on memory and reflection rather than a judgment based on affective experience.

For Peters it is a reflective judgment because he considers that the report of pleasant or unpleasant feelings is based not on the immediate affective reaction to the object but on the knowledge of a person's normal or usual reaction, or on the awareness of what he wants to do if nothing intervenes. But immediate experience cannot be equated with reflection. If such direct here-and-now experience does not determine whether something will be felt as pleasant or unpleasant, we begin to wonder how something new can ever give rise to feeling. It will not do to say that it depends on the judgment that we react to similar objects with approach or withdrawal. There is always a first time. A child will put anything in his mouth; but some things do not taste pleasant and he spits them out again. Here experience has corrected the usual or normal approach.

Peters's definition of feeling would make it impossible to ascribe to the infant and animal feelings of pleasure or pain. But what are we to make of the cat's purring when its fur is stroked, or the infant's gurgling and cooing when it is fed and comfortable? If something bitter is put on the infant's tongue, there are signs of displeasure that remind us of similar reactions in the adult. These signs seem to be expressive reactions, but what do they express? Not the kind of judgment Peters is talking about; yet they are expressions of feeling or emotion. We are quite sure that infants or animals cannot know what their habitual reactions are, nor would they seem to know what they would do if nothing interfered. But are we sure they do not experience pleasure or pain? If we deny such experience to the infant, when and how does it suddenly appear? The expression remains the same—infant, child, adult all smile when they are pleased—but we would have to assume that only the older child and adult have any feelings to express. Unless we want to say arbitrarily and contrary to our own experience that such facial expressions have no connection with what we feel, we must admit that similar expressions should indicate similar experiences. If so, the infant must be able to experience pleasure, even though he cannot report it.

We know from E. B. Hunt's (1932) study that the words *pleasant* and *unpleasant* appear relatively late, much later than words like *good, bad, like* or *love*. Only one out of nine children used the word *pleasant* at age three, and only one out of nine used the word *unpleasant* at age five, while the other words mentioned began to be used between the ages of one and two. This age difference in using words like *pleasant* and *unpleasant* is hardly evidence in Peters's favor. Once a child can say "love dolly" or "want dolly," the chances are that he also knows that he usually loves or wants it, or, at any rate, that he wants it now, which should be sufficient to report pleasantness, if Peters were right. The conditions for report are there and the *word* pleasant is no more difficult to learn than many words the child learns much earlier.

The real reason why these words are acquired so late seems to be that they imply a double conceptual abstraction: first, an abstraction from the object to focus on one of its aspects; secondly, an abstraction from the subject to report on the way something affects the child's functioning. The young child deals with objects rather than characteristics abstracted from the object; and he is able and willing to report his reaction to the object, namely, that he likes or dislikes it. To see that he likes or dislikes something because it affects him favorably or unfavorably needs more reflection than the child can manage. Hence the *report* that something is pleasant is beyond the child's ability, but not the experience of pleasure.

Nor can the judgmental theory of feeling account for the quality of the experience. I can say not only "This is pleasant," but also "I know that I (usually) seek this thing," and these two statements report two different kinds of experience. The mere knowledge of wanting or tending toward something is not an experience of pleasure but a desire to be close to something that gives me pleasure. I may approach an obstacle in impotent anger, may even know that I usually do so, but this action tendency is not pleasant, neither is the thing that has angered me. The introspective reports we have quoted make an even more careful distinction between pleasantness and approach, unpleasantness and withdrawal, than they do between feelings and sensations.

Peters does not seem to distinguish between judgments made on the basis of memory and reflection and judgments made on the basis of immediate experience. The judgment that opium smoking is pleasant is based on the general knowledge of its effects and thus on memory and reflection. But there are judgments based on immediate experience that flatly contradict such knowledge. A man who has been listening to the same simple tune for an hour will judge it unpleasant on the basis of his experience here and now, no matter how well he used to like it. Experiments on satiation show over and over that something normally pleasant may become decidedly unpleasant when a person has had too much of it. Hence immediate experience often contradicts the judgment based on a knowledge of what is our usual reaction.

Finally, the judgmental theory cannot account for the fact that this particular judgment based on memory and reflection is accompanied by various organic sensations, like the bright or dull pressures reported by Nafe. No other reflective judgment has similar bodily effects. According to Peters, such organic sensations accompany emotions that are joined to the judgments of pleasantness or unpleasantness. This may be true for some of the older work which used stimuli intense enough to arouse fear, startle or other emotions in addition to unpleasantness (see Nafe's Investigations, in Ch. 2). It is particularly true of studies in Wundt's three dimensions of feeling: tension/quiescence, excitement/depression, and pleasantness/unpleasantness. Peters's criticism does not hold for Nafe's work and Hunt's studies, where strong stimuli were carefully avoided. Yet it was in these studies employing mild stimuli that bright and dull pressures were reported. There is nothing in the introspective accounts to suggest that emotions were aroused that could account for these organic sensations.

For Peters, the judgmental theory is the only one that provides a clear distinction between feeling and emotion. He says:

According to the judgmental theory, emotions may or may not accompany the feeling judgment. The affective consciousness is probably complicated with bodily sensations during the first encounter with the situation. Familiarity with the situation, however, brings a progressive decrease in the emotional element but leaves the affective judgment constant. This conception of pleasantness and unpleasantness as judgments is the only one that gives to feeling and emotion statuses entirely independent of each other. Otherwise the two are hopelessly confused or feeling is merely a part of, or adjunct to, the emotions. (1935, p. 361)

But evidently the distinction is made at the expense of considering emotions as organic sensations, for as soon as the affective consciousness ceases to be "complicated with bodily sensations," there is a progressive decrease in the emotional element. Apart from such complications, it seems, the affective consciousness is judgmental, and thus cognitive in nature.

The judgmental theory tries to combine two factors connected with feeling: first, that pleasantness goes with approach, unpleasantness with avoidance; second, that feeling seems to include a judgment as to how the pleasant or unpleasant situation affects us. But approach and avoidance are the consequences of pleasure and pain, not their causes; and the judgment that something affects us favorably or unfavorably cannot be reflective as it would have to be if it were based on a knowledge of our usual reaction or even on our knowledge that we would do this if nothing interfered. Such judgment would have to be direct, immediate, as simple as the infant's gurgling and cooing when he is dandled, or the animal's pleasure in warmth or food. We will discuss this judgment in detail in Chapters 4 and 9, together with the role it plays both in feeling and emotion.

FEELING AS SUCCESS OR FAILURE

Successful approach brings pleasure or satisfaction, a fact on which McDougall has based his theory of feeling. When we strive toward a goal, we feel pleasantness or unpleasantness, depending on the conditions under which we strive. We feel "pleasure when the striving attains its natural goal or progresses toward it; pain, when striving is thwarted or obstructed and fails to achieve, or progress toward, its goal" (1923, p. 269). The role of pleasantness is to favor striving, the role of unpleasantness, to hinder it and so divert it in some new direction. Thus pleasure indicates that the conditions are right for attaining one's end; and pain, that they are wrong and the goal is to be attained in some other way. By "striving" McDougall means an instinctive impulse, a native propensity toward some appropriate goal.

To avoid the implication of an inherited behavior pattern connected with the term "instinct," McDougall uses the term "propensity" to denote potential striving which is made actual by the appropriate object. "A *propensity,*" he says, "is a disposition, a functional unit of the mind's total organization, and it is one which, when it is excited, generates an active *tendency,* a *striving,* an *impulse* or *drive* towards some goal; such a tendency working consciously towards a foreseen goal is a desire" (1933, p. 118; McDougall's italics).

In this passage McDougall seems to make the same distinction between feeling and propensity that we have advocated to discriminate between feeling and emotion. We will see later (in Ch. 7) that McDougall ascribes to instinct what is really a property of emotion. As for feeling, he seems to imply that pleasure and pain are exclusively the result of striving, which is patently incorrect. Rest is pleasant, so is dancing, and such pleasure is not the result of trying to reach a goal.

McDougall copes with such difficulties by assuming that every directed activity is a striving. He postulates a special "rest propensity" and "propensities serving simple bodily needs" to account for the pleasantness of sleep and of various physiological functions. Since learning, perceiving, sensing, are directed activities ("strivings"), he can account for pleasant or unpleasant feelings aroused by either simple or complex stimuli, as well as for the pleasure connected with desire. According to McDougall, a patch of color is pleasant if clearly defined because it favors perceptual striving, while an ill-defined blotch which hinders such striving is found unpleasant (1927, p. 179).

There are several areas where McDougall's explanation breaks down. His theory requires definite "propensities" that must be successfully directed toward specific ends before pleasantness can be experienced. To say later that activity does not need to have a specific goal, and that all directed activities are therefore strivings. is but a play on words. There are some activities that are pleasant in themselves, whether they accomplish anything or not. Children enjoy running, shouting, swinging, in fact, any kind of activity as long as it does not require too much effort. When fatigue has made muscular activity difficult, rest restores normal functioning. Rest is pleasant after exercise; but when a man is rested, he finds exercise pleasant also. Psychological activities are pleasant, if smooth and unhindered. Daydreaming is pleasant, but so are planning, organizing, reasoning, as long as no serious difficulties are encountered. There can be pleasure in any activity, even if it is not a "striving."

Moreover, the hormic theory cannot account for aesthetic pleasure. This cannot be an emotion unless we postulate a special "aesthetic propensity," and McDougall has not done that. It cannot be a feeling because, whether we look at a well-defined patch of color or a painting by Van Gogh, there is little difference in the degree of perceptual success. In fact, there are paintings we find pleasant that put far greater obstacles in the way of our "perceptual striving" than does a patch of color.

Similarly, changes in feeling with changing states of the organism are difficult to explain on McDougall's premises. When hunger is satisfied, and there may no longer be any desire for food, the taste of a dish may still be pleasant. In line with his own hypothesis, McDougall explained that the taste of sugar is pleasant only when the hunger impulse is at work and that sugar becomes unpleasant with satiety. But there is a difference between satiety and repletion. A meal may satisfy a man's hunger but leave him far short of satiety. Even after a meal the taste of candy is still pleasant. It becomes unpleasant only after overeating. This was confirmed experimentally by Engel (in: Beebe-Center, 1932, p. 178). His subjects found sugar pleasant even in the highest concentrations; but two men who had overindulged in sweets in childhood found higher sugar concentrations decidedly unpleasant (9 percent and over) though 1 percent sugar solutions remained pleasant. It can be argued that all the subjects were slightly hungry, in which case they should all have found sugar pleasant in all concentrations. Or it may be argued that they were satiated, in which case we cannot explain that the majority found the taste of sugar pleasant.

Similarly, the hormic theory cannot account for changes in the pleasantness of taste in various deficiency states. In chlorosis, for instance, sour foods are found exceedingly pleasant because of the increased alkalinity of the blood. In adrenocortical deficiency, salt is found most pleasant and eaten in quantity. Now it could be argued that the organism needs these particular foodstuffs to supply a deficiency and therefore develops a "propensity" for them. But such a propensity would be acquired and strictly temporary instead of instinctive as McDougall's system would require.

Finally, the hormic theory fails to explain unpleasantness and pain adequately because these must be connected with the difficulty experienced in some striving. Pain, for instance, is supposed to arouse the propensity to flee and thus is really a kind of fear. Sudden pain would be a momentary fear. But if so, what would distinguish it from startle? A sudden pain may startle us, but the two experiences are by no means identical. There are pains that are not sudden and are thoroughly familiar (for instance, a slight headache), and these can hardly arouse fear. But they are both unpleasant and painful. It is no solution to say, as McDougall does, that pain would not be unpleasant if the impulse to withdraw were successful. Pain is unpleasant not because an impulse to withdraw is frustrated but because it comes with excessive stimulation of somatosensory nerves. There is an impulse to withdraw as a result of pain, not before it is felt. It is never possible to withdraw from the pain but only from the thing that gives pain. A man may have successfully escaped from further danger after getting a stab wound and may begin to feel the pain only after he is in safety.

To complete his case for unsuccessful striving as the cause of pain, McDougall claims that pain disappears when it is put in the service of some other striving, as in the case of fanatics, martyrs, and masochists. But there is no evidence to show that pain disappears in any of these cases. The masochist feels pain; but some types of pain are necessary for him to reach orgasm, while he tries just as much as a normal man to avoid other kinds of pain. In the case of the martyr, the pain is disregarded, though he is by no means insensitive to it. To achieve what he has set out to do, he is willing to suffer and even to die.

4. FEELING AS REACTION TO SENSORY EXPERIENCE

We have come to the end of our review of the various theories of feeling. Our conclusion is bound to be that feeling is neither a mental element nor an organic sensation, nor can it be equated with the felt experience of various pressure patterns. Feeling is a direct experience and neither a construct nor an inference. It is a conscious reaction to our experience of things (including our body) and reflects the effect of such experiences on us.

Any sensation may be indifferent, pleasant, or unpleasant. In fact, one and the same sensation may at first be pleasant, then become indifferent, and finally be definitely unpleasant. Hence feeling is not only different from sensation but also indicates how the sensation affects us. Feeling may persist even after the object that aroused it has disappeared; hence the effect of a sensation can outlast it.

Not only sensations but emotions also may be either pleasant or unpleasant, though they ordinarily are so engrossing that we do not stop to see how they affect us. Various experiments mentioned in the last three chapters have shown that pleasantness or unpleasantness is noticed only when a man focuses on the way a particular aspect or quality affects him. When a landscape is called pleasant, we appraise its visual qualities and leave aside any question as to whether we have ever seen it before, and, if we have, whether it recalls gay or sad memories. Nor do we ask ourselves whether we would like to live there. Similarly, when we call music pleasant, we refer merely to its tonal qualities, not to the interweaving of musical themes or to any memories it may recall. When we find it pleasant to sing or dance or skate, we refer to the way our movement feels; we react to the kinesthetic sensations that go with it. If we could move without having any sensation of moving, there would be no pleasure attached to it. In all these cases, pleasantness and unpleasantness are reactions to specific sense experiences.

FEELING AS REACTION TO ENHANCED OR IMPEDED FUNCTIONING

When we find motor activities pleasant, our feeling is based on the realization that these activities go on smoothly, without effort. Dancing, running, skating, or swimming are pleasant only as long as we are rested and vigorous. With fatigue, they become decidedly unpleasant. Similarly, thinking is pleasant when thoughts flow easily and lead to satisfactory conclusions. Imagination is pleasant (for instance, for a creative writer when images and scenes come easily so that the story is almost writing itself). These psychological activities are impeded when their results are meager and unsatisfactory; when thinking does not produce understanding; when imagination will produce neither a credible plot nor interesting dialogue.

Theories of feeling as the experience of enhanced or impeded functioning date back to Aristotle. Later versions, which have been suggested by several psychologists, usually imply that pleasantness or pleasure builds up vital energy and that unpleasantness or pain depletes it. The meaning advocated here is far simpler: any function, sensory, psychological, or physiological, may be enhanced or hindered under certain conditions and thus functioning may be made easy or difficult. When functioning is easy and effortless, it will be pleasant. When it is made difficult, it will be unpleasant.

The arousal of feeling. But it is not enough to postulate the cause of a phenomenon; we must also show how that cause gives rise to a particular experience. Most theorists refuse to commit themselves to any opinion as to how a feeling is aroused. Some of them are content to point to a possible neural mechanism that may mediate it. According to Beebe-Center,

Hedonic tone depends upon a specific type of process in sense organs, namely that which, under sensory instructions or their equivalent, mediates bright and dull pressure. When this type of process occurs under hedonic instructions or their equivalent, it gives rise to . . . hedonic tone. . . . The process in question is invariably proprioceptive. It is aroused by external stimuli—

e.g. visual stimuli—indirectly through the muscular adjustments which they bring about. (1932, p. 413)

Even if we were to agree with the statement that feelings depend upon a proprioceptive process, we would want to know just how this process is initiated. If external stimuli bring it about through a muscular adjustment, we would like to know how they bring it about. Psychologically speaking, neither approach nor avoidance will follow unless the object is perceived as demanding a certain action. We have seen before that approach or avoidance cannot be the origin of pleasantness or unpleasantness; and we doubt whether it can bring about bright or dull pressure.

Other theories specify other mechanisms to account for the arousal of feeling: Lehmann (1914), for instance, considers that pleasantness is aroused whenever assimilation exceeds dissimilation in the activity of any group of central neurones. For Thorndike (1927), pleasantness or, as he calls it, "satisfaction," is experienced whenever neural impulses are channelled through conduction units that are ready to conduct. When such a unit is not allowed to conduct, or when a unit not ready for conduction is forced to conduct, unpleasantness or "annoyance" is the result. For Troland (1928), increased neural conductance is experienced as pleasantness, decreased neural conductance as unpleasantness. Herrick (1918) thinks that normal discharge over nervous circuits that results in free, unrestrained activity is pleasurable, while impeded discharge is unpleasant.

All these theories specify a favorable or unfavorable central state that is experienced as pleasantness or unpleasantness. But none of the theorists informs us just how sheer conductance, whether impeded or unimpeded, can give rise not only to sensations but also to feeling states. Nor is there a clue as to the conditions in which assimilation would exceed dissimilation in central neurones, as Lehmann contends.

Granted that unpleasantness is a reaction to impeded functioning, as most of these authors seem to imply, there must be some recognition or appraisal of functioning before unpleasantness can actually be experienced. The sensory functions themselves, or any of the psychological functions usually recognized, cannot mediate the appraisal of their own functioning. Sensory functions can mediate only an experience of the quality of things, the sight of colors, the hearing of sounds, the touch of something smooth or sharp. Kinesthetic sensations can mediate only the experience of motion or of muscular tension and relaxation. There must be some appraisal that one kind of functioning is impeded, another enhanced; that movement is difficult but seeing or hearing or tasting is smooth and unimpeded. There must be an estimate that one kind of functioning is good, that is, favorable for the organism, another unfavorable, before the one can be felt as pleasant, the other as unpleasant. And such appraisal is beyond the scope of the function that is being appraised.

It would seem, then, that we have to postulate some function that will mediate such an appraisal. The estimate of what is favorable or unfavorable must be direct and immediate, as direct as sense perception, for it is not a deliberate or reflective judgment. The traditional philosophy has called this sense-like process the "estimative sense" and has considered it one of the internal senses, together with memory and imagination. Since it is necessary to postulate such a sense-like process of appraising to account for the facts, we are justified in proposing it as a hypothetical construct.

This appraisal is not only direct and immediate; it is also intuitive and unwitting. We are unaware that we have made such a judgment, a fact that may speak against our inference that it occurs. However, Gasson (1954) has pointed out that we are not immediately aware of the working of any of our functions. We are directly aware only of the results of such functioning. We are aware of our movement, but not of the working of our muscles that has brought it about. We are aware of what we see or hear or think, but not of the way in which we see, hear, or think. Similarly, we are not aware of the way in which this appraisal is performed. We only know the results, feelings of pleasure or pain, of pleasantness or unpleasantness. When we reflect upon our experience of pleasantness and unpleasantness, we are aware of appraising this thing as good (pleasant), that as bad (unpleasant); and we often assume that such evaluation is the *result* of our feeling experience. But the process of appraisal seems to be *inherent* in the feeling experience, just as the process of sensing is inherent in the experience of sight or sound or touch. Reflection on the feeling experience merely makes such appraisal explicit.

Our appraisal evaluates that aspect of the object that is sensed by us, an aspect which affects us over one particular sense modality. It is the objective quality that is appraised; but it is the sense function that is either enhanced or impeded. When it is a movement that is experienced, it is appraised as smooth or difficult and thus must be either favored or impeded. When muscular contraction or relaxation is sensed, it is appraised as it enhances or impedes either particular sense functions or our general organismic functioning. Thus our estimate is either of sense qualities (pleasant or unpleasant sounds, sights, odors, touches, etc.), of the quality of movement (smooth or difficult), of the flow of products of psychological activity (the rate of ideas, images, and insights), or, finally, of enhanced and impeded functioning (muscular tension and relaxation, increased and decreased circulation, digestion, etc.).

Some of these appraisals are reflective as well as intuitive. We may be unpleasantly aware of the difficulty of thinking or writing, the sparse flow of ideas and images. But we are also dissatisfied with the kind of ideas produced with such effort, and eventually decide that we are not up to any serious work today. The sheer awareness of the difficulty in getting ideas is intuitive and results in unpleasantness. The judgment that these ideas are inadequate is reflective. This may be accompanied by another intuitive judgment that such poverty of ideas is bad, which will arouse annoyance, depression, or despair, depending on what we think can be done about it.

Definition and classification of feeling. We can now define *feeling* as *a positive or negative reaction to some experience.* Pleasure and pleasantness are positive reactions, varying only in intensity. They can be defined as *a welcoming of something sensed that is appraised as beneficial and indicates enhanced functioning.* Pain and unpleasantness are negative reactions of varying intensity and can be defined as *a resistance to something sensed that is appraised as harmful and indicates impaired functioning.* What is pleasant is liked, what is unpleasant, disliked.

It should now be possible to state in general what will be appraised in such an immediate and intuitive way as beneficial and what as harmful. We appraise as good and hence find *pleasant:*

1. Sense qualities that enhance a particular sensory function:
   a. Simple sounds, colors, odors, etc.
   b. Patterns of sense qualities: melodies, clangs, pictures, landscapes, etc.
2. Ease and smoothness of bodily movements:
   a. Dancing, running, jumping, skating, skiing, etc.
3. Fast flow of images, ideas; easy understanding, quick insights.
4. Enhanced physiological functioning:
   a. Good digestion, circulation, etc.
   b. Optimal muscular relaxation.

5. Emotions that tend toward something beneficial when such tending is *unimpeded*:
   a. Appetite—when food is available.
   b. Love, friendship, etc.—when requited.
   c. Anger—when freely expressed.

We appraise as harmful and hence find *unpleasant or painful*:

1. Sense qualities that impede or damage a particular sense function:
   a. Intense and excessive stimulation.
   b. Minimal stimulation requiring intense effort.
   c. Discordant or chaotic stimulation: clashing colors, discords, etc.
2. Difficulty in moving body or limbs.
3. Slow rate of images, ideas; difficult understanding; laborious insights.
4. Impeded physiological functioning:
   a. Poor digestion, circulation, etc.
   b. Muscular tension (in voluntary and involuntary muscles).
5. Emotions tending toward something that can be reached only with difficulty:
   a. Fear—urging to seek safety that is difficult to reach.
   b. Anger—if it cannot be expressed or cannot overcome the annoyance.
   c. Love—when unrequited.

Feelings are reactions to experience. This is in most cases sensory experience, but may be the immediate awareness of thinking, imagining, understanding. The type of feeling, whether pleasantness or unpleasantness, will depend on the appraisal of experience as good or bad for us. The quality of pleasantness or unpleasantness will depend on the type of experience that is appraised. Thus we can distinguish sense-bound pleasure, the pleasure of motion or of mental activity, the feeling of physical well-being, and emotional pleasure.

When something is felt as pleasant, it is welcomed. When it seems to be withdrawn, it will be pursued. This accounts for the absence of movement and the muscular relaxation found by Young during pleasantness when the pleasant object was stationary. It also accounts for the pursuit movements when the pleasant stimulus was withdrawn. On the other hand, when something is felt as unpleasant, there will be some attempt to withdraw from it. Both Young and Corwin found that unpleasant stimuli were met with movements of avoidance or aversion (see Ch. 3, pp. 59 f.). We change our activity as soon as it becomes unpleasant. We want to rest as soon as walking or running becomes tiring. The student wants to stop working as soon as studying becomes difficult, the budding writer as soon as words cease to flow easily.

Sense-bound feelings and general feelings. When something is felt as pleasant, this is what seems to happen: sensing (for instance, smelling the fragrance of rose geranium) becomes easy; it is welcomed and felt as agreeable. Next, there may be changes in and around the nose and respiratory passages, probably the result of muscular relaxation that goes with unhindered functioning. Hence feelings aroused by simple sensory experiences are often "localized" at or near the sense organs.

If something affects one particular sense organ favorably, the resulting change in functioning will eventually affect the whole organism or, rather, the living person. If one function is enhanced, there will be less effort and deeper respiration, which will affect the person favorably and may be sensed as "bright pressure" in pleasantness. If some function is impeded, it will result in increased muscular tension which will affect the person adversely and apparently may be sensed as "dull pressure," in unpleasantness. But the primary experience is the pleasantness or unpleasantness of certain stimuli which produce, first, local and next, general changes; and these in turn are appraised as favorable and liked. When attention is specially directed to them, they can also be perceived as localized sensations.

Attention and feeling. We must attend to the aspect of the object that affects us before we can report a feeling of pleasantness or unpleasantness. Without special attention, we deal with the whole object. We treat it as something to eat or throw away, to investigate or disregard, without focusing on any one aspect. Hence it has generally been found that a special attitude to the object is necessary before a person will report pleasantness or unpleasantness. In Beebe-Center's words, the person must assume "a specific evaluative disposition." We would say that he must let one particular aspect affect him and report on it.

Attention does not arouse feelings; it merely allows us to become aware of them. Without attention, the feelings aroused by one particular quality of the object are so faint that they are swallowed up in our preoccupation with the object and its effect on us. In rhythmic bodily movement, as in dancing or skating, we may reach a degree of skill that allows us to forget how to move and what to accomplish so that we are free to enjoy the sheer movement without special attention. As feeling increases and either pain or pleasure becomes pronounced, it compels attention.

Attention can intensify or reduce a feeling just as it can intensify or reduce a sensation. Phelan (1925), for instance, had his subjects taste various liquids while giving them an electric shock. He found that they did not feel the sugar solution as pleasant while the shock lasted. Only as their attention returned to the task in hand did they notice the taste and feel it as pleasant. More pronounced tastes did not suffer such eclipse. Raspberry syrup, for instance, which was ranked as much more pleasant than sugar solution, was usually still noticeable during the shock. But Phelan found also that the unpleasantness of the shock disappeared whenever attention could be concentrated on the taste. The shock was noticed, certainly, and the effect on organismic functioning remained the same. But attention was centered on another appraisal, namely, the effect of the pleasant taste; hence the unpleasantness of the shock was never experienced.

Something similar happens in states of altered awareness. Under hypnosis, a man may not see a knife or feel it prick him, if the hypnotist tells him that he is being touched by a flower. Yet the somesthetic sensations are registered as usual, as shown by the electrical potentials recorded from the somesthetic cortex. There is even an indication that the cut must have been registered as harmful, for the autonomic reactions are the same as if pain were actually felt. During anesthesia also, sensory impulses reach the cortex. Though there is neither an experience of objects nor a feeling of pain, the autonomic reactions occur as they do during pain.

Neither in hypnosis nor under anesthesia is the person able to focus his attention on the situation or its effects on him, nor can he avoid what he judges harmful. We shall see later (in Ch. 4 of the following volume) that the neural mechanism that makes it possible to experience objects and feel pain is not functioning during anesthesia. Perhaps its functioning is reduced during hypnosis, when a man is oblivious of everything except the hypnotist and his commands. When he concentrates on something in his normal state, other activities seem to be reduced, though they are never excluded completely. Intense sensations can compel his attention and so allow the experience of pain.

Qualitative differences in pleasantness and unpleasantness. There seem to be qualitative differences depending on the kind of feeling, either sense-bound or general. There will also be differences according to the type of sensory experience. This is demonstrated nicely in Koch's experiment No. 60 (see Feelings not Localizable, in Ch. 1), where two types of sense-bound feelings are distinguished. On cessation of the musical chord there was a jar, noticeable in the larynx, and an unpleasant feeling like an inner emptiness and protest. Then came the dissonance and with it a hammering kind of organic sensation, and also unpleasantness. Apparently, the first adverse effect was on hearing: the welcome sound dropped out and the dissonance assaulted the ear instead. The jar in the larynx may have been the sudden arrest of unwitting attempts to produce the same tone. Both the chord and the dissonance secondarily produced an organic reverberation which was felt as general pleasantness or unpleasantness. In another report quoted by Koch it appears that there is also a difference between the unpleasantness that comes from detecting a logical fallacy, and that produced by a wrongly used foreign word. We could almost say that there is a different shade of pleasantness or unpleasantness for every function that gives rise to it. Hence we are in complete agreement with Phelan (1925) who concluded from a series of experiments that feeling "takes a variety of qualitative shades according to the quality of the experience as a whole" (p. 260).

Feeling and mood. Since feeling is a reaction to something that affects our functioning, or a direct reaction to enhanced or impeded functioning, it will persist as long as the change in functioning lasts. If one situation affects us adversely and some later experience affects us favorably over a different sensory avenue, the original feeling of unpleasantness will gradually be replaced by a feeling of pleasantness. Here is a rather detailed report from Koch's study that shows the importance of attention and reflection in this change-over from one feeling state to another.

[Experiment 72, Subject Meumann.] The dominant mood before the experiment was that of a strong depressive unpleasantness, aroused by a very annoying letter. I played successively various chords on the piano which usually are very pleasant and arouse great aesthetic delight. Immediately before there was an intense unwillingness to participate in this experiment with musical stimuli because I expected that these stimuli would not agree with my mood. As soon as I sounded the first chord, there was immediately the usual aesthetic judgment: this chord is beautiful. This judgment aroused a certain pleasantness. *But at the same time there was unpleasantness like an undercurrent in the affective life.*

And now there began a struggle between the unpleasantness aroused by my resistance to this acoustic stimulus, and the pleasantness of the sound. The resistance eventually won out. It is not only the aesthetic judgment which aroused temporary pleasantness, but also *the overwhelming impression of the sensory stimulus at the moment of sounding the chord;* it arouses pleasantness, which at first seems to have displaced the unpleasant mood. But immediately afterwards I become aware that the unpleasant mood *was there all the time as an undercurrent.* When the chord died out, the tone itself displeased me and the two causes of unpleasantness combined to an intense depression.

[Several repetitions of the chords.] The mood gradually changed in so far as pleasantness and unpleasantness seemed to be present simultaneously while the chords sounded, but pleasantness gradually became the stronger feeling. There was a noticeable *alternation of attention* between the present content of pleasantness and unpleasantness, but not really an alternation of feeling; both feelings *existed side by side* and only alternatively increased or decreased in intensity.

When suddenly the thought came that these experiments might be able to counteract the unpleasant mood, pleasantness gradually gained the upper hand, though a slight undercurrent of unpleasantness seemed to remain.— This fight between feelings is noticed clearly as a fight between different organic sensations and seems to agree in content with these, so that the total feeling state is constituted by the varying combinations of organic sensations. Physically this struggle was noticeable in breathing, in stomach and intestines and also a little in numerous respiratory muscle groups, also in a change of blood flow to the head. Besides this, there was only an increase and decrease of tension and relaxation. Tension seemed to be produced by the state of unpleasantness, relaxation by reflection and by the stimuli. (1913, p. 39; Koch's italics)

This report demonstrates that a mood can be the result of an emotion and can be influenced by sense-bound feelings, particularly when attention and reflection increase their effect. The effect of the annoyance (an emotion) seems to have been felt as unfavorable and correspondingly disliked. This resulted in a mood of depression. As soon as the chord was heard and felt as pleasant, the secondary effect of this sense-bound feeling on general organismic functioning was favorable and brought about a general feeling of pleasantness. Thus the original depressive mood was first lightened and finally driven out by the gradually increasing pleasantness.

Mood, it seems, is the feeling response to general organismic functioning. It will be influenced by anything that can enhance such functioning or interfere with it. A pleasant surprise or a great joy will induce an elated mood; a disappointment, sorrow, or anxiety will result in a depressed mood. But mood can also be depressed by ill health, by lack of exercise or of congenial activity, by anything that affects us adversely. Even dream emotions will have effects on organismic functioning and will contribute their share to the general mood.

Feeling and emotion. Linguistic usage seems to hint at a progression from pleasantness to pleasure, from unpleasantness to pain. Older writers have usually used the extremes of feeling, pleasure and pain, while psychologists have usually restricted their discussions to the terms pleasantness and unpleasantness, the more moderate feeling states induced in their experiments. Occasionally it has been held that the distinction between feelings and emotions is merely a difference in intensity; yet the extremes of feeling, pleasure and pain, are as intense as any of the experiences of intense emotion, for instance, intense fear or anger, joy or love. No matter how intense, pleasure and pain are not usually considered emotions.

Both feeling and emotion are based upon an intuitive estimate that something is "good or bad for me." But emotion is aroused by an object or a situation as a whole, rather than by a specific aspect of it; and in emotion, this object is appraised as good *for a specific action,* as good to eat or drink or embrace. In contrast, pleasantness of every degree up to the most intense pleasure is aroused usually by a particular aspect of the object and sensed via one sense modality, though eventually the motor system is affected also. The same is true for unpleasantness and pain.

The greatest intensity of feeling, pleasure and pain, is a reaction to somesthetic sensations. Sexual pleasure, for instance, is first the pleasure of touch, next the pleasure of muscular contraction, and finally that of muscular relaxation. All of these pleasures have a specific quality. Pain also is a reaction to somesthetic stimulation: to touch, pressure, heat, cold, or muscular spasm (see Pain, below). Both pain and pleasure do not lead to specific actions, as do emotions, but bring about general effects on the motor system. Pleasure results in relaxation, pain in muscular tension and movements of avoidance.

Degrees of pleasantness and unpleasantness are reactions to various sensations and activities, including emotions. If a man is afraid of snakes or of losing his job, that fear will affect him adversely; he will estimate it as unpleasant. As long as the danger remains, his fear will remain and so will his feeling of unpleasantness. But the fear never merges into unpleasantness.

Since feelings depend on the same sense judgment as do emotions, they should be mediated by the same central structures. At the same time, emotions also include a tendency to specific action and thus would seem to require an additional circuit. The brain circuits mediating both feeling and emotion will be discussed in a later chapter which will be devoted to a careful review of the neurophysiological evidence (see Ch. 2 in the following volume).

There are few experimental findings that demonstrate the difference between the two affective states, mainly because feeling and emotion have usually been taken as different either in complexity or intensity. Few psychologists have designed experiments that would demonstrate a qualitative difference. Gemelli (1949), who proposes a similar distinction, is an exception. He describes "objective feelings" which are reactions to sensations, for instance, feelings of hunger, thirst, well-being, discomfort, anguish, lightness, strength, and others. Emotions, which he calls "subjective feelings," are produced when a person "considers a situation or an object or a person in relation to himself" (p. 207).* Two quotations from introspective reports will suffice to illustrate his meaning:

The odor was disagreeable in itself, but the disagreeable sensation quickly disappeared when the stimulus ceased; immediately in my mind there arose a much greater repugnance, and different because it was not physical, causing an aversion to the source of the odor. I saw that this repugnance was caused in me by the memory of certain parasites, the smell of which had actually been presented to me as a stimulus. I felt also a strong movement of nausea, disgust and repulsion.

The sound was sweet and pleasant; but this pleasure gave way quickly to another pleasure which was more subtle. The sound evoked in me the memory of a particular incident in my recent vacation during which I heard this music; and I felt my soul pervaded with joy. This was something very different from the pleasure caused by the music itself—something more spiritual. I seemed to have become lighter, more active, and a feeling of well-being completely took possession of me. (Gemelli, 1949, p. 211)

In both reports there was first a feeling, strictly a reaction to the sensory experience, to the way in which odor and sound affected the person. Then came, according to the first report, the memory of the parasite that

* An equally good case can be made out for calling feelings "subjective" and emotions "objective": Feelings are reactions to a *subjective* experience, while emotions are reactions to *objects* or situations. Gemelli apparently considers that feelings are in a sense impersonal, the reaction to sensations which the person undergoes; hence he calls them "objective."

Since the terms "subjective" and "objective" can be understood in such an ambiguous way, we refrain from using them to distinguish feelings and emotions.

has such an odor, with an emotion of revulsion and disgust. In the second case there came the memory of an incident that brought great joy. In both cases there was a clear transition from attending to the way in which this particular odor or sound affected the person, to the realization of the object or the total experience and his reaction to it.

These reports exemplify Gemelli's contention that there is first an "objective feeling" which is then followed by a "subjective feeling," the emotion proper. Now it is true that there is always a reaction to the sensory aspect of a situation. But as soon as the person identifies it as coming from some object or being connected with some situation, he focuses on object or situation and feels himself repelled by it or drawn to it; and the feeling is lost in the emotion. Only when there is a clash between the way an object appeals to him and the way one of its aspects or qualities affects him will he become aware of both the emotion and the feeling. A man will seldom notice his wife's pretty new dress, for his affection for her overshadows his pleasure in her dress. But let her wear a hat that offends his taste and she will soon hear about it. It takes a special interest in clothes to notice them when they enhance someone we love and set her off to best advantage.

Gemelli postulates many other feelings besides pleasantness and unpleasantness, such as feelings of hunger, anguish, lightness, and strength. For him hunger and thirst are reactions to organic sensations, and hence "objective" feelings. We shall see later (in Ch. 6 of the following volume) that hunger includes both organic sensations and an impulse to eat. Sensations of lightness or strength can be felt as pleasant or unpleasant; but apart from such feelings, they surely are integrated organic sensations (see Subjectivity of Feelings, in Ch. 1). Feelings of anguish should perhaps be counted among "subjective feelings" or emotions proper, according to Gemelli's own definition, for they are all-pervasive and involve the person in his relation to a total situation. Well-being and discomfort seem to be what we have called "general feelings" of pleasantness and unpleasantness. Hence it seems that pleasantness and unpleasantness are the only dimensions of feeling that stand up to analysis.

EARLIER EXPERIMENTAL FINDINGS IN THE LIGHT OF OUR THEORY

Our theory can account for the facts explained by other theorists and also for those as yet unexplained. It includes the pleasure of functioning as its most important factor and explains pain as the result of greatly impaired functioning. Our definition of feeling can also account for other facts found in years of research by various psychologists, as surveyed by Beebe-Center or reported in later work.

The exercise of any psychological function requires some stimulus that calls it out. Some objects will permit a given function to work according to its natural design: sugar is one of the most important foodstuffs; color is the natural object of vision. Other objects will force it to work unduly: essence of skunk, a saw going through a nail. Hence we would expect some things to be naturally pleasant and thus liked, others to be naturally unpleasant and thus disliked.

Taste. It has been found experimentally that there is a natural liking for some tastes: sweet is most pleasant, sour much less so, and salty and bitter tastes least pleasant. Sugar is a natural food. This fact may be held in general to account for sugar's being considered to have universal pleasantness. But it is not the only food; thus its consumption is limited by satiation and its pleasantness decreases correspondingly under such circumstances. It is found less pleasant by adults than by children who actually need more of it. We have seen before (in Ch. 3) that salty and sour things become pleasant when needed in the economy of the organism. The taste of any food needed by the body is pleasant; but whenever that food is taken in excess, its taste will become less pleasant or cloying. It might be objected here that a drunkard will take far more than is good for him and still like his favorite drink. But he takes spirits not for their taste but for their effects. The connoisseur of fine wines or old brandy knows that these ought to be sipped, not gulped, and appreciates them for their bouquet, not their effects. He is in no danger of becoming an alcoholic as long as he remains a connoisseur.

Such an interpretation is supported by Richter's work on food preferences of rats. In a series of brilliant experiments he and his associates conclude that "nutritive deficits produce physico-chemical changes throughout the entire body, including the taste mechanisms in the mouth" (see Richter, Holt, and Barelare, 1938, p. 742). Young (1948) also agrees on the basis of his experiments that animals may become satiated by specific foods and refuse them. In this way he explains the known selection of a balanced diet by animals and young children when they are given free choice.

While babies and wild animals may depend on this mechanism of satiation, it is a fact that growing children, adults, and even animal pets may develop preferences for foods that are harmful or may eat more than they need. The art of cooking has made some foodstuffs highly appealing by cunning mixtures of tastes and odors. A child would soon stop eating honey and turn to bread or meat instead, but he is unable to withstand the delights of candy and ice cream. The same artificially stimulated pleasure of taste is the reason for overeating. Both human beings and animal pets find it difficult to forego that pleasure, particularly when there are few other pleasures to compete with it and exercise is severely restricted. Soon the sensations that signal stomach distention are no longer heeded. Eventually, the stomach enlarges and allows more eating. Clinicians find that adults overeat when they have few interests and little pleasure in their lives. But they may also overeat when they enjoy the good company that goes with lavish dinners. Even dogs overeat when they have learned to expect morsels from the master's table in addition to their own food. In overeating,* what is sought is not the satisfaction of hunger but the pleasures of taste, eating, and good company.

Smell. The order in which odors are rated as pleasant is also an indication of their effect on general functioning. Fragrant, spicy, and resinous odors are usually pleasant, putrid and burnt odors are usually unpleasant (see Beebe-Center, 1932). Putrid and burnt odors indicate something harmful. If their action is continued, not only olfactory functions but the total vital functioning will be disturbed. A pleasant fragrance means a place where it is good to be, while an unpleasant smell indicates something harmful. What smells putrid cannot be eaten and what smells burnt may threaten danger from fire. Vultures, no doubt, find the smell of decaying flesh attractive.

Hearing. Pure tones are rated as pleasant if they are low and faint, as unpleasant if they are high and loud (Young, 1943). Here it is even more obvious that a tone becomes unpleasant as soon as it threatens to harm the individual by injuring his auditory apparatus. A tone is pleasant as long as hearing is easy and listening requires no effort, but it is pleasant no longer when it becomes intense enough to threaten injury to the most sensitive part of the cochlea. Boilermakers and other workers exposed to intense noise eventually get used to it, but when they do their hearing is

---

* See Ch. 6, p. 177, in the following volume, for a discussion of overeating after brain injury.

no longer normal. Sensitivity to a whole range of sound has been destroyed. Here, also, unpleasantness indicates that the sensory function is disturbed.

Pain. The connection between intensity of stimulation and unpleasantness can be demonstrated in every sense modality. When stimulation becomes excessive, it will arouse pain. It is true, as Piéron points out, that the pain of dazzling light is the result of a spasm of the iris, the pain of loud noise the result of a spasm of the tensor muscle of the tympanum (Piéron, 1950). Similarly, the pain aroused by a pungent odor is produced by the simultaneous excitation of the trigeminal nerve (Elsberg *et al.,* 1935). The pain of heat and cold comes from a simultaneous excitation of nerve fibers mediating heat, cold, and pain (Dodt, 1954); it cannot be produced by stimulating the nerves that convey the sensations of heat or cold (Piéron, 1950). This confirms our suggestion that pain is always the reaction to excessive stimulation.

Excessive stimulation of any sense modality seems to excite somesthetic pathways also, either directly (for example, the trigeminal nerve in smelling ammonia) or indirectly by inducing a muscle spasm which results in excessive somesthetic stimulation. Such spasms guard against possible damage to the retina or auditory apparatus by inducing pain and leading the man or animal to avoid further assaults upon eye and ear. The pain from touch, pressure, prick, or cut may have a similar origin. There is a possibility that several nerve fibers are stimulated so that the combined stimulus amounts to excessive excitation. In the same way, the pain of heat and cold is mediated by the excitation of three different kinds of fibers. The free nerve endings which are held to be pain fibers may simply be additional touch receptors, excited only when stimulation becomes intense. There is evidence that free nerve endings mediate touch when the total excitation is reduced (Bishop, 1949; Sweet, 1950).

In the following volume (Ch. 2) we shall discuss the central structures that mediate the experience of pain. At present, it is sufficient to stress that the functioning of the various sense modalities is threatened by intense stimulation and that such excessive stimulation is appraised as harmful and is disliked. The object or situation that arouses it is called unpleasant or painful. Excessive stimulation produces tissue damage and muscular tension, and feeble stimulation means increased effort; hence both are unpleasant. But optimal stimulation enhances sense functions and induces muscular relaxation. This state of affairs is appraised as beneficial and is liked. The object or situation that induces it is called pleasant.

Touch. Softness and smoothness are more pleasing than stiffness and roughness (Beebe-Center, 1932). When something feels soft and smooth, the sensation can be savored to the full, because nothing threatens to injure the exploring hand.

Color. White is preferred over black, colors over white (and yellow), saturated over less saturated colors (Beebe-Center, 1932). The sense of vision is exercised by seeing colors; the deeper the color, the more agreeably.

There are, however, notable individual preferences. A particular color may be preferred for other reasons than its effects on visual functioning. A redhead may prefer blues and greens for dresses, rather than red or pink shades. Or a particular color may bring back a cherished memory. In the first case the knowledge of being dressed to best advantage, in the second case the memory, may enhance the state of functioning far more than the visual effect of the color.

The experimental finding that there are preferred objects for every sense modality makes its possible to say that a general trait of "readiness to be pleased" could not exist. Young (1943), who investigated this possibility, found that there is no correlation between the degree of pleasantness experienced on perceiving different objects, as there should be if every object would please equally. According to Young, affective responses depend on the circumstances of stimulation and on the sensory avenues that mediate the experience. As we have seen, our theory allows us at least to state the circumstances on which pleasantness or unpleasantness depends.

Form. It has been found that symmetry, balance, and completeness in visual forms are pleasant. According to Beebe-Center, the most important experimental contribution was to establish the general preference for the "golden section." Similarly, rhythm, balance, and completeness in musical forms are pleasant.

Beebe-Center raises the question to what the human being is responding in these cases, for rhythm, balance, and completeness are not given in sense perception. This puzzle cannot be solved as long as we assume that we experience sensations; but as soon as we realize that we experience objects rather than sensations, we see that rhythm, balance, and completeness are features of objects which we can appraise as such. Gibson (1950) has shown that two-dimensional figures are abstractions from the three-dimensional world of objects that we experience. In the same way, rhythm or symmetry in visual forms are special features abstracted from the object.

Many objects around us have shapes that correspond to the golden section, for instance, the heads and trunks of men and animals, leaves, trees, and flowers. The human being is adapted to living in a world of natural objects; he needs and uses them constantly—what wonder that their shapes are pleasing? To experience the golden section as pleasant or to like balance and symmetry simply means that we are at home in a world in which natural objects have balance and symmetry and are complete. Here also, what is beneficial, by and large, is experienced as agreeable. What does not correspond to the usual shape (for instance, deformed and mutilated beings) is thought strange, disagreeable, and, perhaps, even threatening.*) So attuned are we to the harmony found in nature that we try to recreate and even to better it in our works of art. The artist may use disharmony and dissonance, but only as means toward creating an artistic whole that is in itself balanced and harmonious.

Sense-bound feelings compared. It has been found that tones are more pleasant than colors, and colors are more pleasant than syllables (Babbitt *et al.,* quoted by Beebe-Center, 1932, p. 154). Syllables are merely parts of words without much meaning of their own. What they look or sound like may matter in poetry but not in everyday life. We are not interested in them and rarely attend to them because we are so intent on the meaning of the words they form. But we notice colors as they affect us, as they make us cheerful or depressed, as they make a dress look attractive or dowdy. And tones, whether in song or symphony, are appreciated by almost everyone. Hence it would seem that the pleasantness of tones, colors, and sounds depends on their relative importance to us. A painter should think colors more agreeable than tones; a musician should prefer tones—a suggestion that seems confirmed by common experience if not by experiment.

Piéron (1950) gives the approximate values of the relative "affective appeal" of various sense modalities, as contrasted with their "perceptive effectiveness":

* Perhaps the almost universal dislike of snakes has its ground in the fact that the snake, of all animals, departs most decisively from the shape of the golden section.

	Affective appeal	*Perceptive effectiveness*
Burn	10	2
Pinch	9	3
Prick, equilibrium, odor	8	4
Taste, cold, heat	6	6
Touch, audition	4	8
Vision	2	10

Though these affective values include both agreeable and disagreeable feelings, it should be remembered that it is far easier to produce unpleasantness and pain in the laboratory than pleasantness and intense pleasure. The order given by Piéron agrees with the degree to which vital functioning can be impeded but does not indicate the effectiveness of various sense modalities to induce pleasure and enhanced functioning. Burn, pinch, and prick indicate more intense stimulation and hence more interference with functioning than a slimy touch, a jarring dissonance, or a washed-out color. Odors, also, can be extremely unpleasant; so can be suddenly upset equilibrium. But touch (for instance, during sexual stimulation) can be far more pleasurable than taste or odor and can have a far greater affective appeal than a prick or pinch.

Our explanation of feeling seems to stand up to examination when confronted with experimental evidence. We shall see in later chapters that it also fits into a wider scheme in which feeling and emotion are affective responses to the environment, based upon the intuitive appraisal that something is good or bad for us. The only difference is that feeling is based upon the immediate, intuitive estimate of a particular aspect of an object or situation, while emotion is based on the immediate, intuitive estimate of the object as it affects us and demands a particular action.

Part II. THE NATURE OF
EMOTION IN HISTORICAL
PERSPECTIVE

5. PRESCIENTIFIC THEORIES OF EMOTION

Throughout the ages, men have thought about emotion, its nature, and its effects. How does it come about that some experiences have that particular quality we call "emotional"? Seeing a bear in the zoo arouses nothing but interest and curiosity—but seeing the same animal outside the zoo may arouse violent fear. What is the psychological process that turns a perception into an emotional experience? As we shall see, few theories of emotion have tried to explain how an emotion is aroused, yet it is the step from perception to emotion that should yield the clue to the distinctive quality of emotion.

Next, a theory must account for the effect of emotion. From common experience we know that emotion moves us, fills our days with light and shade, makes us actors rather than spectators in the drama of life. The effects of emotion are not always favorable or pleasant. Experimental psychology has shown that emotions disturb skilled functioning, that they interrupt and even disorganize well-integrated behavior. On the other hand, biologists claim that emotions have an emergency function and are useful for survival (Cannon's emergency theory). Clinicians, finally, in particular those psychoanalytically oriented, point out that the forces of love and aggression are the prime movers of human action, though an emotion like anxiety may be harmful. Our discussion of emotion should allow us to come to a theory that resolves these seemingly conflicting views. It should provide some way of distinguishing between various emotions and assessing their value for human life; it should also account for the differences as well as the similarities between human and animal emotions.

Science should explain but also predict and control. In psychology, we not only want to predict what will happen when a man is angry or afraid; we also want to know how these emotions are likely to be aroused and how they can be controlled. Such control must eventually be applied by the person himself—in the last analysis, it must be self-control. To discuss the control of emotion we shall have to discuss the motives for self-control as they apply to a man by virtue of his being human and also as they are adopted by each individual in his particular life situation. Here we shall inevitably be confronted with such norms of self-control as are needed for self-actuation.

what is an emotion?

Warren, in his *Dictionary of Psychology,* gives a variety of definitions of emotion (italics added):

1. An *experience or mental state* characterized by a strong degree of *feeling* and usually accompanied by *motor expression,* often quite intense.
2. *A total state* of consciousness involving a distinctive *feeling tone* and a characteristic trend of *activity.*
3. Non-discriminating or *mass activity* aroused by social situations, either perceived or represented by ideas; i.e. total responses of an organism in which a large proportion of the *experience* is made up of *visceral and somatic elements.*
4. The totality of *experience* during any period in which marked *bodily changes* of feeling, surprise or upset take place.
5. The dynamic *expression* of the instincts which may emanate from *conscious* or unconscious sources (Psychoanalysis).
6. The *conscious* concomitant of instinctive *impulses at work* (McDougall).*
7. A highly complex innate disposition within which instincts are organized as so many sensori-motor dispositions to particular bodily movements (Shand).
8. Affective accompaniments of obstruction of instinctive behavior (Drever).

Of these definitions, the first four emphasize both the experiential quality of emotion and the motor activity, excitement or upset. Definition 7 does not distinguish emotion from instinct but simply considers it as the "totality" of integrated instincts. Definition 8 is circular, using the tautological term "affective." The definitions that really attempt to define always include the experience as well as the motor aspect of emotion. In our further exploration we will try to discover first of all how that

* Another statement by McDougall: "To *experience* emotion is to be excited, to be moved to activity of some sort" (1933, p. 148).

felt experience is related to the extensive bodily upset, and secondly, how such an all-over effect can arise and how that arousal is explained in various theories of emotion. Since emotion differs in this respect from sense experience (which brings about changes in the sense organs and may or may not result in motor response, but never results in a total stirred-up condition), the explanation of the mechanism producing this all-over effect is crucial for any theory. So much so, in fact, that any theory that is silent on this point must be considered as unsatisfactory or at best incomplete.

When we examine the features to be explained in emotion, we find that at the base of every emotion there is some kind of perception or awareness of an object, a person, or a situation, which in some cases becomes emotional, in other cases remains (in the words of William James) a "cold perception." Therefore, it stands to reason that the perception that arouses an emotion must be somehow different from the mere perception of an object as such, which does not arouse an emotion. The felt emotional experience as distinct from the cold perception has often been called *the emotion,* while the observed (and felt) bodily upset has been treated as a separate phenomenon. The two phenomena could then be related causally, by assuming either that the emotion causes the bodily changes or that the bodily changes give rise to the emotion (and, sometimes, that their perception, the being aware of bodily changes, *is* the emotion). Most theories of emotion have accounted for the connection between emotional experience and bodily changes by assuming that one must cause the other; but few have tackled the problem of how the cold perception can cause either the felt emotion or the bodily upset. There has never been any doubt among psychologists, whether of the pre- or postexperimental era, that both the felt experience and the bodily upset necessarily belong together in the total emotional pattern. Psychologists have disagreed only in what they considered cause and what effect.

Aristotle and Thomas Aquinas. Aristotle, the first great systematizer in the field of emotion (as in so many other fields), was well aware that the causal relation could be treated in at least three different ways and that the view of the nature of emotion would vary accordingly. He says:

Now all the soul's modifications do seem to involve the body—anger, meekness, fear, compassion, and joy and love and hate. For along with these the body also is to some degree affected. An indication of this is that sometimes violent and unmistakable occurrences arouse no excitement or alarm; while at other times one is moved by slight and trifling matters, when the physical system is stimulated to the condition appropriate to anger. This is still more evident when, nothing fearful being present, feelings occur as in one who is frightened.

The natural scientist and the dialectician will define each of those modifications differently. Take the question, what is anger? The latter will say, a desire for retaliation, or something similar; the former, an effervescence of blood or heat about the heart. Of these, the natural scientist designates the matter, the dialectician, the form or idea. For this idea is the thing's form. This however must have existence in material of the sort in question; if it is a house, one formula will be "a covering to prevent destruction from wind and rain and excessive heat"; the other, "stones and beams and timber"; another "the form; in these materials; for those reasons." Which is the . . . [natural] definition? That which states the matter and ignores the idea? Or that which states the idea only? Or rather, the compound of both? (*De Anima* 1/1, 403a, b)

Thus Aristotle admits that it is possible to give a definition of emotion either by stating its object, therefore accounting for its arousal; or by describing only the physical symptoms of emotion. But he insists that a *complete* definition must include both: the matter, that is, the physiological changes observed and experienced, and the form, namely, the object to which these changes refer, which includes both the tendency and that toward which it aims—for instance, the desire for revenge and the related tendency to attack for the purpose of revenge.

According to Aristotle's description, the object arouses, say, desire—which is a tendency toward the object. This tendency is a felt attraction and also a physical motion, including bodily changes and facial expression; and it finally culminates in action (which may carry out the desire or resist it). For Aristotle, desire as a psychological experience is not a phenomenon completely separate from its motor aspect. The person sees, and desires. His desire is not exclusively psychological, but is physiological as well—it is a psychosomatic tendency, to use a modern term. Aristotle's terms differ; his meaning is the same:

Sensation . . . is like mere uttering and understanding; but, given a pleasant or painful object, the soul pursues or avoids with, so to say, affirmation or negation. To be pleased or to feel pain is to act in the sensitive mean in relation to the good or the bad as such; and pursuit or avoidance are this operation in act. And the faculties of desire and avoidance are not distinct,—nor distinct from the sensitive faculty; though in essence they differ. (*De Anima* III/VII, 431a)

Thomas Aquinas, commenting on Aristotle's description of desire and avoidance, makes the same point, namely, that emotions (or passions, in the terminology of the time) are distinct from sensation, and that the emotion is one tendency, both psychological and physiological, the movement from subject to object:

The good of the senses,—i.e. what suits them—gives pleasure; while what is bad,—i.e. repugnant and harmful to them,—causes pain. And pain and pleasure are followed, respectively, by avoidance and appetite (or desire); and these are a sort of activity. . . . (*Commentary* par. 768)

Thus the movement from sense-object to sense passes through three stages, as it were. There is first an awareness of the object as being in harmony or out of harmony with the sense: then a feeling of pleasure or pain; and then desire or avoidance. And although desiring, avoiding and mere sensing are different acts, still they are all acts of identically the same subject, though they can be distinguished in thought. (*Commentary* par. 769)

Aristotle, in effect, sees the cause of both the psychological experience and the bodily changes in a man's recognition of an object as good or bad, suitable or unsuitable for him. Desire and aversion (with their modifications) are constituted by the complex of psychological and physiological effects of this recognition. Thomas Aquinas follows him completely in this account. Desire and aversion are experienced by the embodied person and are aroused by objects real or imagined which that person deems suitable or unsuitable. In answer to our problem, how an emotion is aroused, Aristotle (and Thomas Aquinas) would suggest that the "cold perception" is transformed into emotion because the person or animal perceives something as good or bad for him, something that will give him pleasure or pain. This results in an attraction or repulsion that is felt all over; hence the sense estimate affects the whole organism in the resulting emotion.

Descartes' passions de l'âme. Compared with such a definition as that of Aristotle, which is psychosomatic in the best sense of the term, Descartes' fanciful mechanistic explanation is decidedly a step backwards. According to Descartes, "passions" are excitations of the soul referred to itself that are *caused, maintained, and reinforced* by the movement of animal spirits. The picture of the object is projected from the eyes to the pineal gland. If it is very frightening, that is, if it has many associations with things that were harmful in the past, the picture in the brain repels the animal spirits. These not only agitate the pineal gland, so that the soul senses the agitation and feels fear, but also flow

partly into the nerves which turn the back and move the thighs to flight; partly into those which . . . narrow the openings of the heart . . . so that the blood in the heart is thinned in a peculiar way and thereby sends animal spirits to the brain, which maintain and strengthen the fear. . . . For these spirits, by entering these pores, excite a peculiar motion in the pineal gland which is so arranged by nature that the soul feels this passion. (*Les passions de l'âme,* art. 36)

One and the same object may arouse fear in one man, courage or boldness in another; for, says Descartes, the brain is not arranged alike in everyone.

Quite apart from the conception of animal spirits which in Descartes' own time had been proved erroneous * there is a decided retrogression in the notion that mere mechanical association could alter the perceived image sufficiently to repel the animal spirits and agitate the pineal gland, which agitation is then perceived by the soul and referred to itself as something suffered, a passion. Descartes does not explain why the soul refers this agitation to itself, while an agitation aroused by organic pain is referred to the body. Nor does he explain how an object could arouse fear before any associations have been formed. Instead of Aristotle's active tendency toward the object (or away from it) that is felt psychologically and physiologically as a result of recognizing the object as suitable (or unsuitable), Descartes sees a passive soul stirred and afflicted by a bodily upset. This bodily upset is produced by the picture of the object that forms an "impression in the brain." For instance, for Descartes wonder is aroused *by the impression in the brain* that represents the object as rare and therefore worthy of close attention (art. 70). Joy is the pleasure of having something good which the brain impressions represent to the soul as its own. How brain impressions

* Harvey had discovered the circulation of the blood in 1628, a discovery which was accepted by Descartes as early as 1637, while his *Passions de l'âme* was not published until 1649. Harvey had pointed out that the blood is not rarefied by the heat of the heart to flow in the nerves to the brain, as Descartes thought. It was known at that time that the nerves were not hollow and did not transport a liquid substance. Hence Harvey had branded the animal spirits, resorted to for purposes of explanation, as an "asylum ignorantiae" (cf. Gardiner, Metcalf, and Beebe-Center, 1937).

can represent anything as rare or valuable or good, or as the soul's own, is quite inconceivable. After all, brain impressions are there, they are given; as facts of nature they can have no judgment, let alone a judgment of value.

We are sometimes inclined to look indulgently upon such statements, comfortably aware of our superior knowledge, and to excuse such lapses because at that time our knowledge was not available to men. But we must remember that Aristotle and Thomas Aquinas, who wrote long before Descartes and had no more factual knowledge of brain mechanisms, yet arrived at a knowledge of psychological processes far surpassing that of Descartes. Descartes' innovation of an immaterial soul confined in or communicating through a particular organ, the pineal gland, forced him to explain psychological processes mechanically. His expedient has raised the insuperable problem of interaction between soul and body that has dogged our steps to this day, produced contradictions between facts and values, and saddled us with a dualism from which there is no escape as long as we accept his basic premises.

It is idle to speculate how the psychology of emotion would have developed (or psychology as a whole, for that matter) if it had followed the Aristotelian-Thomistic tradition instead of starting afresh with Descartes. Perhaps the break in the religious tradition at first made it impossible to go back past Descrates and use the earlier knowledge, so that, when tempers had cooled, the new Cartesian-Kantian views, now firmly established, had produced the conviction that before Descartes there was nothing but theological prejudice. This hardly made it attractive to study older views for other than historical purposes. Science, as well as philosophy, was unable from now on to profit from the experience of past ages.

Descartes' brave new start, however, was little more than an admission of ignorance in the field of emotion. He declared in his *Passions de l'âme* that he was forced to start afresh because the ancients had contributed hardly anything to the topic, and the little they had provided deserved scant credence. In their extensive and competent historical survey, Gardiner, Metcalf, and Beebe-Center comment on Descartes' declaration:

It can hardly be denied that in the judgment he passes on his predecessors, Descartes shows both ignorance and lack of appreciation. On the purely descriptive side his work shows no advance on that of Aristotle, of St. Thomas, of Vives. His main emphasis is on the physiological conditions of the passions. But this was nothing new. (1937, p. 151)

As we have seen, not only is Descartes' treatment no advance over that of older writers; his psychological analysis is actually inferior to that of Aristotle or Thomas Aquinas. The immediate consequence of his treatment of the soul-body relationship was to accustom his successors to the view of two independent entities, one *res cogitans,* the other *res extensa,* having but the most tenuous connection through the pineal gland. No wonder the soul was soon discarded as so much excess baggage when it was found that the pineal gland has none of the functions Descartes ascribed to it.

In the Aristotelian-Thomistic tradition, the soul was not bound to any organ, nor did it move the body mechanically; hence the objections to the soul that apply to Descartes' conception do not apply here. It was conceived as the center of activity, that which acts in and through the living body, giving it its distinctive character as a stick or stone, flower or beast or man. It cannot be located anywhere, but can only be inferred from its activities—as electricity is not seen directly but is inferred from its effects or actions. That which acts—the agent, the person, the self—is active in knowing, wanting, doing. The acts of knowing, wanting, doing are not caused by something (the soul) that is apart from the body, but are acts of the total embodied person. The hand that grasps is not acting apart from the person who does the grasping. The soul, in Descartes' formulation something added to the body that could easily be discarded, would have proved far more vigorous if the Aristotelian-Thomistic conception had still been a living tradition. To discard something conceived as the center of activity, that which acts, would have been tantamount to giving up the concept of the self.

Although that concept suffered eclipse eventually, it was not given up without a struggle, nor until a considerably later stage. Whenever it was abandoned, this was done at the price of ruthlessly separating theory from practice, science from common sense. In practice, in everyday experience, the personal pronoun and its significance have never disappeared. I, me, and mine are points of reference for every man's thinking. Every man experiences the world in his own way, as it is arranged around him, as he is related to it.

The return of the self, in psychological theory, finally came about through the insistence of psychotherapists, from Freud to Rogers, who realized long before it occurred to academic psychologists that the person, as acting, knowing, wanting, and having goals, emotions, and purposes, is the central object of psychological understanding.

As the soul became a separate entity in the Cartesian formulation, sometimes moving the body but sometimes moved and afflicted by it, so emotion became a motion of the animal spirits disturbing the soul, but sometimes the result of the soul's agitating the animal spirits (when the soul thinks of something by nature connected with their motion). Thus Descartes separated not only the activity of the soul from the activity of the body but also the psychological experience (the "passion") from the physiological changes (motion of the animal spirits to the heart, viscera, and skeletal muscles). With such a complete separation of psychological and physiological causal factors, it is possible to have the emotion cause the bodily upset *or* the bodily upset cause the emotion.

Descartes himself has the body cause an affliction of the soul, and the soul cause a disturbance in the body. Later theorists have been more single-minded, unwilling to concede that an actual object would affect the body, while a thought or memory would be an activity of the soul. Some have held that an object (either seen or remembered) can excite the central nervous system in a specific way, thus arousing emotion which causes peripheral changes (central theory). Others have maintained that every emotional object, whether seen or remembered, excites the periphery directly, thus producing physiological changes that are felt as emotion (James-Lange or peripheral theory). In both types of explanation, the neural process is conceived of as essentially the same, but it is thought to give rise to emotion at different points in its course. As with Descartes, so with central and peripheral theories: the way in which a psychological process (whether perception, thought, or emotion) can produce physiological changes is left to the reader's imagination.

Descartes' position has been treated at some length because his solution (or rather creation) of the mind-body problem by separating soul from body and emotional experience from emotional expression has appealed to many later theorists. In fact, his influence is felt far beyond the specific area of emotion. His attempt, for instance, to derive a strictly deductive system on the basis of experiential facts is a forerunner of recent efforts to construct a mathematico-deductive system in various areas of experience (see Hull in the field of learning).

Descartes' theory of emotion may be unsystematic and even naive, but his influence has been profound. When it could no longer be supposed that the soul resides in the pineal gland, it was simply assumed that the human body can function without a soul, as does the animal body, according to Descartes. In contrast, a carefully worked-out system of emotions like Spinoza's has the advantage of consistency and even of elegance. But it was developed a priori, using facts of observation to illustrate his contentions rather than to verify them. As a result, Spinoza has had practically no influence on later thinking in this field. For this reason, Spinoza will not be discussed in the present survey, which is restricted to tracing the historical genesis of the present state of emotion theory.

Charles Darwin. The first man to deal with the relation of emotion to bodily changes on the basis of a large collection of factual (though anecdotal) evidence was Charles Darwin, whose book on *The Expression of the Emotions in Man and Animals* has long been a classic in the field.

Darwin proposed three principles to explain the origin of emotional expression. The very term "expression" presupposes something that is expressed, but Darwin never explicitly discussed the causal connection between the two. He gave no indication whether it is possible now, or was in prehistory, to have an emotional experience without appropriate bodily expression, or whether the bodily changes in emotional expression are the necessary conditions of emotional experience.

In his first principle, that of *serviceable associated habits,* he assumed that certain expressive actions (clenching one's fist, tensing one's muscles in anger) were originally used "to relieve or gratify certain sensations, desires, etc." by appropriate action. Through constant repetition, they became habits and were passed on from generation to generation. Startle, for instance, was originally a flight reaction. Darwin, after citing his observation of an infant 114 days old who blinked his eyes when someone rattled a box, continued:

It was obviously impossible that a carefully-guarded infant could have learnt by experience that a rattling sound near its eyes indicated danger to them. But such experience will have been slowly gained at a later age during a long series of generations; and from what we know of inheritance, there is nothing improbable in the transmission of a habit to the offspring at an earlier age than that at which it was first acquired by the parents. (1873, p. 39)

Darwin's assumption in this principle that acquired characteristics can be inherited is a little startling; it is an assumption more in line with Lamarckian than Darwinian evolutionary theory. Moreover, this assumption implies that our animal ancestors far back in evolutionary history did not have the startle reflex, but instead had to avoid danger by voluntary action. Similarly, angry expressions are supposed to have gradually developed from the voluntary actions made necessary by attack. This implies that voluntary movement gradually turned into reflex action. Darwin is quite explicit on this point:

It seems probable that some actions, which were at first performed consciously, have become through habit and association converted into reflex actions, and are now so firmly fixed and inherited, that they are performed, even when not of the least use, as often as the same causes arise, which originally excited them in us through the volition. (1873, p. 39)

It appears probable that starting was originally acquired by the habit of jumping away as quickly as possible from danger, whenever any of our senses gave us warning. (1873, p. 40)

Such a hypothesis implies that the early mammals must have been at a decided disadvantage in the struggle for existence, for voluntary movement is considerably slower than reflex action. Moreover, we know today that most expressive movements (smiling, laughing, frowning, and the like, as well as startle) are mediated by extrapyramidal pathways rather than by the pyramidal tracts from the motor cortex used in voluntary action. Similarly, the physiological changes during emotion are mediated by the autonomic rather than the central nervous system. Darwin admits the difficulty of assuming that a habit established through voluntary striped muscle action should become fixed and inherited as a reflex contraction of involuntary smooth muscles. He mentions the ruffled fur of angry animals and says:

If we could believe that the arrectores [pili] primordially had been voluntary muscles, and had since lost their stripes and become involuntary, the case would be comparatively simple. I am not, however, aware that there is any evidence in favor of this view; . . . Another explanation seems possible. We may admit that originally the arrectores pili were slightly acted on in a direct manner, under the influence of rage and terror, by the disturbance of the nervous system; . . . Animals have been repeatedly excited by rage and terror during many generations; and consequently the direct effects of the disturbed nervous system on the dermal appendages will almost certainly have been increased through habit and through the tendency of nerve force to pass readily along accustomed channels. (1873, pp. 102–3)

In this solution Darwin really assumes that emotion and emotional expression are already present and produce piloerection according to his third principle, "direct action of the nervous system." It almost seems as if animals had been attacking their enemies for generations before emotional expression became fixed, and that it must have taken countless additional generations before the physiological changes were properly established. The only alternative to this view is to assume that the emotion (anger) is actually the impulse that urges the animal to attack; but this interpretation is precluded by Darwin's effort to show how attack, flight, and other behavior patterns were originally voluntary and only gradually crystallized into an emotional reaction. He says:

The far greater number of movements of expression, and all the more important ones, are, as we have seen, innate or inherited; and such cannot be said to depend on the will of the individual. Nevertheless, all those included under our first principle were at first voluntarily performed for a definite object—namely to escape some danger, to relieve some distress, or to gratify some desire. (1873, p. 354)

Although the situations that arouse emotions existed then as now, the animal had to perform the correct action without the help of the emotions—which presupposes as great a degree of self-determination as can be expected of ideally reasonable human beings. When Darwin tells us in addition that such voluntary actions were deliberately adopted for some ulterior motive, we begin to wonder whether he does not ascribe more will and intelligence to the first mammals than he ascribes to us. Consider this passage, for instance:

As soon as with animals the power of erection [of hair] had thus been strengthened or increased [by habit] they must often have seen the hairs or feathers erected in rival and enraged males, and the bulk of their bodies thus increased. In this case it appears possible that they might have wished to make themselves appear larger and more terrible to their enemies by voluntarily assuming a threatening attitude and uttering harsh cries; such attitudes and utterances after a time becoming through habit instinctive. (1873, p. 104)

Human beings, as we know to our chagrin, cannot increase their stature by an inch, however much they might want to. But our animal ancestors evidently had a good try and at last succeeded.

Actually, it requires not less but more ingenuity to explain how animals at a low stage of evolution could have carried out a number of extraordinarily complicated actions by voluntary deliberation instead of by the inherent determination of an emotional impulse. To explain the expression of emotion in human beings as the inherited patterns of earlier purposive acts creates more problems than it solves, quite apart from the question whether such habits can be passed on to the next generation. Yet it is a curious fact that this principle of explanation has not only been accepted for many years without question but has been made the cornerstone of at least one comparatively recent theory of emotion (Dewey, 1894).

Darwin's second principle is the *principle of antithesis*. He says:

Certain states of the mind lead to certain habitual actions, which are of service, as under our first principle. Now when a directly opposite state of mind is induced, there is a strong and involuntary tendency to the performance of movements of a directly opposite nature, though these are of no use; and such movements are in some cases highly expressive. (1873, p. 28)

As an example, Darwin gives the instance of a dog who approaches a supposed stranger with a growl and a snarl. As soon as he discovers that the stranger is his master, his whole bearing is instantly reversed. Darwin points out that in this case "the animal is in an excited condition from joy; and nerve force will be generated to excess, which naturally leads to action of some kind" (1873, p. 51). In explaining this principle, Darwin again has to appeal to his third principle, "direct action of the nervous system." Here, as in explaining his first principle, he assumes that emotion produces an excited condition of the nervous system, therefore giving rise to various physiological changes, as well as to action of some kind. If he has to have recourse to this principle for all physiological changes that require the autonomic nervous system and for all movements that are of no use, we begin to wonder just what emotional expressions are left to which the evolutionary principle of associated serviceable habits does apply.

Darwin's third principle, that of *direct action of the nervous system,* is used to make up for the deficiencies of the other two principles. In particular, it is designed to account for the changes in heart rate, circulation, perspiration, etc. during emotion. Yet Darwin always gives primacy to his first principle, insisting that the main reason for bodily changes is to be found in past serviceable acts. He says, for instance:

All these signs of rage are probably in large part, and some of them appear to be wholly, due to the direct action of the excited sensorium. But animals of all kinds, and their progenitors before them, when attacked or threatened by an enemy, have exerted their utmost powers in fighting and in defending themselves. . . . An inherited habit of muscular exertion will thus have been gained in association with rage; and this will directly or indirectly affect various organs. (1873, p. 74)

Here Darwin asserts that the exertion of attack or flight affects various organs and produces changes in them, which must be inherited in turn to explain their association with rage and fear when there is no actual fight or flight.

Summing up, it is fair to say that the principle of serviceable associated habits, the mainstay of Darwin's theory, rests on a very doubtful basis. It cannot be accepted at all unless we have evidence that acquired characteristics can be inherited, and so far we have none. Even if such evidence can be found, we must approach with caution a view that may imply that even instincts (mating, foodgetting, nestbuilding) are remnants of serviceable habits. Darwin's aim undoubtedly was to account for the complicated pattern of emotional expression and associated physiological changes by an evolutionary fixation of habits that started as simple voluntary action. When it comes to instincts, such an account raises doubts. How could the complicated behavior pattern of mating and caring for the young (let alone the physiological changes that go with it) have developed from voluntary action? Without the powerful impetus of instinctual desire, the first mammals would have had an impossible task. Surely these patterns presuppose an inherent impulse that directs them and makes them pleasurable, rather than being the result of voluntary actions that would be neither easy nor pleasant.

It was the impossibility of accounting for physiological changes as remnants of voluntary action that led Darwin to propose his third principle, which really is his main contribution to the theory of emotion. At the stage of knowledge current in his time, an "overflow" of excitation into every available channel was credible and could account for autonomic changes. We must credit Darwin with having recognized the connection of strong nervous excitation with emotional expression, even though his account of the origin of this connection is not convincing. If an overflow of excitation is useful, as Darwin assumes, that usefulness either is another evolutionary acquisition to be explained in turn, or must be inherent in the mammalian economy. Similarly with the physiological changes that go with mating or eating and drinking. Without the mechanisms of reproduction and digestion the acts of mating or eating would be quite useless; and without a natural impulse to mating or eating the animal would never hit upon these actions.

Darwin himself gave priority to his first principle of serviceable associated habits because it fitted in with his evolutionary theory. His second principle, that of antithesis, is not an explanation but a statement of the observed fact that some emotions have an opposite (joy and sorrow, like and dislike). Whether an emotional pattern was explained by his first or his second principle, Darwin always had to take recourse to his third principle, that of overflow of nervous excitation, to explain the physiological changes that go with it. Hence his third principle is the real mainstay of his theory, and it is actually this principle that has influenced thinking in this area to the present day. We shall see that "overflow of excitation" is assumed in many later theories, particularly by psychoanalytic theorists.

6. THE DAWN OF SCIENCE: FROM JAMES TO DEWEY

Darwin's theory did not tackle the question whether emotional experience causes bodily changes or vice versa. Still, his exposition seems to imply that "emotional expression" must have something to express, and that this something is the emotional experience. This view, held for many centuries, was turned upside down by William James and Carl Lange.

THE JAMES-LANGE THEORY

William James. In his famous theory of emotion (1884), William James suggested that the causal relationship between emotional experience and physiological changes goes in the opposite direction from that assumed by Darwin and his predecessors beginning with Descartes: that "the bodily changes follow directly the *perception* of the exciting fact, and that our feeling of the same changes as they occur *is* the emotion" (1884, in: Lange and James, 1922, p. 11). The bodily upset causes the felt emotion which is simply the combination of organic sensations. Of these, the visceral changes seemed to James the most important because most widespread. Like Darwin, James explained the various patterns of physiological changes and changes in facial and postural expression as the evolutionary remnant of once useful adjustments.

In addition, he had recourse to an explanation Darwin rejected, namely the "principle of reacting similarly to analogous-feeling stimuli." He explained: "Winking is the effect of any threatening surprise, not only of what puts the eyes in danger; and a momentary aversion of the eyes is very apt to be one's first symptom of response to an unexpectedly unwelcome proposition" (1922, p. 132).

To say that we react similarly to similar-feeling stimuli is an excellent common sense explanation. But the example of blinking used by James is the only case that fits his theory, and that only because a startle reflex is present in every case of surprise. When there is no reflex reaction, the principle does not explain the analogous-feeling. To avert one's eyes because of an unwelcome sight is one thing; but to recognize that an unwelcome proposition feels similar to an unwelcome sight is quite another. We would have to recognize the disagreeableness of the proposition before averting the eyes—but in James's system the analogous-feeling emotion of distaste can come only *after* the action and the associated physical changes.

James faced the problem that some such recognition or appraisal is necessary between the cold perception and the physical changes, but did not solve it. He admitted that we must recognize or appraise another man's attitude toward us before we react with emotion:

The consciousness of his attitude toward me is the perception that normally unlocks most of my shames and indignations and fears. . . . This being so, it is not surprising that the additional persuasion that my fellow-man's attitude means either well or ill for me should awaken stronger emotions still. What the action itself may be is quite insignificant as long as I can perceive in it intent or animus. That is the emotion-arousing perception. . . (1922, pp. 19–20; italics added).

Such "persuasion" could hardly be called a "cold" perception. Rather, it is the very realization of something good or bad, favorable or unfavorable for the person that is thought by Aristotle and Thomas Aquinas to arouse a felt attraction or repulsion. In a later article (1894) William James put the problem even more concisely, answering some critics:

The same bear may truly enough excite us to either fight or flight, according as he suggests an overpowering "idea" of his killing us, or one of our killing him. But in either case the question remains: Does the emotional excitement which follows the idea follow it immediately, or secondarily and as a consequence of the "diffuse wave" of impulses aroused? (1894, p. 518)

The use of the term "idea" (James's quotation marks) conceals the fact that this idea is not a simple perception as is the perception of the bear as a bear, apart from his intentions towards me or mine towards him. Moreover, that "idea" does not come as a simple associative link, as James implies, but comes as the result of some realization or estimate that this can be fought or this must be fled. Thus a lion will attack but a doe will flee. There must be some kind of an appraisal whether to attack or to flee, for there is a different reaction when the animal's condition changes: a sated bear will avoid a man, a hungry bear will attack him; a rat will ordinarily run from a man, but a cornered rat proverbially fights. In all these cases, the running and fighting are not accidental (whether accounted for by an association of "ideas" or of responses), but are based on some estimate that this thing means harm and, also, that it can be fought or avoided.

William James himself explains the choice of attack or flight as a mechanical association of ideas based on past experience, and insists that this association of present situation with past danger produces the visceral changes felt as emotion. But mechanical association cannot account for the connection of this situation with a past dangerous one. We may have seen bears in zoos or pictures of bears innumerable times, may always have liked them and never thought of danger from them. Yet the moment we encounter a bear in the wilderness he "suggests an overpowering idea" of his killing us or of our killing him—why? Sheer association would bring back only the many earlier perceptions in which there was no hint of either fight or flight—whence this particular idea, and whence its overpowering force? In this explanation James really presupposes an appraisal that the bear is harmful. It is the realization that this bear means danger for us that makes this particular idea of "bear" overpowering by driving everything else from our mind. The appraisal that the bear might kill us is not just an "overpowering idea," it is a practical judgment that arouses emotion and demands action.

James resorted to the mechanism of association only to explain why either one of two serviceable habits may be aroused. The arousal itself is strictly a reflex act for him. But even a reflex requires some sensorimotor mechanism for its arousal. With spinal reflexes, the connection between receptors and effectors is direct, via the reflex arc. But with other reflexes, like the sucking or swallowing reflex, the connection is rather more complicated. When we come to reflexes in which there is voluntary muscle action as well as autonomic excitation (and emotion is such a reflex, in James's view), the "arousal" requires something more than the mechanical connection from receptor to effector. The startle reflex to a sudden loud sound is an example of a mechanical connection. But to turn the typical startle response into flight, it is necessary to recognize the sound as indicating danger. When loud noises are often repeated and no harm results, animals begin to disregard them—which must mean that this particular sound is no longer perceived as dangerous. Similarly, in experiments with human beings, it has been shown that repeated experiences of falling in a collapsible chair always arouse startle responses, but that the emotion of fear occurs only as long as the person thinks there is danger (Blatz, 1925).

James expressly emphasized that it is not the action itself but the simultaneous visceral excitation that is felt as emotion. Hence he refused to recognize as emotion various emotional episodes reported in a fifteen-year-old boy, who was entirely anesthetic, inside and out, with the exception of one eye and one ear. Dr. Strumpell, whose patient he was, reported that the boy had shown shame after he soiled his bed, and grief at the thought that he could no longer taste the flavor of his favorite dish. He also repeatedly quarreled with other boys. James, however, insisted that this case did not contradict his theory because the boy's expressions of emotion might be entirely automatic: "just as he satisfied his natural appetites and necessities in cold blood, with no inward feeling, so his emotional expressions may have been accompanied by a quite cold heart" (1922, p. 107).

James consistently held that the realization of a given object as harmful or beneficial to the person is simply an "idea" like any other, that touches off visceral changes directly by virtue of its association with past actions. If these visceral changes cannot be sensed, James believed, there can be no emotion, even though there is emotional action and expression. One might wonder how anyone could quarrel without emotion or why the "cold" perception that a dish is tasteless could produce even the *expression* of grief in the boy, or why he should *show* shame when he does not feel it, for these emotions are not produced by "naturally appropriate" stimuli.

It seems certain that in the case of Dr. Strumpell's patient his total anesthesia meant also the disappearance of what we have called "sensory feelings." The boy could no longer experience the pleasures of taste, touch, and smell, and could no longer sense the distention of bladder and bowel. But quite obviously he felt the lack, talked about it, grieved over it. To agree with James, we would have to say not only that the boy's emotional expressions were accompanied by a quite cold heart but also that he was a consummate hypocrite, and a first-rate actor.

Finally, James claimed that "the best proof that the immediate cause of emotion is a physical effect on the nerves is furnished by *those patho-logical cases in which the emotion is objectless"* (1922, p. 107; italics added). Yet the occurrence of some condition in disease does not prove that it is a normal condition. When a patient loses his appetite, it does not mean that the intake of food normally occurs without appetite. If there is "objectless" emotion in neurosis or psychosis, it does not mean that emotion normally needs no object. Moreover, as Dewey pointed out some years later, most emotions that seem "objectless" to the observer either have an object from the beginning for the psychotic, or are pro-vided with one as a secondary rationalization. There may well be a "physical effect on the nerves" in some cases, produced either by an im-balance of endocrine secretions (as in climacteric depressions) or by drug injection; in these cases what is produced is a *change in functioning,* not an emotion. Normally every *emotion* begins with the perception of some object or situation, real or imaginary. We cannot assume a direct "physi-cal effect on the nerves" that comes with some perceptions and not with others unless we can state the conditions under which any perception will or will not produce this particular effect.

Carl Lange. Almost simultaneously (1885, one year after James's first article), Carl Lange proposed a similar interpretation of the causal rela-tionship between felt emotion and bodily changes. Unlike James, how-ever, he thought that changes in the circulatory system, rather than visceral changes, were responsible for emotional experience. For him, changes in blood pressure, pulse rate, etc. produce not only felt emotion, but other bodily changes (visceral, postural) and physical action. Lange, as well as James, held experiential evidence in slight esteem when he decided that there is no so-called "mental" emotion apart from perceived physiological changes. Lange, for instance, claimed that it is impossible to distinguish between a "mental" and a "physical" emotion, that there is only "(1) a cause—a sensory impression which usually is modified by memory or a previous associated image; and (2) an effect—namely the above mentioned vaso-motor changes and consequent changes in bodily and mental functions" (1922, p. 64).

Lange considered that the only difference between vasomotor changes produced by physical or chemical means (fever, cold, drugs) and those produced by a sense impression is the *knowledge of the different cause.* The pronounced difference in self-relevance between, say, the knowledge that this is a dog and the realization that this dog can harm me was con-sidered neither by James nor by Lange. Thus Lange can say:

It is not difficult to prove now, and by means of the most ordinary and well known experiences, that emotions may be induced by a variety of causes which are utterly independent of disturbances of the mind, and that, on the other hand, they may be suppressed and modified by pure physical means. . . . It is one of the oldest experiences of mankind that "wine gladdens the heart" and the power of alcoholic liquors to reduce sorrow and fear and to substitute joy and courage has found application, which is in and for itself natural enough, and would be most wholesome, if the substance did not produce other effects in addition. (1922, p. 66)

But surely there is a decided difference between the joy that comes from wine and the joy of the lover when he meets his beloved, a difference that cannot be explained by pointing to the abstract knowledge of a difference in cause. The lover now has what he loves and wants and is glad. But the wine that "gladdens the heart" does so because of its physiological effects, not because its presence brings joy. Under the influence of alcohol, a man's mood is altered so that he is more easily pleased by things that otherwise would not please, and ceases to worry about problems that normally would occupy him. In the first kind of joy, a man has something to rejoice in; in the second, he is more easily pleased. Indeed, if there is little to please a man, alcohol may make him belligerent or maudlin. But the longed-for possession of something he loves will never arouse anything but joy. Alcohol and similar drugs do not *arouse* an emotion, they merely change the way in which things may affect us.

Lange, like James, saw the problem of explaining how an emotion is aroused. He also wrestled with the way a "cold" perception is turned into an emotion, but offered no real solution:

When I begin to tremble, if threatened by a loaded gun, it is evidently not the sense-impression which causes the fear, for a loaded gun looks just like an empty one, which I would not have noticed at all. What, then, happens in the brain, when an affection is induced by a sense impression that can have no direct effect upon the vascular nerve center as can a loud report, etc.? (1922, p. 75)

His solution is demonstrated on a simpler example, that of a child crying as soon as he sees a spoon that has been used to give him nasty medicine. The sight of the spoon, according to Lange, has become associated with the discomfort produced by the medicine; the neural pathway from visual center (sight of spoon) to motor center (weeping from the taste) is opened up by irradiation, to which the pathway producing weeping is most susceptible because facilitated by previous use. The obvious objection to such an explanation is the fact that the child may have been fed with the same spoon for every meal, including his favorite dessert, hence the sight of the spoon could touch off a smile more easily than weeping.

In addition, the use of this example obscures the fact that the very first sight of a gun pointed at us (if we believe it is loaded) will arouse fear even though this particular danger may never have occurred before. A mere mechanical association of sense impressions with previous circulatory or visceral upsets simply will not do, because in many cases mechanical irradition or association may touch off several different patterns with equal ease. Moreover, such an explanation can never account for the first time we feel emotion when we recognize something as dangerous, or pleasant, or annoying. Finally, such an expedient leaves all the intervening steps to the vaguest kind of imagination, and in default of a precise description is always ready to fall back upon the formula: "Of course, the process is much more complicated in most indirect affections" (Lange, 1922, p. 78).

To do justice to James, Lange, and their defenders, it ought to be said that their main intention was to discredit the only alternative they knew, namely the view that the physical changes were the result of "mental" emotions that were somehow interpreted or misinterpreted as "forces which stand outside of the body and control it" (Lange, 1922, p. 79). The psychophysical parallelism of the time, hailing from Descartes and maintaining that soul and body are two distinct and separate entities, certainly gave good grounds for this interpretation.

The James-Lange theory has aroused perhaps more controversy than any theory of emotion before or since. We shall examine its factual basis in Chapter I of the following volume when we discuss Cannon's critique of it. At this point we propose to preserve historical continuity by discussing Dewey's two articles on emotion, in which he tries to make clear the organic connection between the James-Lange theory and Darwin's explanatory principles.

JOHN DEWEY ON EMOTION

Dewey recognized that only one of Darwin's three principles can provide an adequate explanation for the James-Lange theory. This is the principle of associated serviceable habits which can explain how certain situations can arouse a particular behavior pattern that is felt as emotion. If, as Darwin claims, acts that were useful for survival eventually became habits and were passed on to succeeding generations, it is reasonable to suppose that these habits could be called out whenever the original occasions for such acts recur. Neither James nor Lange had realized that Darwin's two other principles postulate an earlier emotion which later arouses the organismic response by association. These two principles cannot explain how the cold perception could directly arouse the bodily response that is felt as emotion, as the James-Lange theory demands.

The principle James had used to supplement Darwin's three hypotheses is similarly unsatisfactory. It is the principle of reacting similarly to analogous-feeling stimuli, and presupposes, as Dewey showed, that something is felt as similar though feeling is a result of the bodily reaction. To be consistent, this principle "must be translated into the statement that activities which involve, in like fashion, the same peripheral structures, feel alike" (1894, p. 554). Dewey even claimed that this principle is an impenetrable mystery to any central theory; but the mystery vanishes when the discharge theory replaces the older view:

Left as Darwin and Wundt state it, all mediating machinery, physiological and psychological, is absent, and we cannot even start a hypothesis as to *how* a feeling (recognizing that it feels *like* another feeling!) sets out along the same afferent paths. Upon the discharge theory the mystery vanishes and we have the practical tautology: like affections of like structures give like feeling, the interest lying in the genetic tracing of the details. (1894, p. 554, footnote; Dewey's italics)

But the mystery is precisely the problem we are discussing here, seen by everybody and explained by none: how do we recognize that this situation feels like another, or, in other words, why does this situation arouse the same emotions, and why (or how) does any situation arouse an emotion? Dewey, finding no mediating machinery or explanation, promptly disregards the problem, yet problem it remains, in his or any other formulation: if "like affections of like structures give like feeling," how does it come about that this particular situation affects like structures? When James suggests, for instance, that winking has become by analogy the reaction to any threatening surprise, or that wrinkling the nose in disdain is connected by analogy "with movements having a perfectly definite olfactory function," how does it come about that situations that reveal no physical threat and in which there is no unpleasant smell affect the eyelids as would a blow and the nose as would a stench? James's own solution begs the question, as we pointed out before; but Dewey's answer simply ignores it.

Darwin's second principle, the principle of antithesis, is completely inconsistent with the discharge (James-Lange) theory, and Dewey accordingly refused to consider it:

There is something intolerable to the psychologist in the suggestion that an opposite emotion can somehow select for itself channels of discharge not already used for some specific end, and those channels such as give rise to directly opposed movements. Antithesis is made a causal force. Such an idea is not conceivable without some presiding genius who opens valves and pulls strings. The absence of mediating machinery, of interlinking phenomena, is even more striking in this case than in that of "analogous feeling." (1894, p. 567)

To explain the facts, Dewey pointed out that the dog's attitude of affection and humility on seeing his master consists of movements that indicate "the attitude of receiving favor and food from another." Dewey also accepted G. H. Mead's suggestion that there may be movements included in this attitude that are remnants of a previous sexual pattern.

Now there may well be something intolerable in the supposition that an emotion can select new channels of discharge; but is it any more intolerable than the supposition made necessary on the Darwin-Dewey-Mead hypothesis that every action (including mating) had to select such channels in the dawn of evolutionary history? If reflexes and instinctive patterns were only gradually built up, then action must have been deliberately selected until it became a firm habit. In reducing Darwin's second principle (antithesis) to his first principle of associated serviceable habits, Dewey seems to imply that every action without exception was, as Darwin thought in the case of fight or flight, the result of deliberation.

But the story is even more complicated than that. According to Dewey, "upon evolutionary principles, the limited, adjusted, and useful discharge must be a differentiation, selected and perpetuated because of its utility in the struggle for life, out of an original more diffuse and irradiating wave of discharge" (1894, p. 561). First in evolutionary sequence, then, is a diffuse wave of discharge as a response to a stimulus, any stimulus;

gradually it is differentiated into serviceable (deliberate) action; finally that serviceable action becomes reflex and is inherited as instinct and emotion. One wonders how the dumb animal could survive if a stimulus simply aroused "a diffuse wave of discharge." Certainly it would be impossible for any animal in one lifetime to learn to convert such diffuse discharges into even one coordinated action, like surrounding and digesting a morsel of food, as does the amoeba. It is commonly agreed that the human being is more flexible, better able to learn than any animal lower in the evolutionary scale. Yet for the human being it is necessary to have some inherently determined patterns of coordination before any coordinated action is possible. We know, for instance, that no amount of teaching will make it possible for a small child to tie a shoelace, or to write, before maturation has made such coordination feasible. And what is maturation but the development of inherited, therefore determined, patterns of coordination? Without any such inherent determination, an organism would be quite unable to learn even the most primitive coordinated movement of fight or flight, let alone hunting for food, or mating.

It almost seems as if during the last century evolution had been made to bear the burden of scientific explanation borne in earlier centuries by natural teleology. Once upon a time it was explained that fishes have fins because they were made to swim. With the advent of evolutionary theory we were informed that they have fins because they developed them during evolutionary history. Now it is possible that either or both of these statements may be true, but they are not scientific explanations. Granted that fishes swim or birds (and airplanes) fly, what is the mechanism that makes swimming and flying possible? Granted that we experience emotion and can observe it in others, what is the design of the living being (the mechanism) that makes emotion possible? There is a more basic question: What was the origin of this design; was it the blind striving for survival or the coordinated plan of a designer? This question is legitimate also and no scientist can ultimately avoid it because it will influence his theoretical interpretations. But the answer will have to come from philosophy and not from the various sciences that seek to find explanations for the actions of their scientific objects within their own field.

Dewey finally left evolutionary explanations when he discussed Darwin's third principle, that of direct nervous discharge (idiopathic response, in James's terms) and reduced it to a breakdown of inherited adjusted movements. Or perhaps we should say that here he dealt with disturbances that have not yet been subjected to evolutionary selection. James as well as Darwin used this principle to explain physical changes in emotion that could not have been serviceable or that could not be explained by other principles. James was tempted to ascribe the visceral changes (which for him are the emotion) to direct action on the nervous system, a drainage of excitation over autonomic pathways. Dewey, however, gave a purposive twist to the principle of direct nervous action: Idiopathic changes represent a disturbance of coordinated action.

Dewey simply postulated different kinds of usefulness. There are the movements that *prepare* serviceable actions (holding of breath, opening of eyes and mouth, strained attention, shivering and crouching). They are felt as fear, caution, anger, and come under the principle of associated serviceable habits. Then there are somatic changes (emotional attitudes in Dewey's terminology), like smacking of the lips, wrinkling of the nose, etc., that are the remnants of an evolutionary *culmination of action* (finding food, etc.); they are felt as satisfaction or disgust, and had been explained by James under the principle of "analogous-feeling." When *expanded and reinforced,* the attainment of the goal results in bodily attitudes that are felt as joy; when *attainment is missed,* the results are felt as grief. These types of excitation, formerly explained under the principle of antithesis, become parts of useful action in Dewey's system. When action is immediate and smooth, when coordination between stimulus and response is complete, there is no emotion. But if the action is delayed and cannot be completed, each phase of it slips out of joint, is exaggerated, and becomes chaotic. This breakdown of habitual coordination results in so-called "idiopathic changes," felt as excessive emotion. Thus Dewey has brought both useful and apparently useless actions under one purposive principle: in the one case, it is the visceral excitation itself that is felt as emotion, in the other it is the interference with action that is experienced as emotion. In his own words:

We thus get an a priori canon, as it were, for determining when, in a given emotion, we shall get symptoms falling under the "serviceable associated habit" principle and when under the idiopathic. Whenever the various factors of the act, muscular movement, nutritive, respiratory and circulatory changes, are co-ordinated and reinforce each other, it is the former; whenever they interfere (the "idiopathic"), the "feel" of this interference *is* (applying the general principle of James) the pathological rage, or terror, or expectation. (1894, p. 564)

This interpretation gives a curious chameleon quality to emotion: now it is the "feel" of action or preparation for action, now it is the "feel" of interference. According to Dewey, when an act has once been useful, though it may not be today, there will be inherited associated changes that are the *normal emotion;* when an action that has once been useful, is still useful today, and can be completed immediately and smoothly, there is *no emotion.* Yet in fact there is the same pattern of muscular, nutritive, and respiratory changes. Why are they not felt alike? On the other hand, when these excitations interfere with one another, then we feel (according to Dewey) not the excitation, but the *interference, as excessive emotion.*

There are two problems here that Dewey does not solve: First, if there is no emotion when the response is perfectly coordinated with the stimulus, there can be no difference between immediate, lusty attack, and an action like hammering in a nail—yet in the one case there is somatic excitation derived from associated serviceable habits, and in the other there is not. On Dewey's own premises there ought to be emotion; and in actual experience there is. Secondly, how is the interference between various reaction tendencies to be felt? In the case of visceral changes there are sensations that *are* the emotion for Dewey; but in an interference we could sense only the end result: if the action lowers blood pressure and the interference raises it, we could sense only the net result, medium high pressure, not the interference as such.

But Dewey claimed that his attempt had definitely made any central theory of emotion impossible:

The fact, if it be a fact, that all "emotional expression" is a phase of movements teleologically determined, and not a result of pre-existent emotion, is itself a strong argument for the discharge theory. . . . If every emotional attitude is referred to useful acts, and if the emotion is *not* the reflex of such acts, where does it come in, and what is its relation to the attitude?

The first half of the hypothesis prevents its being the antecedent of the attitude; the latter half of the hypothesis precludes its being the consequent. . . . I think, then, that logic fairly demands either the surrender of the "central" theory of emotion or else a refutation of the argument of the preceding paper, and a proof that emotional attitudes are to be explained by reference to emotion, and not by reference to acts. (1895, pp. 13–14)

Of course, Darwin's own position was *both* that "emotional expression is a phase of movement teleologically determined" *and* that it is "a result of pre-existent emotion," as we have seen in our discussion. It was

Dewey who reduced Darwin's three and James's four principles to one, that of coordinated or disturbed useful excitations. We have also shown that the mainstay of both Darwin's and Dewey's theories, the principle of associated serviceable habits, (*a*) is not a scientific explanation; (*b*) displaces the mechanism of arousing emotion from ontogeny to phylogeny without explaining it; (*c*) creates two new problems: one of converting voluntary central nervous system action into autonomic habits, the other of explaining how appropriate action can be learned within one lifetime without preformed pathways of coordination; and (*d*) is dependent upon the view that acquired habits can be passed on to succeeding generations, which is not generally accepted. Hence "emotional expression" (or emotional attitude, as Dewey called it) cannot be explained as the remnant of previously useful acts, and therefore is not a fact and cannot be used as argument for a discharge theory.

Thus the argument of Dewey's first half of the hypothesis seems to be fairly disproved. What remains to be found is the proof demanded by him "that emotional attitudes are to be explained by reference to emotion, and not by reference to acts."

This means coming to grips with Dewey's own contribution which he developed on the basis of the James-Lange theory. This is the view that emotion is not only the inherited remnant of once serviceable actions but also the "feel" of disturbed action tendencies. He first found this explanation necessary for grief. The phenomena of grief, he said,

are phenomena of loss. Reactions surge forth to some stimulus, or phase of a situation; the object appropriate to most of these, the factor necessary to coordinate all the rising discharges, is gone: and hence they interfere with one another—the expectation, or kinaesthetic image, is thrown back upon itself. (1894, p. 560)

Here an action in the present cannot be completed because the loved object is lost. But there are other cases where the action cannot be completed because the situation arouses conflicting reactions, and thus a disturbance arises that is felt as *excessive* rage or terror (pathological emotion). In either case, the incomplete reactions or the conflicting reactions must be "instinctive"; but the mechanism of their arousal is passed over in silence, as it is with James. However, the disturbance happens in the present, not in the evolutionary past, thus Dewey's contribution sounds a new note in the scientific explanation of emotion.

But eventually, in his later article (1895), emotion became a phase in a mode of behavior that attempts to coordinate response to stimulus. As long as coordination fails or is not immediate and smooth, there is emotion—hence all emotion (whatever its evolutionary explanation) becomes the sign of a disturbance. Following James, Dewey held that the organic discharge (which *is* the emotion) is an instinctive reaction, not a response to an object or an idea as such. He continued:

Following the lead of this idea, we are easily brought to the conclusion that *the mode of behavior is the primary thing, and that the idea and the emotional excitation are constituted at the same time; that, indeed, they represent the tension of stimulus and response within the coordination which makes up the mode of behavior.* (1895, p. 19; Dewey's italics)

Dewey, then, made action basic to knowing and feeling—so much so that we only know what we do when we do it; only then do we know toward what we are going, and that we like what we approach and dislike what we avoid. To make such a view palatable at all, Dewey refused to recognize any sequence of seeing-running-fearing, and accused James, who did, of atomistic leanings. For Dewey, everything happens all-together-all-at-once. There is an "instinctive coordination" between the act of seeing-touching (which constitutes the object) and the act of running-trembling-etc. (which constitutes the emotion).

Action not only comes before emotion; it even comes before perception. According to Dewey, we do not perceive an object until we move toward it—hence our action constitutes the object: "It is just as true to say that the sensation of sound (or sight) arises from a motor response as that the running away is a response to the sound. . . . Indeed the movement is only for the sake of determining the stimulus, of fixing what kind of stimulus it is, of interpreting it" (1896, p. 362). But how can we move toward anything unless we first see it *as an object,* located somewhere in space, or unless we locate the sound as coming from somewhere? Our movement will not integrate a "buzzing, booming confusion" for the simple reason that there is nothing to move toward; we need an integrated object before movement toward it becomes possible. This can be demonstrated from reports of adults with congenital cataract whose sight was restored by operation. They saw at first not objects but colored patches that seemed to touch their eyes, and the only movement possible was an attempt to protect their eyes (Senden, 1932). If it is not possible to move toward anything unless it is seen as a *thing,* located in space, then flight or fight are also impossible unless there is something to be attacked or something to be fled. If movement cannot constitute the object, then fleeing or fighting cannot constitute it as an object to be fled or to be attacked. This is the difficulty Dewey saw, but could not solve on his premises; hence he was forced to an extreme expedient:

If my bodily changes of beating heart, trembling and running legs, sinking in stomach, looseness of bowels, etc. follow from and grow out of the conscious recognition, *qua conscious recognition,* of a bear, then I see no way for it but that the bear is already a bear of which we are afraid—our idea must be of the bear as a fearful object. (1895, p. 19; Dewey's italics)

Dewey, of course, was absolutely right: if the emotion is aroused by a perception, it cannot be a "cold" perception. But he was wrong in saying that the emotion is already assumed in the recognition of the bear as a fearful object. All that is necessary is that we recognize the bear *as affecting us in a certain way* instead of merely perceiving him as a thing apart from us. As soon as such a recognition comes, it arouses an emotion, though the bodily changes obviously may take considerable time to develop. But Dewey had committed himself to the James-Lange theory, though he recognized its inconsistency in dealing with this particular problem. Logically, he could not admit that the emotion is aroused by an object, once he had claimed that it is merely the feel of bodily changes. So he continued:

But if (as Mr. James' fundamental idea would imply, however his language may read at times) this reaction is not to the bear as *object,* nor to the *idea* of bear, but simply expresses an instinctive coordination of two organic tendencies, then the case is quite different. It is not the idea of the bear, or the bear as object, but a certain *act of seeing,* which by habit, whether inherited or acquired, sets up other acts. It is the kind of coordination of acts which, brought to sensational consciousness, constitutes the bear a fearful or a laughable or an indifferent object. (1895, p. 19; Dewey's italics)

Here again, the only remaining expedient to save the discharge theory is to appeal to *inherited* habit aroused by its *original* object. Dewey to the contrary, acquired habit will not do because on his own premises there is no way in which such a habit could be acquired. If the object is recognized as frightful or delightful only with the action, how would anyone hit upon that action if the object is not one that arouses it instinctively? If any other than a hereditary stimulus is encountered, there is no way short of a recognition that this is to be fled or to be attacked, that could arouse the hereditary pattern of flight or fight. Dewey could not even resort to association, for that would imply some recognition that this object is like a past one—and the object is recognized only with the action.

The more Dewey tried to explain this difficulty, the more involved he became. He insisted that the distinction between a nonemotional and an emotional experience is simply a difference in reflective interpretation:

We have but the one organic pulse, the frightful bear, the frightened man, whose reality is the whole concrete coordination of eye-leg-heart etc. activity, . . . the distinction of cold intellectuality and warm emotionality is simply a *functional* distinction within this one whole of action. We take a certain phase which *serves a certain end,* namely giving us information, and call that intellectual; we take another phase, having another end or value, that of excitement, and call that emotional. . . . But does any one suppose that, *apart from our interpretation of values,* there is one process in itself intellectual, and another process in itself emotional? The eye-touch process gives us information . . . the heart-bowels process gives us the valuation of this information in terms of our own inner welfare,—but aside from this distinction of values within a concrete whole, through reflection upon it, I can see nothing. (1895, pp. 21–22; Dewey's italics)

But the question is wongly put: there is no intellectual *process* as against an emotional *process,* there are two different *types of experience,* one of a thing as it is apart from us, the other of the way this thing affects us.

This, of course, is completely obscured in Dewey's theory, to the point where an action done at the height of emotional experience is equated with a nonemotional action. According to Dewey, emotion disappears as soon as action is fully engaged in. As an illustration, he mentioned his own feeling during a youthful fight. Before the fight, he said, he felt irritation and anger, but during the fight itself he was aware "of nothing but a strangely vivid perception of the other boy's face as the hypnotizing focus of all my muscular activities" (1895, p. 29). Surely, that face was something to be hit hard, and the hitting was not done in cold blood with full deliberation. It was an experience totally different from that of punching a bag, for instance, in which situation he would have been fully aware of everything around him. What Dewey's reminiscence shows is that emotion can become so intense that we are aware only of the object and of nothing else, not even ourselves. During intense emotion, we do not reflect, but that means that emotion is at its height, not that it has disappeared.

Finally, Dewey tried to explain why emotion, upon his own showing "a mere organic repercussation," should have such significance and value for human life. Since emotion occurs when there is tension between two instinctive processes, the significance must be found in that tension:

The tendency to large diffusive waves of discharge is present, and the inhibition of this outgoing activity through some perception or idea is also present. The need of somehow reaching an adjustment of these two sides is urgent. The attitude stands for a recapitulation of thousands of acts formerly done, ends formerly reached; the perception or idea stands for multitudes of acts which may be done, ends which may be acted upon. But the immediate and present need is to get this attitude of anger which reflects the former act of seizing into some connection with the act of getting-even or of moral control, or whatever the idea may be. The conflict and competition, with incidental inhibition and deflection, is the disturbance of the emotional seizure.

Upon this basis, the apparent strangeness or absurdity in the fact that a mere organic repercussation should have such tremendous values in consciousness disappears. This organic return of the discharge wave stands for the entire effort of the organism to adjust its formed habits or coordinations of the past to present necessities as made known in perception or idea. The emotion is, *psychologically, the adjustment or tension of habit and ideal,* and the organic changes in the body are the literal working out, in concrete terms, of the struggle of adjustment. (1895, pp. 29–30; Dewey's italics)

This is the fourth and last change which emotion underwent at Dewey's hands: first it was an inherited habit; then it functioned only if there was no action; still later, it became the tension between two instinctive processes (one the "organic discharge," the other the "idea" or perception) which had to be reconciled in action; now it is the successful reconciliation of this tension. But this time the process of transformation will not work, even with the expedient of making things happen all together all at once. If action is basic and constitutes both the object (in the sensori-motor process) and the emotional attitude (in the vegetative-motor process) how can the perception or idea stand for acts which *may* be done? As long as there is no action upon the object there can be no idea, if we follow Dewey, for the action also constitutes the idea. There is no room for a proposed "ideal" action. The sensorimotor process could at most incorporate previous actions that have controlled the vegetative-motor process, and have overcome the obstacle without fighting. But in that case, how could the vegetative-motor process incorporate the adjustment of the tension between the two processes? If there is control, it must come from the process that incorporates the "ideal," not from the process that "reflects the former act of seizing." And if anger is the felt disturbance or tension between the two processes, that tension surely must become greater as there is an increasingly stronger habit of control—hence the emotion must become more and more violent, or—to speak in the manner of James and Dewey—pathological. Emotion might possibly be the felt tension between habit and ideal, on Dewey's premises, although the mechanism by which it is felt would be doubtful; but it could never "stand for the entire effort of the organism to adjust its formed habits of the past to present necessities." Hence the significance of emotion in the economy of human living remains unexplained.

Dewey's contribution represents an ingenious attempt to make the James-Lange theory self-consistent. But his remedy is worse than the original difficulty. To support James's main contention of the inverted sequence of seeing-running-fearing, he had to obscure the issue by substituting one continuous action that *constitutes* both the object and the emotion. As a result, he could not explain the action, for there is no object that could be acted upon; and he could not explain the emotion, for there is as yet no object to be loved, hated, feared, or attacked.

Emotion can no more be explained as the result of action than can feeling (as we have seen in Ch. 2). Unless approach and withdrawal or the associated serviceable habits are instinctive, they must obviously be aroused by a recognition that action is required and of what action is feasible. Sticks and stones can be aroused to action by mechanical motion, but living beings must *initiate* action when they perceive something they want, or want to avoid. Even if acts are instinctive for some objects (food, water, mate), there must be a recognition that this particular thing is to be approached, that to be avoided, which will initiate both emotion and action. Such recognition must be a sensory function similar to (but not identical with) the perception of an object as an object instead of as disconnected sensations. In addition, the undoubted significance of emotion in human life cannot be explained at all on Dewey's premises, but becomes obvious if emotion follows the *felt* recognition of an object as suitable or unsuitable, harmful or beneficial.

CONFLICT THEORIES

Dewey's theory of emotion has been treated in some detail because its philosophical basis (transactionism) is very much alive today, particularly in social psychology. Moreover, his theory is important in the field of emotion for historical reasons, even though simpler thinking can meet his challenge. Soon after Dewey, the phylogenetic explanations of Darwin and James began to lose their appeal. Even in Dewey's system, as we have seen, they were soon superseded by his preoccupation with emotion as a sign of tension between action tendencies. Dewey had accounted for joy as an expansion of activity in its culmination, and had never quite reconciled this and similar emotions with his later view of emotion as disturbance or tension. But later psychologists began to concentrate more and more on those emotions that could be called more obviously the product of conflict. Eventually the very fact that emotion shows a general bodily upset came to be taken as a sign that it is a product of conflict. Claparède is one of many who take this view. He says:

Emotions occur precisely when adaptation is hindered for any reason whatever. The man who can run away does not have the emotion of fear. Fear occurs only when flight is impossible. Anger is displayed only when one cannot strike his enemy. . . . Analysis of bodily reactions in emotion points to the evidence that one does not make adaptive movements, but on the contrary, reactions which recall the primitive instinct. . . . Far from being the psychic side of an instinct, as McDougall teaches, emotion represents on the contrary a confusion of instinct, "a miscarriage of instinct" as Larguier des Bancels has said. And, as in emotion, we can prove not only the vestige of the ancestral reaction but also the confusion or insufficiency of the acquired reaction, so we can, perhaps, with more justice define emotion as a "miscarriage of conduct." (In: Reymert, 1928, p. 127)

Obviously, this is no improvement on Dewey's theory, whose argument is both more subtle and more persuasive. Similarly Angier (1927), restating Dewey's view, Howard (1928), and others substantially develop the theory of conflict Dewey had propounded three decades before. For all of them, emotion is the result of conflict, of some interference with ongoing action tendencies. The complementary notion, of course, is bound to be that emotion has a disturbing if not harmful effect on the organism. With this aspect we shall deal later in more detail (see Ch. 9, in the following volume). At present we merely note that such a view is a partial development of Dewey's original suggestion. His emphasis on emotion as subordinate to action, and constituted by action, is left aside, and with it his explanation of such emotions as joy. As a result, conflict theorists have had a difficult time explaining emotions like joy and desire. Bentley (1924), for instance, considers emotion the result of a "predicament" and then wonders whether joy is a real emotion, since there can be no "joyful predicament"! True enough, if all emotions are the result of conflict, joy cannot be an emotion. But we too often forget that the premise still has to be proved.

Conflict theorists usually prefer the James-Lange theory in accounting for emotional experience, but are not restricted to it. When it comes to explaining the mechanism by which emotion is aroused, they assume that the arrest of the activity in progress or its disturbance is the necessary and sufficient condition. But an action tendency may be arrested without arousing an emotion: A child may fall asleep over his toys; or he may be busily playing and suddenly see a playmate and run off to play with him. In neither case is there any conflict emotion as the result of the arrested activity. Moreover, although there must be some difference in the way in which activities are arrested to produce such varied emotions as fear and anger, yet this difference is not explained. There is no explanation as to either what occasions such an arrest of action or how it is brought about. It is very rarely a physical restraint that arouses emotion. Most of the time, it is the arrest of an action tendency because of seeing, hearing, or remembering something that is dangerous, annoying, or enjoyable. To state simply that this arrest occurs "under the influence of a stimulus from without," as do Paulhan (1930) and many others, is not an explanation of the process.

The conflict theory postulates a cause of emotional phenomena without specifying the way in which this cause produces its effects. Even on its own terms, the theory can explain the arousal only of some emotions, not of others; and it offers nothing new regarding the direction of the causal connection between emotion experienced and emotion expressed.

7. EMOTION AND INSTINCT AS SEEN BY McDOUGALL AND FREUD

In contrast to the conflict theorists, McDougall sees emotion as a component of instinctive action. Instead of a disturbance, it becomes an ingredient of all action which, for McDougall, is necessarily rooted in instinct. His explanation of the causal relations connecting object, emotional experience, and bodily changes is different both from Darwin's and from the James-Lange-Dewey conception.

MC DOUGALL'S INSTINCT THEORY OF EMOTION

For McDougall, instinct (inherited propensity) and emotion are always combined. The object that arouses the propensity simultaneously arouses the emotion. When a conative disposition (an instinct) is aroused to action, it is experienced as an impulse or desire and associated with an emotion. McDougall takes desire to mean simply the impulse to action and never deviates from this view. For him, desire or wanting is not an emotion but a conation, which, however, is always connected with an emotion according to its special mode of action.

The distinctive quality of the emotion is ascribed to the bodily changes in emotion, but these bodily changes differ according to the instinct they express:

As the primitive appetition and aversion became differentiated into impulses directed toward more special goals and evocable by more special objects and situations, each specialized impulse found expression in some special mode of bodily striving with some corresponding complex of bodily adjustments facilitating and supporting that mode of bodily activity. . . . Each such system of bodily adjustments is reflected in the experience of the striving

organism, giving to each specialized mode of striving a peculiar and distinctive quality. (1928, p. 202)

If the quality of the emotion is determined by the kind of physical
changes induced, the experience must follow these changes. To this extent
McDougall accepts the James-Lange theory, although he insists repeatedly
that it cannot be accepted in its extreme form.

For McDougall, the total pattern of affective changes is aroused together
with the instinct; it is the instinct that makes it possible to be emotionally
excited and to act. An instinctive action is the outcome of

a distinctly mental process, one which is incapable of being described in purely
mechanical terms, because it is a psycho-physical process, involving psychical
as well as physical changes, and one which, like every other mental process,
has . . . three aspects . . . the cognitive, the affective, and the conative
aspects; that is to say, every instance of instinctive behaviour involves a knowing of some thing or object, a feeling in regard to it, and a striving towards or
away from that object. (1926, p. 27)

The instinct itself is an innate disposition that makes the organism
sensitive to special objects and disposes it to appropriate actions. Such objects arouse the disposition or propensity, and with it emotional excitement and action:

We may, then, define an instinct as an inherited or innate psycho-physical
disposition which determines its possessor to perceive, and to pay attention to,
objects of a certain class, to experience an emotional excitement of a particular
quality upon perceiving such an object, and to act in regard to it in a particular
manner, or, at least, to experience an impulse to such action. (1926, p. 30)

Of the three aspects in every instinct, the cognitive and the conative
aspects are held to be modifiable, while the affective aspect remains comparatively unchanged. The primary emotions of the higher animals are
recognizably similar to the corresponding human emotions.

Unlike Dewey, McDougall sees emotion as facilitating action, not as
the sign of a failure of coordinating action with the stimulating situation.
Unlike Darwin, he insists that instinct and emotion belong together, that
both are integral parts of the instinctual pattern, while Darwin implies
that action was originally voluntary and eventually formed a habit pattern that became handed down as a pattern of emotional expression.

The arousal of emotion. When it comes to the arousal of both instinct
and emotion, McDougall is unusually explicit:

Now, the psycho-physical process that issues in an instinctive action is initiated by a sense-impression which, usually, is but one of many sense-impressions received at the same time; and the fact that this one impression plays an altogether dominant part in determining the animal's behaviour shows that its effects are peculiarly favored, that the nervous system is peculiarly fitted to receive and to respond to just that kind of impression. The impression must be supposed to excite, not merely detailed changes in the animal's field of sensation, *but a sensation or complex of sensations that has significance or meaning for the animal;* hence we must regard the instinctive process in its cognitive aspect as distinctly of the nature of perception, however rudimentary. (1926, p. 29; italics added)

Here McDougall recognizes as did Dewey that there is some distinction between ordinary perception and the realization that this is significant or meaningful *to me,* that this affects me. Since this recognition happens in animals as well as in human beings, it cannot be an elaborate inference but must be a sensory estimate. Dewey refused to consider this possibility because he erroneously thought such recognition would presuppose the emotion; McDougall seems to accept it as a process of cognition belonging to the instinct and allied to ordinary perception, though not identical with it. But later, when he explains how other objects than those naturally determined can arouse an instinct, he resorts again to association, as did so many before him. His explanation now becomes as mechanistic as that of his contemporaries who viewed instinctive action as a mechanical reflex. To illustrate the way in which the instinct of fear is aroused by originally indifferent objects, McDougall quotes the example of birds on an uninhabited island. At first they show no fear of man, but when men begin shooting them, they soon fly away whenever a hunter approaches. McDougall points out that a sudden loud sound is a natural stimulus of the instinct to flee with its emotion of fear, and continues:

We may suppose that, since the visual presentation of the human form repeatedly accompanies the excitement of the instinct of fear by the sound of the gun, it acquires the power of exciting directly the reactions characteristic of this instinct, rather than indirectly by way of the reproduction of the idea of the sound; i.e., we may suppose that, after repetition of the experience, the sight of a man directly excites the instinctive process in its affective and conative aspects only; or we may say, in physiological terms, that the visual disposition concerned in the elaboration of the retinal impression of the human form becomes directly connected or associated with the central and efferent parts of the instinctive disposition, which thus acquires, through the repetition of this experience, a new afferent inlet through which it may henceforth be excited independently of its innate afferent inlet. (1926, p. 38)

Thus McDougall assumes that the mere sight of men becomes associated with the sound of their guns, and the instinctive fear of the sound accordingly becomes an acquired fear of men. But only two pages before, McDougall had stated that "on repeated experience of noises of certain kinds that are never accompanied or followed by hurtful effects, most creatures will learn to neglect them" (p. 36), and referred particularly to wild creatures browsing undisturbed by the familiar noise of a railway train. Here the animals surely have learned that the noise of the train does not harm them; similarly, the birds in the first illustration must have learned that the noise made by hunters does harm them.

McDougall refuses to consider this possibility because "such an account would err in ascribing the change of behavior to a purely intellectual process." But if a loud sound can arouse fear by a "rudimentary perception" of it as "something significant and meaningful to the animal," why cannot the sight of the hunters, the sound of the guns, the confusion and noise of frightened birds—the whole picture—arouse such a "rudimentary perception" that this is dangerous, which is aroused again as soon as any part of that picture recurs? Once McDougall is willing to admit that instincts can be modified, that animals can learn to discriminate between harmful and harmless noises, this is by far the simplest explanation.

For McDougall, however, such modification of instinct is a change in the "perceptual disposition, the afferent inlet of the instinct." But he gives us no clue as to just how that change is brought about. Unless the animal can somehow discriminate between harmful and harmless things, either a given object must always arouse its appropriate instinct or it can never do so. Indifferent objects could possibly be connected with naturally coordinated objects by association; but a *natural* object of fear that loses the ability to arouse the instinct cannot be explained so easily.

Moreover, if by some miracle the instinct could suddenly cease to be aroused by its natural object, it would be impossible to explain how the object could again acquire its old power. The same animals that have learned to browse peacefully while the train roars past would quickly scatter on its approach if men began shooting them from the train windows, even though the sound of the guns could hardly be heard over the noise of the train. As far as the natural stimulus (the noise) goes, it would remain the same: unless we grant that the animals realize that the originally harmless train is now harmful, we cannot explain how their fear was restored.

The same reasoning holds for the fear of anything strange. McDougall rightly points out that this is one fact of many that cannot be explained by a mechanical scheme for the arousal of instinctive action; yet he himself offers no explanation. A whole group of things and situations that have nothing in common except that they are *unknown* cannot possibly be naturally coordinated to the instinct of fear. Unless we admit that animals can estimate whether a situation is dangerous or not, and that they can act upon previous experiences and estimates, we have no way of explaining such fears. If we accept the hypothesis that animals are capable of an immediate estimate of things as harmful or beneficial, we can explain not only how they can acquire fears or lose them but also why the young animal has so few fears and can be tamed so easily: the young animal has never had the experience of men that hurt, and of things that jump out from behind a tree or bite in the darkness. Once such an estimate is granted, it is easy enough to explain how it can be modified by experience that confirms or disproves it. Without such an "estimative" function we can never explain how this discrimination could be developed, trained, or changed. We may not know for certain what is the mechanism of this function.* But neither do we know the exact mechanism by which we ourselves, as well as animals, perceive objects as objects.

McDougall, however, cannot explain the arousal of emotion except by assuming that initially certain objects have an innate power of arousing the integrated instinctive pattern. How they can lose that power or how they can acquire the power of arousing an entirely different instinct (as they must do when an unfamiliar and therefore frightening object becomes well known and liked, for instance) is quite inconceivable.

McDougall's theory is further limited by his view that emotions must be connected with particular instincts, and that instincts are the only sources of action. This view forces him, first of all, to make as complete a list of instincts as is possible: in his latest version he lists eighteen. It also forces him to exclude *desire* as an emotion, which is contrary to common experience and usage; to list some instincts without a corresponding emotion; and to call primary emotions many states that are not commonly

* For a tentative description of the "estimative" system see Chapters 5 and 6, in the following volume.

recognized as emotions (for instance, subjection). There is the *propensity to construct shelters and implements* (constructive propensity, No. 12), for which he lists no emotion. Perhaps this propensity could claim "interest" as its emotion, except that interest is shown not only and not even primarily in making things (i.e., in instinctive action) but in seeing, hearing, or knowing things. On the other hand, there is the *propensity to laugh at the defects and failures of our fellow creatures* (No. 14) that has an emotion (humor) but no impulse to action.

Derived emotions. McDougall's assumed connection of instinct and coordinated emotion forces him to classify as "derived emotions" or "complex feelings" many emotions that seem primary in common human experience—much more so, at any rate, than some of the "primary" emotions listed by McDougall. Under secondary emotions, for instance, he mentions joy and sorrow, as well as hope, anxiety, despair, regret. These "complex feelings," says McDougall, are really derived from the simple feelings of pleasantness and unpleasantness, since they are functions of all instinctive striving:

If we strongly desire to attain a goal and if the road to it lies straight and open before us, we do not hope; rather we go forward energetically, with confidence; and, when we attain it, we experience intense pleasure or joy or joyful satisfaction. It is when some shadow of uncertainty lies upon our way that we hope. And when the shadow grows darker, we become anxious. If it deepens still further, so that attainment seems improbable, we despond. And if attainment seems definitely impossible, we despair. All these complex modes of feeling, then, are functions of desire looking forward to its goal; hence they have been called prospective emotions of desire. (1933, p. 157)

These "complex feelings," then, depend on instinct as such and qualify it; they are not connected with any particular instinct as are emotions.

Secondary emotions, or "complex feelings," like the simple feelings of pleasantness and unpleasantness, accompany successful or unsuccessful striving. McDougall considers pleasantness and unpleasantness primary feeling states out of which complex feelings have gradually differentiated.

But we have seen in Chapters 3 and 4 that pleasantness is attached not only to successful striving, unpleasantness not only to unsuccessful striving; the two states indicate quite generally the way in which anything affects our functioning. There is at least this difference between unpleasantness and anxiety, that in anxiety there is no thought of our functioning, however disturbed that may be, there is only disturbance over what obstructs us, concern over the delay in reaching our goal. Here, as in McDougall's "primary" emotions, attention is centered on the object toward which we strive, not on the way in which it affects our functioning. Such a change of regard is hardly credible as a mere differentiation or specialization of one and the same function. Feeling, to put it differently, is concerned with our way of acting or striving, whether smooth or difficult, agreeable or disagreeable. But emotions (whether primary or derived, in McDougall's terms) are *directed toward an object,* and reveal various intensities of striving: greater intensity in hope or anxiety, arrest in despondency and sorrow. Joy indicates cessation of striving and rest in achievement.

Emotion as excitement. Finally, McDougall's view of emotion as "excitement" limits his theory. At first glance such a view makes plausible the distinction between *impulse,* in his scheme the simple tendency toward something, and *emotion* as the felt commotion accompanying this tendency. But in common experience, desire or wanting is itself felt as commotion, very noticeable before action has begun. In its further course, it may be accompanied by hope or anxiety, depending on the conditions we meet, but desire is experienced as an emotion whenever we contemplate the goal. While there is always a generalized bodily commotion, an "all-over" attraction or repulsion, the degree of excitement surely varies with the intensity of striving. Desire becomes overwhelming when possession is possible but long deferred. The excitement of desire is reduced when its goal is easily accessible. But to stipulate that emotion *consists* in excitement is to mistake one of its necessary but variable conditions for its very essence.

Emotion seen as excitement also forces McDougall to the view that emotion disappears if an action is often repeated; this favors the conclusion that tender emotion must disappear when a mother has to protect her child more actively. Since it is obvious that something persists, whether we call it emotion or not, McDougall has to postulate enduring "sentiments" in its place, following the lead of Shand, who proposed this term for "an organized system of emotional tendencies centered about some object" (McDougall, 1926, p. 126). McDougall explains that sentiments include many emotions. So the sentiment of love induces tender emotion in the presence of the beloved object, "fear or anxiety when it is in danger,

anger when it is threatened, sorrow when it is lost, joy when the object prospers or is restored . . . gratitude towards him who does good to it, and so on" (1926, p. 128). But surely the emotions themselves do not change by being included in a sentiment. A threat to the beloved object evokes fear because a threat to what we love threatens us, too; the loss of anything that is ours, no matter how trivial, causes sorrow (in however slight degree) and joy when it is restored to us. What wonder that the intensity of the emotion will be increased if our attachment is strong? But the quality will remain the same; it will still be sorrow or joy.

While there is an obvious difference between an attraction that is fleeting and one that endures, so that the word "sentiment" might well be used to indicate its permanence, there is no reason why a whole host of emotions should be collected together with this lasting attraction, and should even be provided with a common neural substrate, as in McDougall's treatment of sentiments.

There is no need to discuss any others of the many speculative theories of emotion. They have been propounded by psychologists, not philosophers, and are often based upon sound observation and some experimental evidence, but they flower as often into a host of highly speculative generalizations. Such theories as Troland's or Marston's are elaborate hypotheses in speculative neurology, so general as to be unverifiable. It is not our purpose to give an exhaustive historical survey but merely to demonstrate by a few examples the various possible solutions to the persistent question: What is the nature of emotion? and to examine such evidence as we have in order to decide among them. We shall now turn from academic theories to a theory that has grown out of clinical observation and treatment.

FREUD'S THEORY OF EMOTION

Freud's interest was not primarily in emotion, nor in unraveling the causal relation connecting the emotional object, the subjective experience, and the bodily upset. His attention was centered on personality and its disturbances as revealed in clinical observation. No wonder he found that emotional difficulties of one kind or another played a far greater role than purposive activity. To describe this role, he found he had to concentrate on the most powerful driving force in all organisms, the sexual impulse or libido. Like McDougall, he postulated that the sexual impulse is instinctual, experienced as an emotion and leading to action. Unlike McDougall, he claimed that the libido is the only driving force urging to constructive action.

*Instincts.** For Freud, the libido or sexual drive is a constant force that can become attached to many different objects in the course of life. It is not the object that arouses the instinct but the instinct itself that directs the choice of object:

An instinct differs from a stimulus in that it arises from sources of stimulation within the body, operates as a constant force, and is such that the subject cannot escape from it by flight as he can from an external stimulus. An instinct may be described as having a source, an object and an aim. The source is a state of excitation within the body, and its aim is to remove that excitation; in the course of its path from its source to the attainment of its aim the instinct becomes operative mentally. We picture it as a certain sum of energy forcing its way in a certain direction. . . . The aim can be attained in the subject's own body, but as a rule an external object is introduced, in which the instinct attains its external aim; its internal aim is always a somatic modification which is experienced as satisfaction. Whether the relation to a somatic source gives the instinct any specific character, and if so which, is not at all clear. . . . (1933, p. 133)

The aim of the libido is pleasure, and pleasure is equated with quiescence: the instinct has reached its goal and has come to rest. It follows that excitation is equated with unrest, even pain. Hence Freud assumes that there must be a defense against any excitation, whether external or internal. This defense is achieved by the organization of the superego (see Ch. 9, in the following volume, for a discussion of superego formation) which uses instinctive aggressive forces against the libidinal urge. The instinct of aggression works in opposition to the erotic instinct, an opposition deeply rooted in evolutionary history:

If it is true that once in an inconceivably remote past, and in an unimaginable way, life arose out of inanimate matter, then, in accordance with our hypothesis, an instinct must at that time have come into being, whose aim it was to abolish life once more and to re-establish the inorganic state of things. If in this instinct we recognize the impulse to self-destruction of our hypothesis, then we can regard that impulse as the manifestation of a death instinct, which can never be absent in any vital process. And now the instincts in which we

* German: *Trieb,* which means instinct in the sense of *inherent driving force.* It has been translated as instinct, impulse, or drive.

believe separate themselves into two groups: the erotic instincts, which are always trying to collect living substance together into ever larger unities, and the death instincts which act against that tendency, and try to bring living matter back into an inorganic condition. The co-operation and opposition of these two forces produce the phenomena of life to which death puts an end. (1933, p. 147)

Freud found clinical evidence for the fusion of these two instincts: sadism and masochism represent a mixture of love and cruelty, turned either against someone else or against oneself. In masochism, sexual pleasure is found in suffering, which for Freud implies a drive toward self-destruction. Freud commented that there is nothing strange in the idea that an instinct should be occupied with the destruction of its own organic home, for does not the mucous membrane of the stomach on occasion digest itself? (1933, p. 145)

But surely this is not the normal state of affairs. Normally, digestion of the stomach is prevented by the secretion of mucus. Only when there is too little secretion of mucus or too much secretion of gastric juice, or when the gastric juice is too acid, will the stomach lining be damaged. Such damage is the result of a disturbance of the normal process; it is not the result of the normal process of digestion. Similarly, to reach sexual satisfaction by suffering pain is a sign that there is a serious disturbance of the sexual instinct. It cannot be argued that the effect of a disturbance is evidence for the normal working of the instinct. From the fact that the disturbed sexual impulse can be satisfied only when the partner inflicts pain, we cannot argue that the normal person has an impulse to suffer pain or to destroy himself.

For Freud, however, the pathological process is always contained in the normal process. Hence he assumes an instinct of self-destruction checked by an erotic instinct and vice versa. Freud sees life as a system of checks and balances. In his opinion, it is not the outcome, the normally functioning life process, that is naturally determined or instinctual; rather, the individual interlocking parts of that process are instinctive tendencies in their own right, opposing each other, even "raging" against each other. No doubt he realized that such opposition results in cooperation, as the above quotation shows, yet in his description of love and aggression, Eros and Thanatos, we find strife and opposition rather than smooth cooperation.

It is as if we viewed the digestive process as consisting of two opposing

instincts, one the digestive and the other the antidigestive instinct: digestion would become a process bent on death and destruction, and antidigestion would be a defense that holds death at bay as long as possible.
Imagine the complications that would arise from an account of the
digestive process as an opposition between these two instincts! When
digestion is dominant, the result is stomach lesions, ranging from slight
inflammation to perforating ulcer; when antidigestion is dominant, nothing is digested and the patient is in danger of death from starvation. Yet
similar antinomies are the rule in psychoanalytic explanations: The erotic
instinct tends toward life, yet finds its goal in quiescence, and ultimate
quiescence is death. The aggressive instinct tends toward destruction and
death, yet promotes life by attacking anything that obstructs activity. It
is no accident that psychoanalytic explanations uniformly emphasize the
extreme complexity of the problem under discussion. Different explanatory principles might find the phenomena remarkably simplified.

The emotions of love and hostility. The twin instincts of love and
aggression (Eros/Thanatos) carry an "affect charge" which is the psychic
counterpart of instinctual energy. The instinctual energy must be discharged, and this discharge is experienced as the emotion or affect (discharge theory of affect). This was Freud's earliest formulation, as found
in his writings before 1900. There is, however, this difficulty. We have
seen that the dual instincts of love and aggression strive for pleasure,
though they achieve it in different ways, the one by reaching quiescence,
the other by successful destruction. If emotion is the experience of the
instinct in action, no pleasure should be experienced until the instinctual
aim is reached. Yet the emotions of love and sexual desire are experienced
as pleasant long before the goal of quiescence is reached. The mounting
tension of forepleasure is enjoyed as well as the release of orgasm. Later
psychoanalysts have recognized this problem and have suggested that
emotions represent *increasing* or *decreasing* excitation rather than the
sheer discharge of the drive (see Ch. 8). This explanation may account for
the fact that emotion is *felt* during mounting tension, but not for its
pleasurable quality.

In his later formulations (after 1900) Freud came to look upon these
emotions as the experience of autonomic excitation, induced by ideas in
the unconscious. According to this view, the pleasure principle uses autonomic innervations as discharge channels for instinctual tensions, while
the reality principle governs such discharge over the motor system. Thus

affect becomes a pleasurable alternative to action, to be indulged in when action is impossible. It acts as a safety valve when tension is too high and action is delayed. But if the emotion is an alternative to action, and action is *not possible at all,* the emotion felt is frustrated love, impotent anger, or helpless fear, none of which is pleasant. Perhaps Freud meant that the affect is both a discharge and also a possible safety valve. If so, he could account for the pleasurable emotion felt before and during action, but not for the displeasure of frustration. Finally, Freud's theory of emotion as affect charge or an alternative for action does not adequately explain emotion that occurs when there is no urge to action, hence no instinctual energy cathecting an object (for instance, in joy or sorrow).

Anxiety. Anxiety or fear has always held a special place in Freudian theory. It is not the direct expression of any instinct, and hence cannot be an "affect-charge." According to his earliest view (before 1900), anxiety is aroused when the discharge of an instinct is prevented. It is "a sub-cortical deflection of somatic excitation." At a period in Freud's thinking when love and anger were considered the experience of a drive discharge, anxiety was seen as the emotion aroused when drive discharge was impossible; it was "converted libido."

Just as the gradually realized inconsistencies in his discharge theory of love and aggression forced Freud to propound a new version in which emotion became a safety valve instead, so he came to see that anxiety was not invariably the reaction to obstructed libido. In his mature work he traced the origin of anxiety to the birth trauma:

Anxiety is an affective condition—that is to say, a combination of certain feelings of the pleasure-pain series with their corresponding efferent innervations, and a perception of them—but we asserted that anxiety is probably also the trace of a certain important event, taken over by inheritance, and therefore comparable to the ontogenetically acquired hysterical attack. We suggested that the event which left this affective trace behind it was the process of birth, in which the modifications of the heart's action and of respiration, which are characteristic of anxiety, served a useful purpose. The first anxiety of all would thus have been a toxic one. . . . In our analysis of objective anxiety we explained it as a condition of increased sensory attention and motor tension, which we called *anxiety preparedness.* Out of this the anxiety reaction arises. The anxiety reaction may run one of two courses. Either the *anxiety-development,* the repetition of the old traumatic experience, is restricted to a signal, in which case the rest of the reaction can adapt itself to the new situation of danger, whether by fight or defence, or the old experience gets the upper hand, and the whole reaction exhausts itself in anxiety-development, in which case the affective state is paralysing and unadapted to the present situation. (1933, p. 114; Freud's italics)

It is clear that Freud spoke here not of neurotic anxiety but of "objective anxiety" or fear, which he considered basically a reaction to external danger. He used Darwin's principle of associated serviceable habits to account for the physiological changes in fear and implied, at least, that fear is the combination of all the sensations felt at birth and patterned through genetic inheritance (James-Lange theory). But he went far beyond both Darwin and James in his insistence that fear is aroused anew by every perception of external danger and is serviceable even today, as long as it serves merely to alert the ego instead of overwhelming and incapacitating it.

Freud suggested that the ego gradually learns to tame anxiety, by using it as a signal to restrain the id from a dangerous pressure for action. Now the ego no longer must wait patiently until an actual danger arouses an overwhelming anxiety attack. It can apprehend a future danger and arouse slight anxiety, a mere anxiety signal, which prevents the id from precipitating a catastrophe. Thus the ego gradually learns to dominate instinctual forces: controlled by the pleasure principle, the id will withdraw from pain. It might be objected that not the id but the ego suffers anxiety, since anxiety is the result of a clash with reality, and arises in the ego rather than in the id. The id covets pleasure, and experiences pain only when its desire is frustrated; hence the anxiety signal as such can be a signal only for the ego, not for the id. Freud would answer that it is the superego that restrains the id by turning the forces of aggression against it. Once again, the explanation becomes so involved that it is impossible to disentangle the actors in this particular drama or to describe their mode of action.

At any rate, it is clear that Freud assigned to anxiety a special role. Anxiety arises in the ego (not in the id) whenever the ego perceives external danger, whether that danger is actually threatening or merely imagined or expected. Anxiety is newly aroused each time, though the pattern of physiological changes is inherited. It is neither an "affect charge" of a drive, nor a safety valve for it. Anxiety is still a product of conflict, as it was in his first formulation. But now the conflict is between the ego and any situation threatening it, while Freud's first view ex-

plained it as the result of a conflict between the libido and some barrier
to its discharge.

Even in his later theory, danger is in a sense an obstruction for the
libido. Whatever the danger, it always inhibits libidinal gratification for
the time being, even though the exact mechanism of such inhibition is
not made clear. Hence Freud felt justified in continuing to hold that
anxiety is converted libido, and also in saying later that anxiety is the
universal reaction to a danger situation. In his book *The Problem of
Anxiety,* he said:

It is undeniable that in abstinence, in perverted interference with the normal
discharge of sexual excitation, or in the diverting of the latter from its psychic
elaboration, anxiety arises directly out of libido; that is to say, there is brought
about that state of helplessness of the ego in the face of excessive tension arising from ungratified need which results, as in birth, in the development of
anxiety, so that there is again a possibility, which although obvious is of no
great consequence, that it is precisely the excess of unutilized libido that *finds
its discharge* in the form of anxiety. (1936, p. 81; italics added)

All the same, for Freud anxiety is the reaction to a real external threat,
newly aroused each time a dangerous situation is perceived. Love and
aggression, on the other hand, are instincts with an affect charge which
are continually active. Thus Freud's theory gives a different status to
different emotions, a division that is justified only on his assumption that
love and hostility are the affect charges of libidinal/destructive drives,
while anxiety is the reaction to their obstruction. To common human
experience, anger is newly aroused in response to obstruction just as fear
is a reaction to threat. And fear can become enduring anxiety in the same
way as anger can become enduring hostility. For a phenomenological
analysis, there is no fundamental difference between the two emotions.
That Freud himself never felt quite easy over this division is shown
by his often expressed doubts and his attempt to salvage anxiety as converted libido. If he could have done so, all emotions would have acquired
the same status; they would all have become expressions of instinctual
drives.

Are emotions affect charges? Now the question is: What is the evidence for considering love and hostility as the affect charge of constant
instinctual forces, totally different from fear, which is merely an inherited
disposition, aroused by a perceived threat? When we remember that

McDougall defined an instinct as a "propensity" or "innate disposition" that exists only as a *potentiality*, to be aroused and made actual by some present situation, we begin to realize that the difficulty lies in Freud's definition of instinct (see Ch. 11). What for McDougall is a potentiality, a disposition, is for Freud a constant force, an actuality that is sometimes observed or experienced and sometimes not. When it is not consciously experienced it is still active in the unconscious. Lest it be thought that Freud's definition of an instinct as having its source in a state of excitation within the body would permit its temporary quiescence, Freud goes on to say:

Instinctual impulses from one source can join on to instinctual impulses from another . . . and . . . the satisfaction of one instinct can be substituted for the satisfaction of another. . . . The relation of an instinct to its aim and to its object are also susceptible to alterations; both can be exchanged for others, but the relation to the object is the more easily loosened of the two. (1933, p. 133)

Thus the instinct with its affect charge seems sovereign in its course. It cathects an object, discards it again, takes objects belonging to another impulse, can even change its aim. The only thing that remains constant is the instinct itself as a driving force. What happens psychologically speaking when the impulse cathects an object is not at all clear. Freud only says that there is a perceptual process that informs the ego of the environmental object. The choice itself is prompted by the instinct in a way that remains obscure.

Now what is the evidence for such "constant forces"? The sex drive in the narrow sense is obviously not active all the time. In animals it is aroused seasonally and in human beings there is the "latency period" even in Freudian theory. As a matter of common experience, the sexual drive is in abeyance for longer or shorter periods even in adults, noticeably during periods of illness, concentrated work, or absorption in some other activity. But for Freud the libido is not restricted to the impulse toward sexual gratification. Every kind of sensory gratification is libidinal in the wider sense of the term. We cannot discuss here the justice of such an extension in meaning, but we must point out that once such an extended usage is preferred it follows naturally that the libido must be a constant force. There is probably no instant during which a normal human being cannot long for or feel sensory satisfaction of some sort; and it is only a small step beyond the facts to say that therefore the drive is active all the time, merely changing its object.

The case becomes a little clearer when we turn to aggression. Here we must distinguish first between the *emotion anger,* the Freudian *instinct of aggression,* and *aggressive action.* Very often these three factors are hopelessly confused in discussion. Now anger is not present all the time, nor is open aggression; but according to Freud, at least, the aggressive instinct is active continuously. It is true that psychoanalytic investigations often uncover a good deal of hostility. But it is an open question whether such hostility that is gradually observed during analytic treatment is the release of "repressed" aggression. It could be that the patient was much too fearful in the past either to show *or to feel* anger. For Freud such anxiety is the cause of *repression;* but it could also be that repression was not necessary because anxiety *prevented* anger in the first place. Now Freud would point out that anxiety prevented the *expression* of the aggressive drive, *that is, the emotion,* but the drive itself remained. But this argument assumes that it has already been established that such a constant drive exists. This problem will be discussed in more detail in Chapter 12. Here it is sufficient to point out that the evidence for aggression as a constant instinctive force is based on the psychoanalytic *interpretation* of facts, rather than on the facts themselves.

We might distinguish emotions from affect charges of instincts by their somatic source. It is usually assumed, and Freud agrees, that the source of an instinct is a state of excitation within the body (see Ch. 11). The sexual drive is rooted in the excitation produced by the gonadal endocrine system. There is no such certainty of an endocrine source for an instinct of aggression, though Freud's successors have speculated about a possible endocrine basis (Hartmann and associates, 1949). Fear or anxiety is certainly not somatically based in the Freudian system, because it arises in the ego rather than the id; nor does Freud ever mention such a possibility. Cannon (1915), however, did suggest that both fear and anger are accompanied by adrenaline secretion and excitation of the sympathetic nervous system (see the discussion in Ch. 7, in the following volume). If adrenaline secretion were taken as the source of physiological energy for aggression, the same source would be present in fear; hence both fear and anger would be instinctual, a possibility which Freud explicitly rejects for fear.

In our discussion of instinct (Ch. 11) we shall see that both fear and anger can be distinguished from true instincts. In instincts the somatic state induced by endocrine secretion has its own periodicity (hunger, sex) and sensitizes perception. In emotions the endocrine secretion *comes with* the perception and appraisal of an object. Instincts are aroused *even without a suitable object* (we become hungry whether or not we see or think of something edible); emotions are *aroused by an object* (we do not become angry unless we are up against an actual, imagined, or remembered frustration). Hence the somatic state comes before perception and appraisal of an object in instincts, but after such appraisal in emotions.

8. THE MODERN SCENE

To complete our survey, we will discuss the more recent theories of emotion, even though the yield of the last quarter of a century has been comparatively meager. During these years a great deal of effort has been devoted to experimentation and clinical research without much concern for integrating or explaining the data. Recent surveys that are primarily experimentally oriented can be found in H. Helson, editor (1951), *Theoretical Foundations of Psychology,* the chapter on "Feeling and Emotion," by J. G. Beebe-Center, and in S. S. Stevens, editor (1951), *Handbook of Experimental Psychology,* the chapter on "Emotion," by D. B. Lindsley. There are earlier surveys by Hunt (1941), Lund (1939), Ruckmick (1936), and Young (1943), while an exhaustive historical treatment of theories of feeling and emotion by Gardiner, Metcalf, and Beebe-Center dates back to 1937. The two symposium volumes, *Feelings and Emotions,* edited by M. L. Reymert (1928, 1950), provide a good cross section of the field during these two periods. The present survey will deal primarily with theories of emotion, though experimental facts will be quoted whenever they are relevant to theory.

In this chapter only psychological theories will be mentioned so as to set the stage for a careful discussion of the psychological factors in emotion (Ch. 9). Earlier chapters have shown that emotion must be aroused by the individual's perception and appreciation of some situation, while physiological changes, though important, play a secondary role. Since such physiological changes are not reflexes, they themselves must be initiated by perception and appraisal. For this reason a discussion of the psychology of emotion must necessarily come before an examination of the way in which physiological changes are brought about in emotion. Neurological and physiological theories of emotion will then be discussed in Parts I and II of the following volume, together with the important new evidence brought to light during the last few years.

Later analysts have developed one or the other aspect of the Freudian view, though none of them can be said to have worked out a consistent theory.

Fenichel. In 1945, for instance, Fenichel proposed that increased ego mastery in genetic development results in a change in the character of the affect. At the time that id impulses reign, early in life, they are expressed as emotion. But later the child learns to control the discharge: "Affects are originally archaic discharge syndromes that supplant voluntary actions under certain exciting conditions. Now the growing ego learns to 'tame affects and to use them for its own anticipating purposes' " (1945, p. 43).

Fenichel thus substitutes a safety valve theory of emotion for a discharge theory. But such a theory cannot deal with pleasant emotions, nor can it account for emotions as yet untamed. Fenichel claims that emotion breaks through such taming only when ego control fails, and hence full emotional expression represents a regression to an earlier stage, before ego mastery was complete. This theory, however, could be applied accurately only to anger and fear, the typical conflict emotions. It can obviously not be held that the full expression of sexual love is a throwback to an archaic and infantile stage.

Jacobson. Later on, Jacobson (1952) criticized both the discharge and the safety valve theories of emotion and pointed out that ego functions, as well as instinctive activities, are accompanied by emotion. Hence she suggested that affect is the experience of an increase or decrease of drive tension rather than the experience of a drive. These drive tensions may be either *within the id* (sexual emotion and rage) or *within the ego* (fear and interest). They may be *between the ego and the id* (fear of id impulses, shame, disgust), but they may also be *between the ego and the superego* (guilt feelings, depression).

Jacobson's theory implies that emotion is the experience of an increase or decrease of excitation. While it is true that psychological processes are never stationary, it is by no means certain that changes in the intensity of excitation will give rise to qualitatively different and sometimes opposed emotions. Passionate interest in a hobby may represent just as much of an increase in excitation as does fear, yet the psychological experience is completely different. In addition, it is difficult to explain how drive tensions may arise not only within various structures but also between them. If we employ the simile of "drive," these drives must be anchored in some structure; but in the analogy with the tensions in a field system, the tensions between structures are obviously of a very different type from the "drives" within each structure. To call both "affects" is stretching the analogy to breaking point.

Rapaport. In 1953 Rapaport recognized that these later theories cannot be contained within the Freudian system and proposed to extend Freud's own views in such a way that the fruits of his earlier as well as his later insights would be combined into a systematic theory of emotion. Historically, Freud's views of emotion represent three phases. Rapaport attempted to integrate them by applying each phase to a different stage in phylogenetic and ontogenetic development. To begin with, he explained, affects use *inborn channels of discharge;* hence Freud could call emotions "inherited hysterical attacks." During infancy, at a time when the pleasure principle reigns unopposed, drives tend towards immediate discharge. Emotions are the experiences of these drives, their *affect charge,* and act as safety valves when the object is out of reach. At this second stage, emotions are felt as "massive affect-storms" which allow internal discharge when action is impossible. Gradually, the growing ego develops "counter-cathexes" and so is able to delay action, which results in more intense and more varied affect discharges. Since affects partake of the general development and become attached to developing part-drives or countercathexes, a hierarchy of drives and affects is eventually established together with the developing ego structure. Thus new, more complex, and more subtle discharge channels are created. In this third phase, the ego, which originally had to endure affects, now can use them as *affect signals,* and so control action. Massive emotional outbursts still happen, either as the result of weakened ego control or a "regression in the services of the ego." Since emotional expression may arouse further tensions (anxiety), emotions themselves may become motives of defense.

While Rapaport has faithfully combined the three phases of Freud's exposition, he has not succeeded in making psychoanalytic affect theory either more lucid or more consistent. What has to be explained is how the specific affect charges of a libidinal/aggressive drive can later be attached to counter-cathexes and finally become the signal of an affect and its underlying drive. Perhaps a drive can split into many part drives, and perhaps the very drive energy itself can be used to counteract the drive—but what are the means by which such transformations are brought about? What is the psychological or physiological mechanism that accounts for all these changes? According to Rapaport (and Freud) emotions and feelings are the experience of the drive in action, its affect charge; and drives have their source in the id. How, then, could the ego *produce* an affect signal for its own purposes?

No doubt there is a "hierarchy of motivations ranging from drives to interests and preferences," as Rapaport says. But if the ego can produce the drive underlying the affect signal, why not the "drives" usually called interests and sentiments? If, on the other hand, the id is the sole source of drives, the problem of how id energy can be converted into sentiments and interests is not solved by postulating sublimation. Sublimation is no more than a label for a process that awaits description. And if all emotions are affect charges of drives that have their source in the id, how does it come about that we experience at least one emotion, anxiety, as a reaction to external danger rather than the affect charge of a drive? (see Ch. 7)

Freud himself obviously was not satisfied with his own explanations, or he would not have attempted over and over to refine his views, particularly as regards anxiety. Perhaps it would be better for modern theorists to make a fresh start instead of engaging in the herculean task of forging links between different phases in Freud's explanation in an attempt to reconcile irreconcilables.

PSYCHOLOGICAL THEORIES

If the psychoanalytic theory of emotion has made little progress since Freud, academic theories have not gone very far either. Some variants of the conflict theory of emotion have sought to explain emotion either as an inability of higher brain centers to deal with the situation (Hodge, 1935), or as "functional decortication" produced by a conflict of impulses (Darrow, 1935). Darrow, like Dewey, recognized that conflict can account only for some emotions, not for others. Hence conflict theories, like psychoanalytic theories, explain only some emotions consistently. Others they leave unexplained; or they admit a dichotomy in emotion without explaining its necessity.

Georges Dumas. One of the most interesting variations of the conflict theory is the theory proposed by Georges Dumas (1932, 1948). He suggested that a situation may lead to an arrest of tendencies and attitudes that is experienced as an *emotional shock*. This can be mild, the result of a loud noise, a handclap, a shot, or any stimulus that has no great significance for the individual. Or the shock may be more intense, followed by an emotion as soon as the significance of the situation is realized (e.g., reading the death notice of a close friend in the paper). Finally, the shock may be very intense, the result of powerful stimulation (scenes of carnage, danger of death, and the like), causing a widespread physiological inhibition. Such a shock is followed by intense debilitating emotions. The shock itself seems to be primarily a physiological reaction, some aspects of which are consciously perceived.

The emotion proper, on the other hand, "constitutes an organic and psychological combination which, despite the diversity and often instability of its constituent elements, has a certain physiological individuality, a certain psychological coloring" * (Dumas, 1932, p. 349).

But Dumas warns us that we must not let language deceive us into thinking that emotions are separate entities. For him, emotions are psychological states, different from instincts because they are not tendencies to action. If fear is an emotion, he says, it is emotional rather than instinctive, because it is not the tendency to flee. McDougall, in Dumas' opinion, made the mistake of conceiving emotions as action tendencies, which forced him to join emotions to instincts and exclude joy and sorrow from his list of emotions.

Dumas' expedient, however, is little better. Conceiving of emotion as static, he is unable to explain why joy should urge the person to attach himself to what brings him joy and why he should be reluctant to turn away even when its loss has brought him sorrow. Still less can Dumas account for the strong impulsion of fear or anger. He is forced to postulate separate instincts that are joined to some emotions but not to others. Unless we see emotion as a felt tendency toward something good, away from something bad for us, we cannot explain how emotion can take us captive and make us oblivious to everything else. Such a tendency may be no more than an inclination toward the object or away from it, and does

---

* "Chaque emotion constitue un ensemble organique et psychique qui, malgré la diversité et souvent l'instabilité des éléments constitutifs, a une certaine individualité physiologique, une certaine coloration psychologique."

not necessarily lead to action. Love as well as joy implies an inclination toward something desirable. Fear as well as sorrow indicates an aversion toward something undesirable that is about to befall us or has already happened. Only some emotions urge to overt action (e.g., fear, anger, desire) while others simply urge to remain where we are: joy, because we have what we want and nothing else is needed; sorrow, because we have lost what we love and nothing else is wanted. This will be discussed at length in Chapter 10. Here we merely note that Dumas saw the problem. His solution is neither the only one nor the best one.

Dumas distinguished between passive and active emotional states. *Passive sorrow* is a slowing of vital functions, joined to the meaning of its cause. *Passive joy* is a mild facilitation of psychological activity without any effect on other activity (as seen temporarily in dreams, permanently in happy idiots). *Passive fear* results from the perception of a serious danger and is accompanied by immediate inhibition of heart and respiration, a general decrease of muscular tone and, in extreme cases, paralysis. *Passive anger* is the result of strong competing and conflicting tendencies to action that cancel each other out and inhibit action. These four passive emotions have an inhibiting effect, while their active forms facilitate action. The passive form of each emotion is an intensification of its active form.

Dumas may be right in saying that anger and fear are more intense when passive (white anger vs. red anger, paralysis of fear vs. fear that drives to flight). But it is doubtful whether passive sorrow (depression) is more intense than active sorrow (agitated depression) unless we change our notions of what is an intense experience. According to Dumas, the man who is depressed feels little, says little, does little; surely his experience cannot be as intense as during agitated expression when he laments and wrings his hands, bewailing his fate. Passive joy seems to be a contradiction in terms, as Dumas admits, because joy means movement, life, action. Dumas' examples, the happy idiot and the joy of ecstasy, do not prove his point because these are not examples of the emotion of joy. The idiot is smiling though inactive not because he feels more intense joy but because he has so few wants that minimal care will prevent distress. Mystic ecstasy by definition is beyond sensory experience or even intellectual knowledge; hence the joy experienced cannot and need not be expressed in physical or psychological activity.

Dumas' great contribution to a theory of emotion is his careful distinc-

tion between what is essentially a physiological startle response and emotion proper; and his insistence that different emotions are different psychological experiences with different bodily sensations. His insight that
excessive fear and anger (passive fear and anger) are paralyzing is illu-
minating. But his further distinction of passive vs. active joy and sorrow
is not confirmed by facts. Passive joys and sorrows are not necessarily
more intense than their active forms, and passive joy is not necessarily
inhibiting. In mystics, ecstasy leads to inactivity not because it is joy but
because it is super-sensory joy.

Behavioristic theories. Logically enough, behaviorists of all persuasions
consider emotion as an aspect of biological drives. From Watson to Skinner and Hull, emotion is a modification of drive. For Watson, emotion is
"a hereditary 'pattern reaction' involving profound changes of the bodily
mechanism as a whole, but particularly of the visceral and glandular system" (1919, p. 195). He claims that the innate emotional patterns are
anger, fear, and love; they are aroused in the newborn by restraint
(anger), loud sounds (fear), and stroking (love). Gradually these instinctive patterns become modified in the course of development. In the adult,
emotion is recognized in most cases merely in the facilitation or inhibition
of responses.*

Hull and Skinner are fairly close to Watson in their formulations. For
Skinner (1938) emotion represents changes in reflex strength; Hull
(1943) does not use the concept of emotion but apparently subsumes it
under increase and decrease of drive strength.

For Tolman (1932) feelings and emotions are "immanent determinants
of behavior," which occur in sequence:

(a) sign-gestalt expectations of resulting physiological goods and bads as
"promised" and "threatened" by the immediate stimulus-situation; (b) incipient movements and visceral activities resulting, in physiological fashion,
from the release of these sign-gestalt-expectations; and (c) resultant organic
and kinesthetic stimulations. (1932, p. 264)

Interestingly enough, the sign-gestalt expectations of promised "goods"
and threatened "bads" is a fairly close equivalent of what we have called
the estimate or appraisal of a situation. However, this expectation arouses
visceral activities and incipient movements, but no felt attraction or repulsion—an omission to be expected in a behavioristic account. For Tolman

* For a discussion of emotional development, see The Genetic Development
of Emotion, Ch. 10.

as for William James, "the emotion, as 'conscious feeling,' is but the complex of resultant organic and kinesthetic 'sensations,' which enter 'conscious awareness'" (1932, p. 266).

Behavioristic theories assume that the stimulus arouses the response through some organismic linkage which it is not the task of psychology to investigate. This conceals the further assumption that the linkage is either physical (mechanical) or physiological. This assumption may be harmless in experimental work with animals where the stimulus arouses an inherent drive (hunger, thirst, mating, avoidance of pain) in which emotion can be assumed to be a factor. But not all emotions are aroused together with inherent drives (e.g., fear of strangers), for their object can come to arouse quite a different emotion (when the stranger becomes a friend of the family, the child may now greet him joyously). Hence emotion can occur without a drive, particularly in human beings. More-over, to conceive emotion as a variation in drive strength does not reliably distinguish emotional from nonemotional behavior in human beings, where deliberate effort may substitute for emotion.

The attitude theory. Nina Bull (1945, 1951) makes a careful analysis of the sequence perception—emotion—action, also from behavioristic premises. She suggests that the distinction between emotional experience and emotional expression is but a crude approximation to a whole series of changes. The individual reacts to an emotional stimulus with a prepara-tory motor attitude which gives rise first to feeling, and then to action. "We feel angry as a result of *readiness* to strike, and feel afraid as a result of *readiness* to run away" (1951, p. 6). Here, as in the behavioristic account, it is assumed that perception gives rise immediately (through some organismic linkage) to motor activity. The innovation is the view that this motor activity is incipient, rises to awareness as an affect, and eventually ends in action.

This readiness or attitude is a neural *disposition;* when activated by the stimulus, it results in an *actual* motor attitude which is then experi-enced as an affect. The accompanying diagram (Bull, 1951, p. 9) will illustrate this sequence:

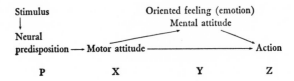

This analysis makes a careful distinction between the *neural organization,* which determines emotional expression; its activation, that is the *motor attitude;* the felt orientation toward or away from something, which is the mental component or *affect;* and the *action,* that follows upon attitude and emotion and can be influenced by thinking. There is no doubt that all these components can and should be distinguished in emotion; hence Nina Bull's analysis is a real contribution. However, the experimental evidence does not prove the contention that the felt orientation stems from the motor attitude. In her experiments, Nina Bull found that emotions produced on command during hypnosis were accompanied by objectively distinguishable motor attitudes. If one such attitude was "locked" by hypnotic command, the person could feel no other emotion. Now we do not question the fact that a motor attitude goes with the felt emotion, but we doubt that it produces the emotion. If an emotion is a tendency to action based on the appraisal that something is good or bad for the person, as we shall argue later (see Ch. 9), this action tendency would be felt as an orientation toward or away from something and would organize the muscles in readiness for action. If the motor attitude is "locked" during hypnosis, the whole action tendency is frozen and no other emotion can be either felt or expressed.

For Nina Bull, however, the psychological orientation comes only if and when the motor attitude rises to awareness. The mental attitude is "the orienting part of [sequence] Y, and corresponds . . . to feelings of direction and intention" (1951, p. 9). If the awareness of intention (i.e., the emotion proper) comes only after we become aware of the motor attitude, the stimulus must activate a particular neural predisposition mechanically; but a given stimulus does not always arouse an emotion, nor does it always arouse the same emotion.

The theory seems to imply that the stimulus has a special affinity to a given neural predisposition; in old-fashioned terms, that the stimulus arouses an instinctual pattern or biological drive. If that is so, it would be difficult to explain conflicting emotions or "objectless" emotions. Nina Bull sees this difficulty and comments upon it:

We are now in a position to consider briefly these *un-*oriented feelings coming from the various organic changes (in heart action, breathing, gland secretion, etc.) which necessarily accompany any preparation for bodily exertion, regardless of direction and intention. In poorly oriented emotional reactions, various feelings of organic preparation tend to obtrude themselves in consciousness as vague suspense, excitement, tension, restlessness, nervousness, etc., without an adequately oriented mental component *to whip the process into shape and give it point.* For it is only in their relation to the mental attitude with its awareness of intention, that any such feelings (of organic changes) can become intelligible. In short, a clear-cut mental attitude is necessary to give the sense of aim and purpose, so that the crudely oriented feelings of suspense and restlessness acquire meaning.

The process of sharpening the focus of mental attitude, by bringing the *orienting aspects* of subconscious motor attitude up into cortical awareness, is part of modern psychotherapeutic method. It is the sharpened focus that gives the person insight into his hitherto submerged behavior patterns and enables him to become self-critical, both as regards his aim and manner of pursuing it. (1951, pp. 9–10; italics added)

It seems that the mental component whips the organic process into shape, and also that the motor attitude has orienting aspects that must be brought into awareness; yet these two statements are contradicory. If the motor attitude is simply a generalized excitement given direction by the mental component and shaped into fear or anger or love, then we may frankly doubt whether the organic motor attitude has any "orienting aspects." If the "readiness to strike" is felt as anger rather than any other emotion because the motor pattern is specific to begin with, no mental component need whip it into shape. If it is felt as anger only when "a clear-cut mental attitude" gives it aim and purpose, the motor attitude is reduced to generalized excitement—which contradicts Nina Bull's own experimental evidence.

The attitude theory of emotion in its present form is a refinement of the James-Lange theory in which motor attitude determines feeling, thought, and action. If a similarly careful analysis had been made of the determinants of the motor attitude, there is no doubt that the present ambiguity in the assumed connection between motor and mental attitude would have been resolved.

The energy release theory. Emotion had been called a disturbance, an awareness of drives, a complex of sensations, or an ill-defined behavior pattern. What wonder that in the end some theorists refused to consider it a separate phenomenon altogether. Meyer (1933) and Duffy (1934, 1951) in short succession insisted that emotion had been little more than a chapter heading which should be superseded by more basic categories, now that psychology had come of age and no longer depended on common sense categories.

Duffy pointed out that the energy released in human behavior is customarily conceived as channeled through specific sources. Separate driving forces are needed to account for these channels: drives, instincts, motives, emotions. Since there is a common factor in all these forces, because energy is released and directed toward specific objects, Duffy suggested that all these terms, including emotion, should be discarded and replaced by "energy mobilization and direction." Then behavior could be classified according to its degree of energy mobilization and direction. In her opinion,

The degree of energy mobilization . . . is the extent of release of the stored energy of the organism through metabolic activity in the tissues. This appears to occur in a continuum, from a low point during deep sleep to a high point during frantic effort or excitement. . . . The extent of the energy release is determined by the degree of *effort* required by the situation as *interpreted by the individual*. For example, difficult tasks require more energy than easy tasks; situations which the individual regards as significant in relation to his goals release more energy than those interpreted as lacking this significance. (1951, p. 32; Duffy's italics)

There is no doubt that energy mobilization and direction can be inferred in every emotion. But there is also no doubt that the same can be said of every other psychological activity, not only of so-called "dynamic" processes. We could not perceive unless we focused our eyes on the object. Nor could we think or plan unless energy were available, mobilized, and properly directed. Yet we could not successfully distinguish perceiving from remembering on the basis of energy mobilization and direction. If energy mobilization and direction are common to every psychological (and even physiological) process, then they cannot serve to distinguish one from the other.

To understand various kinds of behavior, we must make distinctions. We cannot hope to understand or quantify behavior in general. The obvious distinctions are those given by immediate experience: sense perception differs from remembering and thinking, and both differ from wanting and striving. To reduce all these activities to one dimension of "energy mobilization" is hardly helpful. Degrees of energy mobilization are not readily distinguished in experience, nor are they easily observed. Even if we could refine our observation, such a procedure would blur available distinctions and lose the information we have already acquired. Extreme effort and emotional excitement may have the same measurable energy output and even the same direction, but effort is laborious while excitement is not. Where Duffy assumes a continuum of energy expenditure, to be measured by physiological indices, there are actually qualitative differences that can be both experienced and observed. These differences change the conditions of energy release (effort as compared to excitement), and should be taken into account for prediction.

There are also qualitative differences between various emotions, and these cannot be reduced to differences in direction of overt action, or to differences in energy mobilization. Anger and love both result in approach; but the quality of that approach is rather different even where the amount of energy remains the same. Fear and anger, as measured by energy output during fight or flight, might release the same amount of energy; yet the difference between them is more than a difference in direction.

When emotion is reduced to "energy," as is the rule in psychoanalytic and behavioristic systems, it is assumed that physiological energy acts like physical energy, which always increases the force of overt movement. But Dumas has noted that excessive fear paralyzes and thus prevents flight, while extreme anger locks action in an excess of uncoordinated power. If physiological indices are to be used instead of muscle tension or overt action, we must first examine the physiological effect of autonomic excitation. Sympathetic and parasympathetic excitation have opposite effects that may cancel each other out if both systems are excited equally in every emotion. On the other hand, if some emotions excite the parasympathetic and others the sympathetic system, some indicators might not show any effect in a given emotion. For this reason we must first examine what is the effect of different emotions on various physiological systems as well as on overt action. This we will do in Part II of the following volume.

While the problem of measurement is admittedly difficult, it will not be solved by oversimplification. To discard traditional categories of emotional experience in favor of Duffy's quantitative distinctions will bring us no nearer to scientific precision. Hebb (1946), for instance, reported that emotions of chimpanzees could be reliably distinguished and their behavior predicted if "frankly anthropomorphic concepts of emotion" were used by the observer. An objective description of behavior (which certainly included intensity and direction) yielded a meaningless series of specific acts useless for prediction. And Nina Bull found that hypnotically induced emotions could be easily recognized and distinguished in human beings even without overt action. Hence we are bound to conclude that common experience and terminology yield valid distinctions and should not be discarded unless we have something better to put in their place.

The motivational theory. The concept of emotion found a defender in R. Leeper (1948), who tried to restore it to its rightful place in the life of living beings. Perhaps he realized that emotion was bound to be suspect as long as psychologists saw it only as a disturber of the peace. At any rate, he insisted that emotion is itself purposeful, that fear urges to flight, anger to attack.

In a spirited criticism of the concept of emotion as disorganized and disorganizing, Leeper pointed out that organization of one process always implies some disorganization, namely a disorganization of interfering processes. The emotional process itself is always organized: viscerally, because the visceral changes are favorable for behavior consistent with the emotion; behaviorally, because emotional action is organized toward fight or flight or a friendly approach; experientially, because attention is concentrated on the object of emotion.

Leeper admitted that emotional organization may not always be useful to the person. (Stage fright is organized toward withdrawing from a situation despite conscious intention.) But the term organization means simply harmonious function of all parts of the emotional process without any implication that it must harmonize with every other process. Of course, extreme emotion (such as terror or extreme rage) may disorganize emotional action. But Leeper insisted that any process must be assessed according to its normal effects. In the same way, normal amounts of salt included in a balanced diet have a favorable effect, while excessive salt intake is harmful.

For Leeper, all emotions normally have an organization which directs and sustains action. Hence "emotional processes operate primarily as motives. It means that they are processes which arouse, sustain and direct activity" (1948, p. 17). As motives, emotions are aroused in a psychological situation:

It is quite a possible hypothesis that the perception of the emotion-producing situation produces the emotional process (which may have a conscious aspect to it, and which may produce also an autonomic discharge, either directly or via some subcortical centers, and which may then be reinforced or supported by widespread bodily changes). And it is quite a possible hypothesis that this emotional process . . . then operates to motivate behavior. (1948, p. 18)

According to Leeper, the interpretation of the situation arouses emotion consisting of emotional experience and expression, which then motivates action. Leeper pointed out that this explanation is usually rejected by modern psychologists as naive common sense, because of the supposedly unsound assumption of mind interacting with body which is implied in it. He made the obvious point that such interaction is implied also when the James-Lange or Thalamic theory is used as an explanation of emotional experience. We might point out in addition that such interaction could be implied even in the simple statement that the driver steps on the brake because he sees a red light. But on the modern assumption that the human being is a psychosomatic unit instead of the possessor of two separate entities, mind and body, there can be no objection to assuming a connection between experience and behavior.

Leeper's insistence that emotion is organized toward action has been timely and constructive. However, a theory of emotion must also take account of the disturbance in the ongoing action often produced by emotion. True, emotion is an organized process; and some emotions urge to action, but that action may not be what the person had intended. Anger urges to attack, fear to flight, but it is not in the best interest of the person to attack everyone that frustrates him or to flee from everything that may threaten. Emotion cannot be trusted to give direction to human life. In fact, a man's reasonable goals may easily be forgotten in the fascination of a momentary attraction. Hence emotion may make action easy, yet hinder the action that had been intended and so stand in the way of achievement.

Young's eclecticism. P. T. Young (1949) answered Leeper's criticism by appealing to Leeper's own distinction between emotions that are organized and that organize actions (normal emotions) and emotions that disorganize actions (excessive emotions). Young concluded that therefore a distinction between organizing and disorganizing emotions is legitimate.

But the disorganization that comes with excessive emotion is not a disturbance of ongoing action, it is a disorganization of the very action to which the emotion urges. Such an effect could be explained only by examining the physiological changes in excessive emotion as compared with mild emotion. In Chapter 7 of the following volume we shall see that excessive sympathetic stimulation reduces muscular contractions and so accounts for the paralysis of terror; excessive parasympathetic stimulation during rage results in massive muscular contractions and hence makes for incoordination. Emotion may urge to action, but the physiological excitation that accompanies it may become so extreme that effective action becomes impossible. Young is right in maintaining that emotions may disturb ongoing action, but they need not always do so. Even when they do, such disturbance is not the disorganization of action that comes with excessive emotion.

Young's own theory of emotion (1943) is an eclectic's expedient. He defines emotion as one of many affective processes that represent a class of their own, presumably in contrast to perceptual processes. Emotions properly so called (emotional upsets) occur when a highly organized activity is blocked, when a release of tension is achieved suddenly, and when danger threatens. Thus emotions would include anger, sudden joy, and fear. But this classification does not distinguish between an emotional upset and a sudden release from tension that is a mere cessation of effort (for instance, rest after lifting a heavy load). Emotions are defined as follows: "An emotion is an acute affective disturbance within the individual as a whole, arising from psychological situations and manifest in conscious experience, behavior, and especially through bodily changes which are regulated by the autonomic nervous system" (1949, p. 189). This definition includes the usual triad of experience-expression-action, but, also as usual, does not explain how the psychological situation arouses an emotion.

According to Young, emotions do not motivate; they are the result of motivated action. "In every emotional upset some motivating factor is thwarted, or satisfied, or excites the individual" (1943, p. 392). And a motive is any factor that arouses, sustains, or changes bodily activity. At best, an emotion seems to be only a sign that overt action has been aroused in some way.

Emotion is only one of a number of affective processes, according to Young. They include feelings of pleasantness or unpleasantness, moods, attitudes, sentiments, interests, organic aches, hunger, thirst, fatigue. We note that these affective processes are not necessarily disturbances (e.g., feelings of pleasantness or a cheerful mood), do not have to be aroused by a psychological situation (e.g., hunger and thirst), do not necessarily accompany motivated action (e.g., organic aches), and do not obviously excite the autonomic nervous system (e.g., interests). Hence the distinguishing marks of emotion do not fit these processes. Young included them under affective phenomena together with emotion because they all have a polarity not found among other psychological processes. Such a polarity is undoubtedly present in pleasantness/unpleasantness, elation/ depression, love/hate, and the like. But the opposite of fear (courage) is not necessarily an emotion, and there is no opposite of anger. Organic aches also have no such polarity. On the other hand, if polarity were sufficient to classify an activity as affective, then judgments of right/ wrong, good/bad, straight/crooked, would have to be included as well.

Young's theory makes emotion an incident in motivated action, satisfying, disturbing, exciting, but does not account for emotion which occurs without overt action (e.g., our annoyance when we remember that we have forgotten an appointment). It provides no criterion by which affective phenomena can be distinguished from other psychological activities. In its very breadth of scope Young's theory only illustrates the difficulties encountered by a comprehensive theory of emotion instead of solving them.

THE EXISTENTIALIST REACTION

Jean-Paul Sartre (1948) tellingly criticizes psychological theories of emotion.* Psychologists, he says, are so fascinated by objective facts that they seek the laws of emotion in the emotional process itself. Yet the fact of emotion, like any fact, cannot be its own explanation.

For him emotion is a way of experiencing reality. Since we as human beings are aware of this experience and can reflect upon it, the objective approach discards the most valuable evidence. For Sartre:

The emotion signifies, in its own way, the whole of consciousness, or, if we put ourselves on the existential level, of human reality. . . .

That being so, it is impossible to consider emotion as a psycho-physiological disorder. It has its essence, its particular structures, its laws of appearing, and its signification. It cannot come to human reality *from the outside*. On the contrary, it is man who *assumes* his emotions, and consequently emotion is an organized form of human existence. (1948, p. 18; Sartre's italics)

Sartre sees the "signification" of emotion in its unique relation to reality. Emotion always has an object reference. A man is always afraid *of some-*

---

* Sartre's theory of emotion, a philosophical rather than a scientific inquiry, is discussed here because existentialist thought is beginning to have a marked influence on modern psychology.

thing, angry *at something.* As long as the emotion lasts, it maintains that focus on the object. Emotional consciousness is an unreflective awareness of the object, not a person's awareness that he has an emotion.

For Sartre emotion occurs when the world becomes too difficult. When all ways to action are barred yet we must act, we transform the world by magic. This transformation of the real world into a world of magic is made possible by emotion. Action, which has first become impossible, now becomes unnecessary. Flight is "a fainting that is enacted." It is a way of forgetting or denying one's danger.

Sartre uses the same principle to analyze joy. Here the magical transformation becomes necessary because the possession of something we love can never be instantaneous or complete. Joy is an attempt to make it so. Thus emotion sets up "a magical world by using the body as a means of incantation." At the same time, the physiological disturbance testifies to the sincerity with which the magical belief is held. Emotion originates in a "spontaneous and lived degradation of consciousness in the face of the world" (1948, p. 77). Consciousness endows the world with magical qualities as a last resort when it becomes impossible to cope with reality. In this helplessness, consciousness sinks to a lower level of awareness, into passivity. Passive, it is taken captive by the world. Objects first attract it, then trap it. Once consciousness is enmeshed in emotion, emotion tends to take over altogether.

Emotions enmesh consciousness and overwhelm it because the magical quality they confer upon the world seems to be enduring:

The horrible is now within the thing, at the heart of the thing. It is its affective texture; it is constitutive of it. . . . The horrible is not only the present state of the thing; it is threatened for the future; it spreads itself over the whole future and darkens it; it is the revelation of the meaning of the world. (1948, pp. 80–81)

According to Sartre, this magical quality is an aspect of the world that penetrates all our relations with reality. It is not only conferred by emotion; it is given in reality itself. In fact, only because there really is magic in the world can emotion seize upon it, diffuse it, or concentrate it on a given object.

Sartre posits a world of instruments for action that is strictly deterministic, and another world of magic which "acts upon consciousness immediately," offers no instruments for action, and can only be combated by "absolute and massive modifications of the world" as they are possible in emotion. Hence emotion is "the return of consciousness to the magical attitude, one of the great attitudes which are essential to it, with appearance of the correlative world, the magical world" (1948, p. 33).

In his insistence that emotion can be understood only as a special relationship of the human being to the external world, Sartre's theory is a much needed corrective. There is no doubt that any emotion refers to an object and clings to it as long as it remains an emotion. It is also true that the emotional awareness is unreflective, immediate, object-bound. Nevertheless, it remains a reaction to the object, and therefore is active, not passive.

Not all emotions are reactions to difficulties—that would be but another version of the conflict theory of emotion. Since emotion itself signifies "the whole of consciousness, of human reality," it is really poetic license to speak of consciousness as being passive, degraded to a lower level, when this same consciousness has to *establish* a wholly different magical world. The compelling character of emotion is sufficiently explained by showing how emotion forces us to believe in the apparent permanence of the harmful, the horrible, the enjoyable aspects of the world. To call it a "magical attitude" is to label without explaining. It may be magic that anything in this world can have significance for us, can aim at us personally, so to speak; but it is magical only if we assume that human beings are unrelated and isolated monads living in an alien and fragmented world.

Since an emotion clings to its object, it cannot "deny" it. If it did, not only the need for action but the emotion itself would be over. If flight is "a fainting which is enacted" and fainting is an effective denial of the object, as Sartre says, that is also the end of the emotion. In human experience emotion urges to action: fear urges us to flee, anger to attack. To turn such action into a denial that makes action superfluous is to do violence to the very experience, the emotional consciousness, to which Sartre appeals in his analysis.

It is interesting to reflect that Sartre's approach is at the opposite extreme from the behavioristic account. While behaviorists ignore human experience and awareness altogether, Sartre makes consciousness explain itself and even posit itself. At both extremes the system must be maintained by anthropomorphic interpretations. The behaviorist makes the various conditioned stimuli, linked to inherent drives, act like a person in initiating, selecting, and directing action. The existentialist makes

consciousness act or be passive like a person, or confer qualities upon
objects, and existence upon itself. In the pursuit of both extremes
theorists tend to forget that it is always the human being who acts, who
does not create either himself or his consciousness, but who also is not
merely the inert plaything of his environment.

Our survey has shown that theories of emotion seem to concentrate
on one or a few aspects of the phenomenon at the price of neglecting
others. Some theorists emphasize the sensations of bodily changes, others
the relation of emotion to instincts and drives; still others concentrate
on the source of emotion in conflict, or its character as a disturbance.
Whenever one facet of emotion dominates in this way, the theory becomes
one-sided and incomplete.

FUNCTIONAL THEORIES

There are some modern theories that take the middle road, neither
disregarding the significance of emotion for the living being, nor making
the emotional consciousness magically ascendant over the physical world.

Gemelli. Having done considerable experimental work on the physi-
ology and psychology of emotion during the last thirty years, Gemelli has
recently (1949) worked out a consistent theoretical formulation on neo-
scholastic lines.

He first distinguishes feeling from emotion by suggesting that feelings should be called "objective" because they seem to adhere to the
object, while emotions are "subjective feelings" because they involve the
person as a whole. Objective feelings are the reaction to some sensation
(for instance, feelings of hunger, thirst, well-being, discomfort, anguish,
lightness, strength, etc.). They are elementary and primitive and cannot
be further defined. Emotions or "subjective feelings" are produced when
the person "considers a situation or an object or a person in relation to
himself" (1949, p. 207).

To illustrate the difference between objective and subjective feelings,
Gemelli quotes some introspective reports, of which only one will be
given here: "The sound was sweet and pleasant; but this pleasure gave
way quickly to another pleasure which was more subtle. The sound
evoked in me the memory of a particular incident in my recent vacation
during which I heard this music; and I felt my soul pervaded with joy"
(1949, p. 211). The two types of feeling have a distinctive character;

"objective feelings" depend on sensations, while "the so-called subjective feelings which can also be initiated by a sensation are largely dependent on another content of consciousness, a memory evoked by the sensation, an idea or even a perception or an image" (1949, p. 210).

Both objective and subjective feelings are regulators of action. There is an intimate relation between feelings and action tendencies (instincts) so that they can both be "produced conjointly—a sensation being sufficient to touch off the entire biological complex of which they both are parts" (1949, p. 300). In someone who is fond of sweets, for instance, the sight of candy immediately touches off an objective feeling of pleasure, "and the awakened pleasure stimulates him to react by helping himself" (1949, p. 300).

In the same way, subjective feelings or emotions are joined to instinctive tendencies that either aim at the satisfaction of organismic needs or evaluate objects, situations, and people. Though feelings regulate actions by making us aware of action tendencies aroused by the object, these action tendencies may not always urge to the most effective action, nor may the action toward which they urge always be in the best interest of the person as a whole.

The feeling reaction must be complemented by an intellectual appraisal of the situation. The action which is finally decided upon may either implement the felt tendency or be contrary to it. Hence feelings are only one of several factors in deliberate action.

The action tendencies themselves (often called instincts) are evoked when the object is seen as affecting the person in some way:

A knife seen by the subject does not by itself alone awaken any biological complex; it is purely an object of perception. But if the subject in perceiving such an object, has also knowledge that it has a dark significance, because of the special circumstances in which he sees it, so that it constitutes a menace, immediately there will occur in him a movement of repulsion, with a general feeling of disgust, resulting in the still more general feeling known as fear. (1949, p. 305)

It seems that for Gemelli there is always an objective feeling which is then followed by the emotion proper (the subjective feeling). But it is very doubtful whether there would be first an objective feeling at the sight of the knife itself and only later the emotion of fear. If the significance of the knife as a threat is appreciated at all, that recognition of a threat would arouse fear immediately. Our attention will be drawn from the visual aspect of the object to its significance for us. Hence the objective feeling could hardly become conscious. In the same way, we do not feel discomfort when we are angry or afraid or even greatly interested in something. Emotion takes precedence over objective feeling and does not necessarily grow out of it. The transition from objective feeling to emotion seems to require a change in regard which may occur in some emotions but is not a necessary condition for emotion (see Ch. 4).

For Gemelli the action tendency is organized as a neurological pattern, an inherited predisposition which is activated when a situation is perceived as desirable, menacing, or annoying. Gemelli mentions that this is the same "neural predisposition" postulated by Nina Bull in her attitude theory of emotion. However, it is important to realize that Gemelli's theory provides for an activation by a *psychological* appraisal of the situation by the person, while Nina Bull has the mental attitude follow the activated motor attitude. Hence Nina Bull sees her analysis as a refinement of the James-Lange theory, while Gemelli points out that emotion must be understood from a functional point of view, as the result of a *perceived special relationship* between object and subject which also arouses the appropriate action tendency.

It is clear that Gemelli's "objective feelings" are identical with the "sense-bound feelings" discussed in Chapter 4. Gemelli's formulation, however, makes it impossible to distinguish accurately between feelings and emotion, for instance, between joy and the pleasantness of joy, or between the emotion of fear and the unpleasant feeling we have when we are afraid. In Gemelli's terms both are "subjective feelings." This difficulty may have contributed to Gemelli's view that objective feelings are always present before subjective feelings arise. For him there is evidently a progression from feeling to emotion—yet it has been shown that a special attitude must be assumed before feeling will be noticed, while emotion tends to compel attention.

Michotte. In 1951 Michotte reported some interesting experiments with colored rectangles moving along a slot, which have a bearing on views of emotion. His observers rarely gave a purely objective description but interpreted the movement as attack, escape, friendly approach, and the like. Evidently each observer interpreted the movement of one rectangle as somehow affecting the other, expressing some emotion toward the other. Michotte pointed out that this "functional connection" between the observer and the object becomes even clearer when the observer's own

movements are involved, when he himself approaches something or withdraws from it, pushes or is being pushed. Here he is no longer an observer, he is the agent, and the movements appear no longer as the
expression of someone else's emotion, they become the expression of his
own.

For Michotte emotion is a functional connection between subject and
object, established by a reaction of the person:

> It is *I* who repels, who embraces, who avoids, etc. For the observer the reac-
> tions which he witnesses are conveyed by an object distinct from himself; it is
> that person whom he sees over there who goes toward the other and shakes
> his hand. In the case of the agent, on the other hand, the action is not that
> of another person, nor is it properly speaking the action of his own body (as
> a thing); it is *himself* who acts in such a way toward such and such a person
> or thing or who feels this affective reaction for this person or thing. (1950,
> p. 124)

The other person's movement toward him is similarly interpreted as being caused by the other and affecting himself.

Thus emotion depends on an estimate of the function of the object in
relation to the subject. It is a felt functional connection. Michotte pointed
out that such an estimate is possible to animals as well. In man, however, there is an additional factor,

> for he is not merely a being which "feels," but also one which "thinks," and
> "knows," so the emotions he experiences usually have an intellectual aspect.
> Onto the felt connection is superimposed the knowledge of the *abstract* rela-
> tion implied in that connection. A man "feels" himself attracted or repelled
> by an object, and at the same time he "is aware" of the attraction or repulsion,
> he knows it is happening. (1950, p. 126)

For Michotte the functional connection between subject and object is
established by an intuitive judgment which may be supplemented by
reflection but is not itself reflective. But for the human being who does
reflect on his emotion, the sheer emotional experience ceases to be a
transitory episode and takes its place in his whole scheme of life, to be
intensified or suppressed according to his wider goals.

For Michotte, as for Gemelli, emotion as a "functional connection" or
a "perceived special relationship" between subject and object can explain
how emotion is aroused. An object is seen in a special relationship to the
person, it affects him in a particular way; hence he feels emotion toward
it which may or may not culminate in appropriate action. What arouses

emotion is no "cold" perception but a practical estimate that demands some kind of action. Both Michotte and Gemelli have given an adequate psychological explanation. Theirs is a balanced theory of emotion, even though it is not complete.

To have a balanced theory, we must have a description and explanation of all three aspects of emotion: *emotional experience, emotional expression, and emotional action*. A balanced theory must explain the nature of emotional experience and how it differs from unemotional experience; the arousal of emotion and bodily changes; and emotion as a factor in goal-directed action. There are other problems that must be tackled before a theory will be complete: the differences, both psychological and physiological, between one emotion and another; the relation of emotion and feelings; the neurophysiological mechanism that mediates the experience and expression of emotion; and the significance of emotion for personality integration.

Part III. THE PSYCHOLOGY OF EMOTION

9. PHENOMENOLOGICAL ANALYSIS OF EMOTION

As we have seen in the last four chapters, the causal relation between perceived object, emotional experience, and bodily upset has been a problem to theorists throughout the ages. From the time when psychology became a science, three main solutions have been advocated: (1) that perception arouses emotion and emotion then causes bodily changes; (2) that perception induces bodily changes that are felt as emotion; (3) that perception arouses both emotion and bodily changes. There have been many psychologists who have seen the problem involved in the causal relations of these three factors, but none of them has solved it adequately or consistently.

Darwin's account (see Ch. 5) transferred the problem from ontogeny to phylogeny without solving it. James and Lange (Ch. 6), reversing the accepted sequence of experience-expression, tried to account for emotional experience as the result of physical changes. They explained the arousal of these changes on the basis of Darwin's principles, which created new problems. As a partial remedy, James added the principle of analogous-feeling, thus in effect contradicting his own theoretical formulations, as Dewey was the first to see. Dewey (Ch. 6), attempting to restore consistency, substituted for the causal relation a simultaneous "tension" in which action produces and contains all the causal links. Compared to this counsel of despair, McDougall's view (Ch. 7) that impulse and emotion are aroused together by the object looks like a return to common sense. If he had followed through his suggestion that both are aroused by a rudimentary instinctive perception, this would be the most satisfactory explanation achieved up to that time.

With Freud, finally, the problem was shifted to different ground altogether. Though anxiety (fear) was still thought to be aroused by the perception of a threat, love and anger became the affect charges of the libidinal and aggressive drives. As such, they are not aroused by an object, but are experienced when the drive cathects the object. Whatever the merits of this explanation for personality theory, for a theory of emotion it is unacceptable because it makes an unjustifiable distinction between emotions aroused by objects and emotions that are the experience of a drive cathexis.

Later theorists hardly touched upon this problem. The behavioristically inclined (including Jacobson, Bull, and Duffy) assumed that emotion is drive strength, energy mobilization, and the like. If it is experienced at all, it would have to be experienced as kinesthetic sensations. Others were noncommittal about the connection between emotional experience and expression (Young) or ignored it altogether. Only Michotte and Gemelli insisted that an object must be appraised before an emotion can be felt; and they implied that emotion is accompanied by physiological changes but does not cause them.

The only approach that promises a solution of the problem of how perception arouses emotion is a careful phenomenological analysis of the whole sequence from perception to emotion and action. Sartre attempted such an analysis, but his fascination with the way in which emotion changes the world, seemingly for all time to come, sent him into bypaths where we cannot follow him. His antithesis of emotion and action makes of emotion a magical wand that transforms reality into a fantasy world where action is suspended altogether. We hope to examine emotion as a human experience and trace the link that connects emotion with action.

FROM PERCEPTION TO EMOTION

In emotion, as in perception, there is not only someone who experiences but also someone or something that occasions the experience. We are afraid of something, we rejoice over something, we love someone, we are angry at something or someone. Emotion seems to have an object just as sense perception does. To say that emotion may be vague and objectless, as in neurotic anxiety or in depression, is to confuse the issue. These are departures from normal functioning. Normal emotion carries with it the reference to an object or situation that is known in some way.

The object of emotion. The object or situation may be actually present, as in the reunion of lovers after long absence. It may be in the past, as a remembered injury done to a friend. It may be the anticipation of some future event, as an impending automobile collision. Emotion may even be aroused by something merely imagined, as the possible loss of a job, or winning the Grand Prize in the Irish Sweep.

To have an emotion, it is necessary to perceive or know the object in some way, though it is not necessary to know it accurately or correctly. In fact, we may ascribe to what we love or fear qualities that exist only in our imagination. We may love or fear something for reasons that have nothing to do with its physical nature or with the way it affects our sense organs.

What arouses our emotion need not be a single concrete thing or person. It can be a group of people, like one's family, or a complex situation, like an examination, or a state of affairs, like the danger of atomic war. It can be a complex state of mind, like gloating or feeling inferior, like being praised or being scolded.

Emotion distinct from perception. How, then, can emotion be distinguished from sense perception? Both perception and emotion have an object; but in emotion the object is known in a particular way. To perceive or apprehend something means that I know what it is like as a thing, apart from any effect on me. To like or dislike it means that I know it not only objectively, as it is apart from me, but also that I estimate its relation to me, that I appraise it as desirable or undesirable, valuable or harmful for me, so that I am drawn toward it or repelled by it.*

To arouse an emotion, the object must be appraised as affecting me in some way, affecting me personally as an individual with my particular experience and my particular aims. If I see an apple, I know that it is an apple of a particular kind and taste. This knowledge need not touch me personally in any way. But if the apple is of my favorite kind and I am in a part of the world where it does not grow and cannot be bought, I may want it with a real emotional craving. Similarly I may know that two cars traveling at right angles will reach a point of intersection at

---

* In our context, the term perception is used for the simple apprehension of an object as an object rather than a bundle of sensations. Before anything can have "meaning" for us, it must be seen as a thing (must be *perceived*) and must also be seen in some relationship to us (it must be *appraised*). Meaning comes with appraisal.

the same moment. But only when I realize that in these cars there is someone I love or someone who belongs to me in any sense of the term (a member of my family or my species or even a fellow vertebrate) will I feel emotion.

Emotion distinct from appraisal. Since emotion has an objective, something to be gained or avoided that is appraised as good or harmful, desirable or undesirable, the question arises whether this appraisal itself could be the emotion. If I love somebody, does loving consist merely in estimating him to be good for me? Surely not, for it is possible to form an estimate that is entirely unemotional. Often enough we do realize that a given person would make a good friend, husband, or wife, that a given association would be both desirable and profitable—yet we feel no attraction and make no move toward closer friendship. Emotion seems to include not only the appraisal of how this thing or person will affect me but also a definite pull toward or away from it. In fact, does not the emotional *quale* consist precisely in that unreasoning involuntary attraction or repulsion?

If I merely know things or persons as they are apart from me, there is no emotion. If I know them and judge them theoretically and abstractly to be good for me, there may still be no emotion. But if I think something is good for me *here and now,* and *feel myself drawn toward it,* sometimes even against my better judgment, then my experience is, properly speaking, nonrational; it is other than just cold reason; it is an addition to knowledge: it is *emotional.*

Appraisal direct, immediate, intuitive. The appraisal that arouses an emotion is not abstract; it is not the result of reflection. It is immediate and indeliberate. If we see somebody stab at our eye with his finger, we avoid the threat instantly, even though we may know that he does not intend to hurt or even to touch us. Before we can make such an instant response, we must have estimated somehow that the stabbing finger could hurt. Since the movement is immediate, unwitting, or even contrary to our better knowledge, this appraisal of possible harm must be similarly immediate.

Animals and very young children seem to be able to judge things that are harmful and things that are good to have, for they avoid the one and approach the other. They may have to learn, of course, that some judgments are mistaken. Small children or kittens may well reach for a candle flame the first time they see it and will be burned. Once burned, they avoid it. Such learning is possible only if child and kitten remember the flame and hurt and in addition realize the next time they see the flame that it will hurt again. There must be a psychological capacity of appraising how a given thing will affect us, whether it will hurt or please us, before we can want to approach or avoid it. To call upon mere "learning," "past experience," or the "conditioned reflex" for an explanation is futile. Without such an appraisal learning would be impossible and past experience useless.

Appraisal in learning. In every formal learning situation * there is a goal set by the experimenter or the person, to which the experimental subject has to find his way (see Arnold, 1954). In such learning, the present situation must be appraised as similar to a past one, promising a similar satisfaction or demanding a similar action. In classical conditioning, for instance, the animal learns that the conditioned stimulus announces food, and salivates in expectation of food; or that it announces pain, and withdraws. In instrumental conditioning, the animal learns that the lever in the Skinner box, when manipulated, brings food. The animal learns to expect food, water, or pain, either immediately the conditioned stimulus is perceived or upon pressing the lever. Hence the animal remembers, recognizes, *appraises:* unless the buzzer is *appraised* as meaning food or electric shock, the animal will neither salivate nor withdraw. Unless the lever is appraised as bringing food, the animal will not press it. The conditioned reflex is always a reaction to the *un*conditioned stimulus, based on the animal's realization that the conditioned stimulus *announces* or *belongs to* the expected food or shock.† Hence

* Of course, learning is not restricted to formal learning situations. Most of the time, we learn without deliberation, without setting a goal. Whatever we perceive adds to our knowledge, just as every movement we make adds to our general motor skill. But this learning is *incidental;* it is not deliberate or formal learning. Such incidental learning does depend on memory but it does not require the *recognition* that the present situation is like a former one, nor the *appraisal* that it can be approached in a similar way.

Animals also learn incidentally by exercising their functions. In formal learning situations (deliberate learning) the deliberation is that of the experimenter who sets up the problem. For the animal, all such learning is really emotional learning: the buzzer is appraised as bringing food which is wanted and expected, and this expectation results in salivation; the lever is appraised as bringing food, and the animal "wants" it (i.e., it has a tendency toward it) and manipulates it. (See Ch. 11, on emotion initiating animal action.)

† See Walter's (1953) penetrating analysis of conditioning that enabled him to build *machina docilis.* In this machine, the appearance of food initiates a short electrical impulse, and a neutral stimulus an impulse lasting for some time. When food appears shortly after the neutral stimulus, it intensifies and prolongs that impulse until, after many presentations of neutral stimulus and food, the

conditioning occurs if the conditioned stimulus is given before or with food or shock but does not occur if it follows food or shock. Without the *appraisal* that buzzer or lever brings food or buzzer brings pain, no conditioned reflexes could be formed at all. In concentrating exclusively on the conditioned response we have overlooked the experiential factors that make such responses possible.

Direct and reflective perception and appraisal. Perception is often discussed as if it were a unitary global process, without distinguishing between simply apprehending an object, recognizing it, understanding or making judgments about it, arguing, and the like (see Blake and Ramsay, 1951, Ch. 1). However, for our discussion of the genesis of an emotion it is necessary to make some distinction between different kinds of perception and different kinds of judgment.

Psychologists of an earlier generation distinguished between direct apprehension like the *simple seeing* of a color (e.g., blue), *recognizing* it when seeing it on different occasions, and *reflectively knowing* it to be blue. They called both direct and reflective recognition (both of which imply judgment) *apperception,* and distinguished this from *direct apprehension.* But they did not distinguish direct recognition which does not involve rational judgment from reflective recognition which does. Similarly, no great attention was paid to the difference between judgments that *connect* concrete particular sense data with concrete particular objects or events in a given sense experience, and judgments that *generalize* from these sense data or events. Thus it has come about that "sense" judgments, which merely *find* the relation between sense data, and reflective judgments, that *understand* them, are both called judgments, and often included in the term "perception." * Yet there is a significant

---

electrical impulse is intense enough to activate *machina docilis* to approach. What we have called "sense judgment" in living beings is obtained in Walter's machine by having a set threshold for motor activation and having a memory unit to preserve the electrical impulses set up by earlier combinations of neutral stimulus and food. Whatever the neural mechanism in animals and men, we know from firsthand experience and from reflection that our perceiving and appraising the situation touches off motor action. For this reason, it is more fruitful to start from these psychological processes and look for the neurological mechanism that mediates them rather than the other way round. After all, a model that will give the same response need not be built on the same principles.

* It is sometimes said, for instance, that the animal can perceive "triangularity" because it can distinguish between a triangle and a square (cf. Lashley, 1938). But the animal merely makes a sense judgment that this thing is different from that, a judgment that requires neither reflection nor learning and is possible

difference between the two, between sense judgment and reflective judgment. When the elephant tests the ground with his foot, he makes a sense judgment. When the physicist tests a hypothesis by an experiment, he makes intellectual judgments.

What we call *appraisal* or *estimate* is close to such a sense judgment. In emotional experience such appraisal is always direct, immediate; it is a *sense judgment* and includes a reflective judgment only as a secondary evaluation. Perhaps an example will illustrate the difference. When the outfielder "judges" a fly ball, he simply senses where he is going and where the ball is going and gauges his movements so that he will meet the ball. If he stopped to reflect, he would never stay in the game. We ourselves are constantly making judgments of this sort without paying much attention to them. Now the judgment that the ball is too far or too close or just right for catching is no different from the judgment we make in appraising an object as good or bad, pleasurable or dangerous for us. Such sense judgments are direct, immediate, nonreflective, nonintellectual, automatic, "instinctive," "intuitive." The terms "instinctive" and "intuitive," whenever they were used to describe such sense judgments, had the meaning of *direct, immediate, nonreflective,* as, for instance, in the phrases: "he shrank back instinctively," or "he knew intuitively that he had met a friend." This usage is still common in literature but has been banished from psychological writings because of the mistaken conviction that "instinctive" must mean a mechanical behavior pattern and "intuitive" must have the character of a hunch. In the context of this book, the term "intuitive appraisal" will mean the direct, immediate sense judgment of weal or woe.

Appraisal and reflective judgment. In the human adult and the older child, the estimate of weal or woe is both intuitive and reflective. But the intuitive judgment is immediate; the reflective judgment follows. This is shown by the fact that the intuitive appraisal is often supplemented or corrected by later reflection. When this happens, the emotion changes with the new intuitive estimate which follows the corrective judgment.

---

to a rat reared in blindness on its first exposure to light (Hebb, 1949). The judgment that this is a *triangle* requires not only reflection and an abstraction of the essential feature of "triangularity," but also an opportunity to identify the same feature in various kinds of triangles. For this reason such a judgment is impossible for the animal which cannot reflect or for the human being born blind, immediately after he gains his sight (cf. Senden, 1932), who has not yet learned to identify and abstract the essential feature in visual objects.

A child may start and run when he sees something that looks to him like a ghost moving in the dark. But as soon as he remembers that this is wash day and realizes that the object is only a sheet flapping in the breeze, the fear that sent him running will turn to laughter. Whenever there is no intuitive appraisal of an object or a situation but only a reflective judgment, the matter becomes strictly speculative—there is no emotion. This seems to happen in the emotional flattening of the schizophrenic ("schizophrenia" means a split between reason and emotion). When the schizophrenic tells us with a vacant smile that he is much distressed because his mother has died, he makes a strictly speculative reflective judgment that a mother's death is a source of grief for a son. But he does not or cannot make the intuitive appraisal; hence he neither feels nor shows sorrow.

Perception completed by appraisal. To know or perceive something and to estimate its effect on us are two distinct processes, and appraisal necessarily presupposes perception. The perception of an object requires the integration of sense impressions even within one sense modality, for we perceive objects, patterns, or shapes, not simply a collection of colors, tones, or touch impressions. It also requires the integration of impressions from various sense modalities, for we know that the sound we hear comes from this bell we can feel as hard and smooth and see as golden and shining. To estimate how it affects us personally (for instance, when someone threatens to toss it to us) seems to require a further step beyond perception which cannot be the function of any one sense modality nor of all of them together. At the same time, as we have seen, this appraisal is instant and intuitive; hence it cannot be the result of reflection but must be the work of some integrative sensory function. Following upon perception and completing it, appraisal makes possible an active approach, acceptance or withdrawal, and thus establishes our relationship to the outside world.

The process by which isolated sensations are integrated so that we perceive things and people is not open to introspection. We know that such integration must occur in all living beings with sense organs and we assume that it is the result of some integrative nervous function. Only in special cases can a pure sensation be experienced apart from the object and its meaning for us: for instance, people born blind, who regain their vision after an operation, at first see patches of color instead of objects (Senden, 1932). For anyone who is not blind, sense impressions are immediately and automatically ordered into objects; only when the sensory cortex is destroyed is this integration disturbed. After injury of the visual cortex, for instance, the patient sees colored patches instead of patterns or objects (Goldstein, 1948).

The process by which we estimate whether a thing is harmful or good for us is similarly direct and intuitive, hidden from inspection. A fear or anger reaction follows so quickly upon a sudden threat that it may be all but impossible to separate perception, appraisal, and emotion. In other cases, there is no perceptible time interval between grasping the meaning of the situation and feeling the emotion, but there may be a perceptible interval between perceiving the situation and realizing its import for us. The fact that perception and appraisal can be thus separated shows that sense perception alone is not sufficient for an emotion.

FROM EMOTION TO EXPRESSION AND ACTION

The connection of perception to action requires some link or links that can initiate action. This link cannot be a mechanical switch-through from receptor to effector systems. Such a switch-through would be invariant, yet action varies according to circumstances. In fact, this variation is the very basis for distinguishing action from reflex. The link must consist in some psychological activity that leads to action; it cannot be either perception or appraisal. To perceive something and estimate its effect on us merely completes the information we collect, hence theoretically still belongs to the receiving system.

As soon as we appraise something as worth having in an immediate and intuitive way, we feel an attraction toward it. As soon as we intuitively judge that something is threatening, we feel repelled from it, we feel urged to avoid it. The intuitive appraisal of the situation initiates an *action tendency that is felt as emotion,* expressed in various bodily changes, and that eventually may lead to overt action.

Normally, the sequence perception-appraisal-emotion is so closely knit that our everyday experience is never the strictly objective knowledge of a thing; it is always a knowing-and-liking, or a knowing-and-disliking. There is hardly any object we simply note as such without appraising it. Whether a thing is pleasing to the eye, delectable to the palate, useful as a tool, or a treasure to possess, it is never simply there, apart from us, it is always seen in some relationship to ourselves. In fact, strictly objective observation has to be carefully taught and meticulously acquired to make so-called "scientific method" possible at all.

This fact is at the bottom of Bergson's and Dewey's notion that reflective knowledge is secondary to action upon the environment, that we first perceive and do, and much later think about the object of our perceiving and doing. But there is a link left out in thus telescoping perceiving and doing into one action sequence. Without this link, we are at a loss to explain why the same perception results sometimes in one and sometimes in another emotion and action. The link left out is the intuitive appraisal of the object, its "demand-character," as Lewin would say. The emotion, as well as the action, follows the intuitive estimate that establishes this demand-character. First I see something, then I realize that it is dangerous—and as soon as I do, I am afraid and run. Since this appraisal is almost as direct as sense perception and immediately follows and completes it, it can be known as a separate process only when we come to reflect upon it.

In the past, psychologists have analyzed the sequence emotion-expression-action rather than the sequence perception-appraisal-emotion. As a result, it has often been claimed that perception and emotion follow upon each other immediately, that they are always associated and should be considered as one. Every perception, it is said, is accompanied by some feeling tone, hence perceptual and emotional processes cannot be separated. It is quite true that perception and appraisal (and therefore emotion) normally occur together, but there are obviously some instances where emotion is at a minimum, and others where emotion is so intense that it blots out all incidental perceptions. In between there are all shades of intensity, unrelated to the intensity of sensation. Since the two processes, perception and affect, do not vary together, they cannot be identical, though their connection in time is exceedingly close.

Bodily changes implied by sequence emotion-action. The attraction or repulsion felt in emotion is not a mere psychological state; it is an impulse to action that brings with it a host of physiological changes. Anger brings an urge to strike and tear, to use the muscles poised for action, to express the tension that threatens to smother us. To act as anger prompts us to act, so that we crush or destroy what annoys us, not only removes the obstacle but also brings relief from unbearable physical tension. Similarly with other emotions. Their physiological effects are such that action must follow under pain of considerable discomfort. Fear is intensely unpleasant. To flee as fear prompts us means not only escape from danger but relief from internal discomfort. Longing for something we cannot have may become a torment when it is intense. To act as we feel urged to act, so that we finally reach the goal we desire, brings not only the possession of what we long for but also alleviates physical discomfort.

Since different emotions urge us to different actions, and the physiological symptoms are relieved when we give in to this urge, we might expect that the physiological changes, taken by and large, will be as different as are the emotions. We know from personal experience that the physical sensations we feel are different in different emotions. Dumas (1932) has recognized these differences in emotional experience, while Cannon (1915) insisted that all emotions have the same physiological state (cf. Ch. 8, for a discussion of Dumas's theory of emotion, and Ch. 7, in the following volume, for a discussion of the physiological changes in various emotions).

Patterns of physiological changes. For each emotion, there is a distinct pattern that remains more or less constant and is recognized as characteristic for that emotion. Whether we are afraid of a bear, a snake, or a thunderstorm, our bodily sensations during these various experiences are very much alike. When we are afraid, we tremble, our heart races, we feel chilly, have clammy hands, and suffer from general malaise, the more pronounced the longer it lasts. When we are bubbling over with joy, we have quite a different bodily experience; and never would we mistake the one for the other. It may be difficult to describe these differences accurately even to our own satisfaction (let alone to the satisfaction of the psychologist) but subjectively we feel quite sure of it. In any experience of the same emotion, the same pattern is repeated and is more or less widespread and intense, according to the intensity of the emotion. True, two different people may show and experience fear or any other emotion in individually different ways; nevertheless, there will always be a core that is similar from person to person or even from man to animal. Unless there were such a core, we would never recognize emotions in another human being, let alone in animals (see Ch. 10).

Since the felt tendency to approach or withdraw comes in full strength as soon as we have appraised the situation, while the physical disturbance takes an appreciable time to reach its peak, the felt emotion cannot be identical with the physical upset. Both may start at the same time; both are the result of appraisal: but the physical disturbance requires the conduction of nerve impulses from brain to periphery while the experience of emotion evidently does not. Lehmann (1914), Newman and associates (1930), and others have found repeatedly that an emotion is reported before any peripheral changes can be felt or observed.

Secondary appraisal. The physical changes that come with emotion are sensed and appraised in turn. They may be evaluated as having a meaning, indicating some physical condition that affects the person in some way. If a man is afraid without paying attention to his fear (as happened, e.g., time and again to pilots during bombing missions) the physiological effects of fear may be noted with surprise long after the threat is over. The weakness, tremor, fast heart rate, will be an occasion for alarm if their connection with the earlier fear (an automatic reaction to a situation appraised as dangerous) is not recognized, and may then be interpreted as signs of a serious illness.

As an example, let us analyze the complete sequence as it might occur in a bomber pilot:

1. Observation: "There are fighter planes coming up."
2. Appraisal: "There is danger; they may catch up with me and hit the plane."
3. Fear (not attended to because the pilot is fully occupied, evading the fighter planes).
4. Physiological changes: Increase in heart rate; tremor; fatigue, which becomes cumulative until the mission is finished.
5. Awareness of these changes (will be delayed until the necessity for action is past and attention is free to notice the physiological state).
6. Secondary estimate: "I am chronically tired, trembling, irritable—I must be ill."
7. Secondary emotion: Fear of illness, heart disease, etc.
8. Physiological changes: Reinforcement of fatigue, tremor, etc., increasing the malaise.

In this way, emotion can grow in intensity and the physical effects can become cumulative, though they may not be felt until some time after the first appraisal. A man may be confronted with a dangerous situation and may act immediately and effectively. If he is completely unaware (does not remember) that he has felt fear, he may later misinterpret the physiological effects of fear as symptoms of an indisposition or illness. It is generally recognized that it is preferable to have men exposed to danger realize that fear is a natural and inevitable reaction, rather than to let them disregard their fear and become a prey to organ neurosis, battle fatigue, or effort syndrome (cf. Grinker and Spiegel, 1945).

The secondary estimate accounts for the fact that an adrenaline injection sometimes produces a genuine emotion but at other times is reported as a bodily upset that feels *as if* there is an emotion. Cantril and Hunt (1932) have studied the psychological effects of adrenaline injection and have quoted very different reports from men who claimed to have felt a genuine emotion and from those who felt an "as if" emotion.

Typical for a "cold" emotion are the following remarks:

Decided predisposition to an emotion. Only a constant conscious attempt to keep calm prevented an emotion. It was an effort to keep calm. (Cantril and Hunt, 1932, p. 304)

Feel as though I had had a big scare, not fright but like a reaction after a tremendous fright. Don't feel unpleasant. If there is any affective state it is somewhat pleasant. Certain bodily restlessness but no worries, cares, or mental anxieties. (p. 303)

The following two reports are typical for genuine emotion:

Extreme fear was present, but no content for it at the time. Probably an unconscious reason but at the time nothing but fear. . . . I found myself shaking, chest trembling, building up rapidly in intensity, whereupon I abruptly recognized that I was intensely afraid. (p. 303)

I seem oppressed with a vague fear of something—feeling much the same as when I'd lain awake all night, frightened that Bill might die. (p. 303)

The difference between the two kinds of statement is a difference in appraising the bodily state. In the first two reports the individual simply noted a "predisposition" to emotion or a bodily restlessness, but he knew of no object that could have caused an emotion, hence he did not identify it as such. In the third report the bodily state was again noted but here the symptoms were finally added up and recognized as characteristic for a state of fear. In the last case the bodily state was immediately recognized as similar to that experienced earlier during intense fear; hence it was identified as fear. Here we see very clearly that the physiological effects of fear will be recognized in cases where the person has had a similar experience, and the whole pattern will be identified as fear even though there may be no object that arouses it.

Definition of emotion. We have seen that emotion is an experience in which the person appraises the object as affecting himself. Such an appraisal of the object results in a felt attraction or aversion, and eventually (if no other motive interferes) in approach or avoidance. Perception is completed by an intuitive appraisal that arouses emotion. Hence the sequence perception-appraisal-emotion comes before the sequence emotion-expression-action, which so far has been emphasized almost exclusively in psychological theory. It is the sequence perception-appraisal-emotion that alone will explain the conditions necessary for arousing emotion.

Since emotion is experienced as an action tendency, it must excite brain circuits that give rise to emotional expression and action (see the following volume, Parts I and II). These expressive patterns then allow us to recognize emotions in others, both in men and animals. In human beings, bodily changes may be appraised in turn when they are felt, particularly when the connection of appraisal with emotion and autonomic changes has escaped attention because the person was otherwise occupied.

Summing up our discussion, we can now define emotion as *the felt tendency toward anything intuitively appraised as good (beneficial), or away from anything intuitively appraised as bad (harmful). This attraction or aversion is accompanied by a pattern of physiological changes organized toward approach or withdrawal. The patterns differ for different emotions.*

RESIDUAL EFFECTS OF EMOTION

While the appraisal of the object is immediate, the felt attraction or repulsion lasts as long as our attention is centered on the object. Because we feel the attraction or aversion all over, our attention may be kept riveted to what arouses it; thus we discover new reasons for liking or disliking it. The new appraisal reinforces the emotion. Feeling attracted, we see only the attractive side; feeling repelled, we center all our attention on the distasteful aspect. Sartre rightly emphasizes that the object of our emotion fascinates us and takes us captive. This peculiar bondage is the result of our appraisal arousing attraction or aversion, that is, *action tendencies* that organize later perception and bias later appraisal.

Constancy of perception and appraisal. Sartre has seen also that emotion changes the world around us. What is horrible is so not only now but "spreads itself over the whole future and darkens it." But that need not mean that emotion somehow confers a magical quality upon the world, as Sartre claims. There is a much simpler explanation. Just as there is a constancy of perception,* so there is constancy in our intuitive appraisal of the world around us. When we see what we recognize as an apple, we expect it to remain an apple. When we say we like apples, we expect that they will keep their apple qualities and that we shall go on liking them. If a child is hurt by a dog or burnt by fire, he will expect the dog and the fire to remain dangerous. More than that, just as we expect that all apples will have apple qualities, be they russets, greenings, or Northern Spies, so the child will expect all dogs to be dangerous, from bulldog to Pekinese. When he gradually realizes that other animals are like dogs in some way, he may expect them to threaten harm as well.†

In our experience with things and people, the expectation of their constancy remains indefinitely until another experience contradicts it. Once a child knows what a table is, or a doll, he is not likely to forget it. The little girl will recognize a doll and play with it whether it is big or small, black or white, a baby doll or a bride. She may even dress up a stick and croon over it. The child has abstracted the constant factor, the essential feature, has grasped it into a concept, and now looks for this constant feature in many individual dolls. Human beings expect concrete indi-

* This constancy is more than the constancy of color, shape, weight, etc. investigated by psychologists. We form a notion of the object from seeing, hearing, touching, handling, hefting it, so that we expect the object itself to remain as we have learned to know it. For this reason, drawing in perspective, for instance, has to be laboriously acquired in much the same way as is scientific method. When we draw from perspective, we must disregard our earlier perceptual expectations derived from combined sense experience and must concentrate on the actual visual impression as the image on the retina portrays it. In scientific method, we must disregard earlier appraisals which have led us to expect a certain effect, and must concentrate on the characteristics of the experimental object as we observe it, apart from its effects on us personally. (Cf. Heider, 1958, on the constancy of person perception.)

† Animals also act upon such constancies of perception and appraisal, but they merely expect *concretely similar things* to be similarly harmful or beneficial. Human beings extend such expectations to all members of the same class of objects. This accounts for the fact that we find phobias in human beings but not in animals. While a person suffering from claustrophobia is as much afraid in a large auditorium as in a car if the doors are closed, the animal may be afraid of a particular cage in which he has been shocked but is not afraid of a different cage or another compartment in the same cage.

vidual objects to remain constant, and also those objects they have recognized as members of a class.

Similarly, the appraisal of something as good or bad for us and the emotion that follows it will be generalized to the whole class of objects rather than be confined to an individual instance. The little girl not only knows dolls but likes them, though she may prefer one doll to another. Once she has taken a liking to her first doll, she will expect to like all other dolls. Any intuitive appraisal, once made, brings with it the expectation that this object, and all other members of the class to which it belongs, will be good (or bad) for all time to come. The greater the good it promises or the harm it threatens, the more intense will be the emotion that follows such appraisal. "Emotional conditioning" is the inevitable result of the expectation that a situation threatening extreme harm will keep its harmful qualities. No repetition of the threat is needed because the emotion had maximum intensity the first time.

There is one important difference between our appraisal of the physical world around us and our estimate of our fellow beings. Because we expect that the physical world is constant, we can act with assurance, confident that things will remain as we expect them to be. Whatever we expect does not change the qualities of the physical world, though it may affect our appreciation or use of the things in it. But what we expect of other people influences our approach to them, and our behavior in turn affects their attitude toward us, so that we often provoke what we expect. When a boy is bullied by an older brother, he expects that his brother will go on bullying him, and he will go on resenting it. He will also expect that every boy, and later every man, who is in some way like his brother will try to bully him. If that is what he expects, he will at first be aggressive toward every pseudo-brother and later, when the other's anger is provoked, he will give in because he also expects the other's victory.

The expectation that others will act toward us as people resembling them have done in the past is an essential feature of the process by which we appraise others and their effect upon us. Hence we often provoke what we fear, even without any special "need for punishment." This constancy of appraisal is as necessary as the constancy of perception if we want to deal with things and people effectively. What needs to be explained is not why our appraisal of a situation (and therefore our emotion) remains the same, but why it ever changes. Our emotion changes when the thing itself or its effect on us has changed, but the fact of change can be known only as we experience a different effect.

Normally, the changes to which we continually expose ourselves in daily life will serve to correct our appraisal. But if the emotion aroused is strong and urges avoidance, (as do fear and dislike), this situation and even all thought of it, will be carefully avoided until the very memory of the experience is no longer available. Intense emotion is so harmful in early childhood because the expectation it creates cannot be easily corrected by a rational estimate. For all the child knows, the dog that approaches him is a ravening beast. The adult has encountered friendly as well as vicious dogs and has seen vicious dogs tamed by kindness. He can appraise the threat in its true perspective, but the child cannot.

For the child as well as for the adult, an immediate corrective experience is needed to prevent such set expectation after an intense fear experience. Hence the advice to people who have had an accident flying, driving, or canoeing that they should immediately get back into a plane, car, or canoe before the fear has "set." Once a man has relived the experience in imagination, has savored all its dangerous possibilities over and over, he can no longer conceive that the actual situation will be different next time. The mere reflection that it will not necessarily hold the same danger or that he will be able to meet it is not enough. Once his expectation has become set, it will be difficult for even a corrective experience to dislodge it. And his willingness to try again, itself the result of a new appraisal, will be based on desperation in the face of inevitable defeat rather than on the confidence that he can master the danger. Hence his fear will once more provoke what he expects.

This is illustrated by a case recounted by a colleague: a young man, an excellent driver, swerved to avoid a car that had suddenly swung out across an intersection, and ran his car into the ditch. The car turned over and the friend who sat beside him was killed, though he himself was unharmed. After some years during which he did not drive at all, he was counseled to try again. The first time he took the car out he overlooked a sign "No thoroughfare" and ran into a wall. The second time he went through a red light and ran into a car. This time two men who were with him were injured, though he again escaped with minor scratches. Since then, he has not driven again and one would hesitate to persuade him to try. In driving, fear creates hazards, and even a willingness to take the risk cannot turn fear into confidence, which alone could bring about a corrective experience.

Emotional attitudes. We must not assume that the expectation of constancy in the object and the effect of this expectation on us are the only results of an intuitive appraisal. Since such appraisal is automatically followed by emotion, emotion itself will leave a residue. Again, this is no isolated phenomenon. Any organismic function is improved by exercise. A movement once made can be repeated more easily; an unfamiliar selection once read can be read fluently the second time; an appraisal once made is repeated more easily in similar situations; and an emotion once felt is reexperienced more quickly with a similar stimulus. In every case, the disposition to move, to remember, to appraise, to feel an emotion, is intensified with exercise. This has been explained as "facilitation of nerve conduction." Whatever the actual neurological changes, such improvement of function with exercise is a fact of experience. It has been called *change in adaptation level* in touch, color, or weight perception (Helson, 1947); it is called *skill* in coordinated movements; it can be called *attitude* in appraisal and emotion. Such an attitude is the residue of the experience of emotion and of the physiological changes that go with emotion. Both the experience and the bodily changes are facilitated and occur more easily, more quickly, a second time. Hence each emotion facilitates the experience and expression of that emotion and eventually results in a stable emotional attitude. Thus timidity is accompanied by blushing, while aggressiveness goes with a confident bearing in every situation.

Every emotion is the root of an emotional attitude. The stronger the emotion, or the more frequent it is, the more stable will the attitude be, and the more will it spread to similar situations. Hence intense emotions or emotions aroused repeatedly will mold the child's approach to the world around him. He will gradually come to meet new situations with definite attitudes, derived from his early experiences that others like him or dislike him, that he is ugly, helpless, and inferior, or that others admire his every word and gesture. Whatever he decides to do about it, his attitudes dictate his appraisal and determine his emotions.

The effect of a traumatic experience is so serious because it begins an attitude that may affect a person's approach to the world around him for a long time to come. It is not necessary that the trauma should occur in childhood or that it should be repressed. If it is intense enough, the effect of the emotion it arouses may incapacitate the person even though the traumatic incident is well remembered. What is remembered is the actual experience, though a man may not be aware that the psychological and physiological effects of that experience still linger on and cause his difficulties. To give an example:

A young man of twenty-five consulted me because of his excessive anxiety whenever he had to speak to the director of his department. He felt that he not only made a poor impression but also that his fear made progress in his profession almost impossible. He could not bring himself to ask for a raise in salary, could not voice the most reasonable suggestions or complaints, in short was reduced to a quivering bundle of nerves as long as his employer was in the room with him. After every such occasion, he felt completely exhausted, so weak he could hardly walk, and was almost convinced that he was suffering from a severe and progressive disability.

I asked him when he had first experienced a like feeling in his life. He thought for a while and then recounted an experience he had had as a boy of seventeen. He had worked for a friend of the family during every vacation all through high school, had been treated almost like a partner, and had felt a great sense of achievement and responsibility. He had intended to make this occupation his life work as soon as he should graduate. During his last summer before graduation, however, he noticed some serious irregularities in his employer's business. At first he tried to draw his friend's attention to what he believed to be an oversight, but with little result. Later during the same summer a business friend of the firm, apparently with his employer's tacit consent, asked the boy to take his daughter to a dance. The boy did not want to take the evening off from work but finally decided to oblige his employer's friend. Next day he was called into the office and dismissed on the spot for his neglect of duty—in spite of his explanations and in spite of the unclouded and cordial relationship that had existed before. This was a severe blow to the boy, who saw not only the summer's job disappear but also the opportunity to be accepted into the firm and establish himself. In addition he lost a personal friend whom he had admired and idolized. His world was in pieces—no wonder that he had all the signs of a severe fear reaction. This reaction with its full complement of physiological symptoms was repeated afterward every time he had to talk to an employer again.

In this case, the original traumatic experience did not happen in infancy and, far from being repressed, was one of the young man's bitterest memories; yet it continued to affect him. He had a set expectation that every employer would act as his friend did and would in the end disappoint him. The fear of such an outcome lingered on, an emotional hang-over that was not recognized as such. The young man did know that he was afraid and recognized on reflection that this fear (and the physical symptoms that accompanied it) was unfounded in the present situation; he did not realize that his earlier traumatic experience had forced his present appraisal and intensified his present emotion. In the nature of the case, the more congenial and friendly a new employer, the more would he seem to resemble the once idolized friend, and the more surely would the young man expect a similar disappointment. Hence a corrective experience was impossible unless he could realize the connection between his old shock and his present exaggerated fear reaction.

In this case, such insight was acquired in a very short time. Over and above this understanding, there had to be a deliberate decision, supported by his confidence in the therapist, to suffer the discomfort of these fear experiences and act in spite of his fear until he could come to *realize* emo-tionally (what he had always known reflectively) that his present em-ployer was not a replica of his former friend. Reflective reappraisal gave him the opportunity to approach the situation with a new attitude until eventually his intuitive estimate was changed as well.

Less intense experiences of fear, disappointment, or helplessness, all pointing in the same direction, have a similar effect. They induce an atti-tude of fear, distrust, or suspicion in a child that gradually vitiates his ap-proach to everybody and everything (Adler's "life style"). Heroic meas-ures are needed when the fear has been severe or long continued. Ordinar-ily, no one is willing to take the risk of exposing himself again to an imminent danger. Thus he can never learn by experience that the situa-tion has changed or that he is now more competent to cope with it.

Yet, over and above his ironclad expectations, a child has the possibility of trying again as long as the hurt has not been so severe as to incapacitate him completely. Some children may be more sensitive than others and so feel fear more intensively; but some children surely are more courageous than others and respond to the challenge in spite of their fear. Not every child is scarred for life by a traumatic experience or by an unfortunate family situation. Not every rejected child becomes a rebel, a criminal, or a neurotic. On the other hand, some children develop a neurotic attitude on the flimsiest of grounds, interpreting as parental rejection what others would interpret as indulgence (see May, 1950). Whatever the child chooses, to persist in his old expectation or to test it by new experience, such choice is the result of reflection and reappraisal. He must acknowledge that his old expectation has not been verified, and either act in spite of his intuitive appraisal and his fear or work out defenses that will allow him to avoid reflective reappraisal.

Intellectual attitudes. There are some attitudes that do not necessarily grow out of emotion, though emotion may play a part in forming and maintaining them. Such phenomena as the individual's attitude to religion, to prohibition, to censorship, to education, to a political party, and the like seem to indicate that conviction and willingness rather than sheer emotion should have created them.

Conviction is based on appraisal, but an appraisal that includes much more than a simple practical judgment about a present circumstance. Rather, it is a studied evaluation of the available evidence on a wider issue. The judgment so arrived at is held for future reference because we are convinced it is correct—whether we believe that certainty can be reached in this matter or not. The conviction itself may be held with considerable emotional fervor. We call that man open-minded who is willing to revise his judgment when new evidence is brought to his attention. But even an open-minded man is attached to his opinions, changes them reluctantly, eyes with suspicion evidence that seems to contradict his convictions, and is sad when at length he persuades himself that they will no longer do. Intellectual attitudes may contain strong emotions, as strong as the convictions that give rise to them. But they do not spring from these emotions.

At the same time, forming attitudes from conviction (by reflection) does not mean that we simply adhere to a self-evident truth. We have no attitudes toward what is self-evident (e.g., two and two are four), or what is factual (the sun shining in the daytime when there is a cloudless sky). We have attitudes not toward self-evident or universally recognized truths but toward values. And a value can be called anything regarded as good by human beings, whether found in something concrete or something abstract, whether regarded as good by nearly everyone or by only a few. A value becomes an object of emotion when the individual appraises it as something good for him *here and now.*

Other writers (Allport, 1937, 1954; Young, 1943) seem to include under the term attitude both emotional and intellectual attitudes as we have defined them. There is no objection to such usage for general purposes. But as soon as we try to find the origin of our attitudes, it becomes desirable to distinguish between those that are the residue of sense judgments (emotional attitudes) and those that stem from a reflective judgment (intellectual attitudes).

Attitude and habit. We have seen that an emotional attitude is a habitual emotional reaction. We call it an emotional attitude rather than a habit to distinguish it from emotions that not only are felt habitually but also lead to habitual action. Of itself, an emotional attitude does not include a habit of action. A man may be timid, and hence have an attitude of fear; but if he manages to do what is required in spite of his diffidence, it does not develop into a habit but continues simply as an attitude, alleviated or intensified depending on the result of his action. But if he gives in to his timidity on every occasion, it may develop into a habit of neurotic withdrawal.

An emotional attitude becomes an emotional habit only when it is given in to and acted out.* When such a habit is fully developed, it may force actions that go against another emotion or even against a man's deliberate goal. A boy, passionately interested in flying, may have the chance of meeting a famous pilot. But he is painfully shy and so refuses to be introduced to his hero. He must have given in to his fear of talking to strangers for a good many years before his shyness could have become a powerful enough habit to prevent him from approaching a man whom he really wanted to meet.

When a habit is formed that yields pleasure, it is even more difficult to resist. The craving for drink or sweets, or for praise and recognition, is a habit that has developed from an initial pleasurable experience. It may even happen that an initially neutral if not unpleasing experience is sought for some other reason (a boy starts smoking because he wants to

---

* Lest it be thought that this is mere speculation, it should be noted that our analysis always begins with empirical situations.

We find that a habitual action has implicit in it a constant mode of appraisal and a habitual emotional response. In another action, we find a constant mode of appraisal and a habitual emotional response which does not always lead to a constant action pattern. The first combination we call an emotional habit, the second an emotional attitude. This mode of analysis is analogous to qualitative analysis in chemistry. We take a solution and discover that it is $H_2NO_3 \cdot 2H_2O$. We take another solution and find that it is $NH_4 \cdot 2H_2O$. The first combination, apart from the two molecules of water, we call nitric acid, the second, apart from the two molecules of water, we call ammonia. (It is obvious that we do not mean to imply that attitudes and emotional habits are compounded in the same way as chemical substances; we merely want to illustrate our point of departure.)

show he is a man) until its pleasure-giving qualities are discovered. From then on, the potentialities for addiction are given, precisely because of the expectation of constancy confirmed with every indulgence. It is quite true that the average person is interested in so many things that he will not concentrate on this one pleasure so exclusively as to develop addiction. But if he is bored or depressed, or if his circumstances make indulgence easy (as in the case of a salesman who is offered a drink by every customer) the danger of addiction is multiplied. The physiological effects of tobacco, drink, and drugs then reinforce the craving.

Such a habit is not learned, properly speaking; it is given in to. The tendency to develop it is acquired in the first experience of feeling or emotion, whether it be pleasure, fear, anger, or any other. To break an emotional habit it is not enough to turn the coveted pleasure into temporary misery (for instance, by using "antabuse" which produces nausea when a drink is taken), or to reduce the physiological effects of addiction by sedation and the like, although such procedures will help. So too, a habit of shyness or gruffness or anxious withdrawal cannot be broken by merely recognizing its presence or its roots in the past (through insight therapy), even though such realization does help. In addition, breaking emotional habits requires a strong motive to ensure a deliberate decision to stop the indulgence or to act contrary to the emotion. It also requires a willingness to forego the pleasure of indulgence, to suffer the discomfort of thwarted desire, to take the risk fear urges us to avoid, to put up with the annoyance anger urges us to combat.

There are also habits of deliberate choice and of rational thinking. To break an emotional habit, a habit of acting from rational motives must be substituted. Every action decided on after reflection on rational grounds leaves an inclination to a similar action, just as every action that indulges emotion leaves an inclination to do the same next time. There is a habit of acting according to what is held right, and one of acting contrary to it —what used to be called virtue or vice. It is also possible to develop a habit of incisive logical reasoning, for every human being is inherently capable of reasoning within the limits of his ability. Within the limits of his understanding, a man can train himself to think logically, or he can indulge in verbiage and get lost in confusion. Logical thinking is a habit that must be learned but is strengthened with every successful attempt. This can be demonstrated by every teacher who has tried to lead his students to such thinking (see Wertheimer, 1945).

Emotional attitudes and habits in animals. The distinction between emotional attitudes and habits is based on the observed fact that human beings do not always give in to their emotions, even when these have developed into an emotional attitude (see our discussion of human motives, Ch. 11). Animals, on the other hand, do not exhibit any goal-directed actions that are not dictated by emotion or instinct. The dog that is taught to hunt and to bring the prey to his master is motivated by the fear of punishment and the expectation of reward. In animals, one emotion can be used by man to defeat another emotion, or even an instinct, but there can be no goal-directed action without some emotion. For this reason, there can be no distinction between emotional attitudes and emotional habits in animals. Whenever an animal has acquired a disposition to a certain appraisal and emotional reaction, it will act out the emotion unless a stronger emotion or mechanical interference (internal or external) prevents it from doing so.

IO. BASIC EMOTIONS

While some emotions, like jealousy, seem exceedingly complex, others seem to be simple experiences of attraction or recoil. Though complex emotions may often defy analysis, it should be possible to classify simple felt action tendencies. Since the *quality* of every emotion depends on *how* we appraise the object, while the *intensity* of an emotion depends on *how much* the object affects us, it should be possible to arrive at some systematic scheme by discovering the way in which an object can be appraised, whether it is a thing or a person, a single aspect of a situation or its total effect.

CLASSIFICATION OF EMOTIONS

There are a limited number of conditions under which any given object can affect us. These can be fitted into a scheme of three dichotomies: the object is either good or bad for us; * it is either present or absent; and finally, it is either easy or difficult to attain (or avoid). We call those emotions basic that occur as a reaction to these basic conditions. These emotions are episodic emotional tendencies, the result of an intuitive appraisal made here and now, though they may become organized eventually into attitudes, habits, or sentiments. These basic emotions represent a simple unambiguous relationship between the person and the object or situation he appraises.†

* If it is neither good nor bad for us, it will leave us indifferent, hence will not arouse an emotion.

† In substance, this analysis goes back to Aristotle and Thomas Aquinas. Much later, Shand (1896) pointed out that there are certain emotions that always occur under given conditions. He said: "In the love of an object or interest in it, there is pleasure in presence and desire in absence, hope or despondency in anticipation, fear in the expectation of its loss, injury or destruc-

When we appraise something as good for us, we *like* it. When we appraise something as bad for us, we *dislike* it. We like what helps to maintain and perfect us in some way; we dislike what harms us or detracts from us. Since pleasure means enhanced functioning, and discomfort impeded functioning (see Ch. 4), we also like what is pleasant and dislike what is unpleasant. We must live, maintain ourselves, and develop, before anything can detract from us or threaten our development. Hence liking is primary, dislike secondary. This is true for every other negative emotion also. We must like something, must want or possess it before our aim can be frustrated or our possession disturbed so that we feel anger or fear.

If what we like is not with us but is easily accessible, we *want* or desire it. If what we like is present and we possess it, we are *joyful,* we delight in it. If what we dislike can be evaded easily, we simply turn from it, we feel *aversion.* But if it is actually upon us, we are *sad* or depressed, we feel *sorrow.* Liking and dislike, desire and aversion, joy and sadness, are aroused by something we have or something that is easily accessible. They represent a simple tending and could be called impulse emotions.

Sometimes what we want can be reached only with difficulty. Since emotions are action tendencies, felt impulses to action, their impulsion must increase when action becomes difficult. From simply tending toward something that attracts or away from something that repels, the impulsion increases until it is felt as an urge to *contend for* anything that is difficult to reach and to *contend against* anything that is difficult to avoid. If what we like and want is not easily accessible, we feel an urge to overcome all obstacles, we *long* and *strive* for it. If these obstacles are considered insuperable, hope is replaced by *hopelessness* or *despair.* If what we dislike becomes an immediate threat that is difficult to avoid, we may appraise it as something we can cope with, and feel an urge to contend with it: we show *daring,* we feel *courage.* Or we may appraise it as too difficult to cope with and have the urge to flee: we feel *fear.* If what we dislike is actually upon us, if it frustrates and obstructs us and we feel it can be

---

tion, surprise or astonishment in its unexpected changes, anger when the course of our interest is opposed or frustrated, elation when we triumph over obstacles, satisfaction or disappointment in attaining our desire, regret in the loss, injury or destruction of the object, joy in its restoration or improvement, and admiration for its superior quality or excellence. And this series of emotions occurs, now in one order, now in another, in every sentiment of love or interest, when the appropriate conditions are present" (1896, p. 218). Shand spoke here of sentiments, but the same conditions apply to simple basic emotions.

overcome, though with difficulty, we have the urge to attack it: we feel *anger*. Longing, courage, fear, and anger are contending emotions.

In this way, we can classify the basic emotions according to their direction toward or away from an object, as *positive* and *negative* emotions. We can also classify them according to their degree of impulsion, as *impulse emotions* and *contending emotions*. The accompanying chart shows this twofold classification.

Not only are impulse emotions and contending emotions distinguished in experience (as shown by different names); a contending emotion can become intense and may give rise to a new distinction. Wanting is a simple tending toward what we like, while striving means a forceful contending for it. When this is further intensified it becomes a craving which will brook no delay. Similarly, anger becomes desperation, fear becomes terror, and daring becomes rashness.

MODALITIES OF EMOTION

Activity changed or continued by emotions. It is obvious that emotions can move to action and speed action. Fear prompts us to flee, anger to strike and attack. By definition, *contending* emotions tend toward vigorous action. When an obstacle hinders our approach to what we want or our enjoyment of it, anger urges us to attack and overcome it. When we are in distress, we hope for improvement and actively strive to bring it about. We strain to avoid what is harmful; we precipitately escape from danger. Hence emotion leads to action when our present state is harmful or undesirable and we feel we can change it, though perhaps not without difficulty.

Impulse emotions need not always lead to action. When we possess what we want there is no reason for further action. Possessing something we like brings joy without any desire to change this state; rather, there is a tendency to prolong it. We decide on further action only when our joy is threatened. Similarly, when we have lost someone we love, there is no urge to action. What we have loved and lost completely occupies our mind and heart, and nothing else is wanted until in the course of time the distractions of everyday life arouse new interests and heal our sorrow. In sadness, we tend to dwell not only in but on our state, while in joy there is an aura if not a conviction of permanence ("rest in possession"). On the other hand, desire carries us into action, to change the present state

BASIC EMOTIONS
CLASSIFIED ACCORDING TO THEIR DIRECTION AND DEGREE OF IMPULSION

Emotions differ according *to their object and its conditions* (appraised as beneficial or harmful). Therefore we distinguish *positive emotions* (tending toward good objects) and *negative emotions* (tending away from harmful objects). Emotions also differ according to their *degree of impulsion*. Therefore we distinguish *impulse emotions* (tending toward or away from an object when conditions are favorable) and *contending emotions* (contending for or against something when conditions are unfavorable).

IMPULSE EMOTIONS

	Emotion Toward Object (*whether present or absent*)	Emotion Toward Object Not Present (*tendency toward or away from*)	Emotion Toward Object Present (*rest in possession*)	Kind of Emotion (*based on direction*)
Object suitable (beneficial)	love, liking	wanting, desire	delight, joy	positive
Object unsuitable (harmful)	hate, dislike	aversion, recoil	sorrow, sadness	negative

CONTENDING EMOTIONS

	Degree of Difficulty in Attaining or Rejecting Object	Emotion Toward Object Not Present (*tendency toward or away from*)	Emotion Toward Object Present (*rest in possession*)	Kind of Emotion (*based on direction*)
Object suitable (beneficial)	if judged attainable	hope		positive
	if judged unattainable	hopelessness, despair		negative
Object unsuitable (harmful)	if to be overcome	daring, courage (rashness)	anger (desperation)	positive
	if to be avoided	fear (terror)	dejection	negative

of lack, just as aversion implies an inclination to be removed from the harmful object ("tendency toward or away from"). This distinction between emotions that tend to continue the present state and emotions that tend to change it is also shown in the chart above.

Emotional polarities. From a consideration of this scheme we come to see that opposite emotions can develop toward one and the same object, depending on the aspects we appraise and the way in which we appraise them. There is a polarity in emotions either because they refer to different objects, suitable or unsuitable; or because they refer to the same object under different conditions, favorable or unfavorable; or because unfavorable conditions are either estimated as yielding to attack, and therefore to be mastered, or as insuperable, and therefore to be avoided. We either like or dislike something; we either wish for something or strive to attain it, we either fight for it courageously or flee from it in fear. In every case, the emotion will differ according to precisely defined conditions which depend on the way we appraise the object.

These polarities in emotion are very different from the emotional polarities discussed by Freud. For him, emotion is the experience of instinct in action; hence opposite instincts will arouse opposite emotions. Since love and death instincts are fused, one restraining the other, love and hostility will occur in close association. Hence love is always ambivalent and may erupt into hostility at any time (cf. Ch. 7).

There is no doubt that emotional polarities exist; but in any given case the one *excludes* the other. One and the same object cannot at one and the same time and under the same aspect be both liked and disliked, desired and avoided by the same person. What we like we like for its attractive aspects that promise to benefit us in some way; if we also dislike it, we dislike it for the harm it has done or can do. Since objects and particularly people have many aspects and can affect us in many ways it is quite possible for us both to like and to dislike them. But our liking is the result of judging a person attractive in some respect, and our dislike is the consequence of appraising him as hateful in another. Our estimate of him may oscillate, and so will our emotion. While we can say superficially and inaccurately that we both like and dislike *him,* we like and dislike him for entirely different reasons, whether or not we explicitly acknowledge them.

Simple and complex emotions. A simple emotion is aroused when an object or situation is appraised under a single aspect. It is a simple, unambiguous tendency of the person toward or away from the object. Basic emotions (see the chart above) are all examples of simple emotions.

A complex emotion is a compound of many emotions, all directed toward the same object, but aroused by various and often conflicting aspects of the object or situation. An emotion like jealousy, for instance, includes love, a fear of loss, anger at the beloved (and the third party) for disturbing secure possession, and many other emotions, all of which depend on the various aspects of the situation that are emphasized and evaluated. The more complex a situation, the more ways there will be in which it can be appraised; hence the more varied will be the emotional complex.

The jealous husband may consider that he has taken his wife for granted for a long time and has perhaps given her reason to feel neglected and to look for affection elsewhere. Then he may come to think of her as he used to during their first years together and may find that she is as lovable now as she was then. With this realization, his love for her will be rekindled and he may again show a lover's affection and consideration —until it seems to him that she does not respond in kind. At this point he may begin to think of her lack of affection for him, the bitter injustice of it, and may indulge in an outburst of angry vituperation, only to realize suddenly that his behavior will alienate her still further. The sudden fear that follows this realization may then lead him to plead with her in abject misery and drive him to do something desperate if he fails to move her.

Obviously, all these emotions are born of jealousy. In a sense, jealousy contains them all, for none of them would be possible without it. This means that jealousy is neither a single felt action tendency, nor can it have a single expressive pattern. Many other emotions contain similarly complicated elements, depending on the various ways in which the situation is appraised. Since emotional expression and physiological changes follow the changes in appraisal (as does the emotion), it is impossible to isolate and describe accurately either the experience or the expressive pattern for such complex emotions. One man's jealousy may contain more anger than fear, another's may include fear of loss and hurt pride but no love at all. In such complex emotions we must know how the matter is appraised and how that appraisal changes before we can describe the emotion.

Episodic and enduring emotions. When an object, a person, or a situation affects us for good or ill, it arouses a transient emotional tendency. This emotion leaves a residue which may become an emotional attitude; the attitude when acted out, may become an emotional habit. Hence an emotional episode may generate an enduring emotional state. Both emotional attitudes and emotional habits may spread over a whole class of objects (e.g., arrogance, timidity, confidence, shyness, and the like). If emotional habits are restricted to a given object, they become highly stereotyped actions (smoking, drinking, etc.). In emotional attitudes and habits, we are really dealing with the long-range or cumulative effects of emotion rather than with emotions themselves.

Sentiments. A single basic emotional reaction may endure and develop into a sentiment, provided that the emotional object has enduring value beyond its immediate sensory appeal. Such an object may be concrete, either a person or a thing (e.g., one's childhood home) to which a man is bound by many ties. It may be abstract: a cause, a virtue, a value, or a relationship to which he is committed. In a sentiment, the objective is always well-defined, whether it is concrete or abstract. Love of country, of family, of justice, love of friend or spouse are sentiments. So is enmity toward another person or toward a country at war with one's own.

Sentiments are enduring tendencies to react emotionally and overtly when the opportunity is given. Such action is never stereotyped; it is infinitely variable, according to the ever-changing condition of the object. When someone we love is with us, we may express our affection in word and action; when he is absent, we write to him or think of him; when he is ill, we care for him, when he is lost to us, we grieve for him. All these actions and emotions are motivated and activated by our love. A sentiment is a core of either love or hate (and variations of these emotions) which gives rise to other emotions and actions, depending on the presence or absence of the beloved and other conditions affecting his relationship to us.

That core of love or hate which is the sentiment remains identifiable throughout the various emotions and actions that grow out of it. For McDougall and Shand, the sentiment includes both the core and the emotions clustering around it. We would prefer to apply the term to the core, the underlying basic tendency of love or hate, which is the enduring reaction to the good or evil seen in the object. The emotions that cluster around this core depend on the conditions under which the object is appraised, in the same way as the various episodic emotions depend on the basic emotions of liking and dislike. This usage allows a sharp distinction between sentiments and emotional attitudes and habits. All basic emotions can generate emotional attitudes and habits, whether they are reactions to the object itself or to the conditions under which it is appraised: liking can become an attitude of friendliness; dislike, surliness;

hope can become an attitude of confidence; fear, timidity; sadness may develop into depression; and anger, into hostility. But only the basic tendencies of liking and disliking can generate sentiments, for only these two tendencies respond to the good or harm in an object regardless of its presence or absence, its loss or possession, or any other condition.

A sentiment is a disposition to react with love or hate, activated by an actual intuitive and reflective appraisal; and the appraisal itself depends on the conditions under which the object appears. A sentiment, unlike an emotional attitude, directly leads to action because it is a disposition that is accepted, endorsed by reflection, and implemented by deliberate choice. Hence a sentiment is necessarily conscious, but it is not always active. The lover is aware of his love (though he may misjudge its intensity), but he may not always want to hug or kiss. Moreover, the conditions of appraisal may often obscure the underlying sentiment. The jealous husband may be aware of his love only by the agony caused by the threatened loss.

Interests. Interest is to knowing what sentiment is to liking. Just as the impulse to love may become organized around one person or cause, so the impulse to know and understand can become organized around one object and develop into an interest. Interests, like sentiments, may center around persons, situations, abstract causes, but the characteristic mark of interest seems to be a desire to *know* rather than to have or possess. In some cases, possession seems to diminish interest. An uncompleted task is more interesting than a completed one; a new acquaintance is more interesting than a childhood chum. Sentiment, on the other hand, grows with possession. The more a man feels himself a part of his family and country, the more he loves them. The more something hateful bears in upon him, the more intense his dislike.

McDougall (see Ch. 7) has postulated a special instinct of curiosity, coupled with emotional excitement, to account for the desire to know. And Maslow (1954) has suggested that the desire to understand and reason is an "instinctoid" need. A simpler solution is to postulate an inherent impulsion in knowledge functions as in all psychological or even physiological functions (see Arnold and Gasson, 1954, Ch. 6). We want to see, hear, touch, know, and go out toward the world to meet it halfway. Anything new will be appraised as *good to know* and lead to more concentrated exploration. Such a desire to know may develop into a stable interest if endorsed by reflection and implemented by deliberate choice.

Clearly, the desire to know may be deliberate (a will impulse) as well as spontaneous (an emotional impulse). In abstract interests (music, art, literature, science) choice plays a greater part than emotional attraction. Such interests require some effort and application before a stable disposition is formed, while sentiments merely demand a steadfast regard.

Interest and attention. The first movement of the desire to know seems to be attention. *Involuntary* attention is attention attracted by the object. Attention may also be directed toward it, either *spontaneously* or *deliberately,* in *voluntary* attention. The dog exploring a new place, the rat exploring a maze without a food box, a woman window-shopping, all show spontaneous attention, indulging their desire to know. An experimenter checking his experimental controls, a man listening for the footfall of someone he is expecting, a night watchman on his rounds, all show deliberate attention, based on a reflective judgment that this is something they want to know. Since attention is initiated by an estimate (intuitive or reflective), it is a form of wanting rather than of knowing.

If attention were a form of knowing, we would expect it to be part of the sensory function it initiates. It would be part of looking, listening, reading, or even of playing the piano; yet attention is clearly different from these functions. But if, as we suggest, attention is a form of wanting that focuses and initiates perception or action, we would expect it to be different from the activities it accompanies. In that case, it should be mediated by a separate neural circuit, different from the sensory or motor system. More than that, the same circuit should be activated whether attention is paid to something seen or heard or touched, or even to our own movements. We shall see in our discussion of the felt impulse to action (Ch. 3, in the following volume) that there is actually evidence for a neural circuit mediating attention which is different from the pathways employed in sensory or motor functions.

THE RECOGNITION OF VARIOUS EMOTIONS

In our everyday living we take for granted that we can recognize other people's emotions. We know when looking at our friends whether they are sad or happy, angry or afraid. We never doubt that we can tell when something moves them, and that we can within limits predict their emotional response. We have reacted to their emotions as far back as we can remember and we never doubt our ability to do so until the scientist questions it (cf. Heider, 1958).

Interestingly enough, the so-called mentalistic psychologist never doubted that such recognition exists. He, like everybody else, assumed that anyone who is afraid or angry, or feels any other emotion, will show it in face and manner unless he is a master at dissembling. Conversely, psychologists used to take for granted that we can recognize when another person feels fear, anger, or any other emotion. But with the objective behavioristic trend came an insistence, first, that only behavior can be accepted as evidence, and later, that certain behavior patterns are the only clear signs of emotional disturbance. Next came the search for such established behavior patterns; and when none were found, the conclusion was inevitable that there are no emotions that can be recognizably distinguished and described.

Experimental studies. A glance at the studies designed to test the recognition of emotion reveals the dubious grounds on which such a conclusion was based. Landis (1924), for instance, aroused emotion in students by having them listen to music, read the Bible, smell ammonia, hear a loud noise, look at pictures of skin diseases or pornographic material, handle live frogs, see a rat decapitated. He photographed their expressions and tried to distinguish emotions by the amount of movement of facial muscles. He found that there were wide individual differences: no facial movement made by a single muscle group could be considered characteristic for an emotion. There was most facial expression in pain, less in surprise, still less in anger, gradually decreasing through exasperation, crying, disgust, until least was found in revulsion and sexual excitement. Landis also found that each person had two or three facial patterns he used in all situations.

Now it is hardly reasonable to expect a fixed pattern of emotional expression if emotion depends on the appraisal of a given situation. With each different aspect noticed, there is bound to be a change in emotion and emotional expression. In addition, a man may either abandon himself to the emotion or restrain it. Only as long as it was assumed that emotion is a reflex pattern called out in response to particular stimulus situations could it be expected that the measurement of facial movements would distinguish emotions. To say, as Landis and others do, that adults have developed "conventionalized" expressions, and that we recognize these rather than a native pattern, begs the question. If the measurement of muscular contractions could distinguish between emotions, it could have distinguished the expressions of the students, who as members of their culture surely must have acquired the same "conventionalization." Moreover, facial expression is not brought about by deliberate learning or imitation; it depends on autonomic innervation, and is therefore involuntary. We cannot imitate emotions—an imitation smile deceives no one. Even the best actor cannot portray emotion by deliberately arranging his gestures and expression; he can do so only by living in the situation, so that imaginatively he *is* the wronged husband, the insulted father, the rebellious son. Only the ham actor tries to arrange his face and posture the way he thinks it ought to look; and nobody mistakes his emotion for the real thing. Social conventions may permit emotions to be expressed or insist that we conceal them by immobilizing all expressive muscles; but such conventions cannot add to our emotional repertoire.

This reflection also tends to make us doubtful of the earlier studies of Féléky (1914) who tried to test the recognition of emotion by showing a series of photographs of herself, in which she assumed various emotional expressions. There is no guarantee that she was a great enough actress to express an emotion as it really occurs, without exaggerating emotional expression to the point of grimacing. There is also no assurance that either posed or real emotion can be judged from a picture which freezes one moment of a continuous movement. The same objection applies to the experiments of Langfeld (1918), who let his judges use artists' sketches of posed emotions. He found among other things that positive suggestions helped in judging these sketches, while negative suggestions interfered so markedly that the judges evidently must have distrusted their own judgments. This is understandable enough if the judgment is intuitive and immediate, rather than an inference based on reasoning.

The notion that the emotional expression of adults is "conventionalized" led to studies seeking to test the recognition of infant emotion. Sherman (1927) asked psychology students, nurses, and medical students to judge the emotions of infants shown in moving pictures. He found no agreement. This result is contrary to the experience of every mother who recognizes what her infant wants and manages to satisfy him by either changing his diaper, feeding, or cuddling him. It also disagrees with Wolff's report (1943) that a child expresses various emotions in a way that can be readily recognized, though with individual variations; his emotional expressions keep their individuality from infancy to later childhood (and presumably to adulthood). There is no contradiction in admitting that each person expresses fear or anger in a way characteristic for him and also that fear or anger can be reliably recognized in different individuals. One must know a person before all his individual variations on a common theme can be reliably recognized; but various moods and emotions can within limits be recognized even in strangers because there is a common core of emotional experience and expression.

Students and nurses cannot be expected to recognize emotions accurately in babies they have never seen before: first, because they are not familiar with the differences of emotional expression in infants as compared with adults, and second, because they do not know the individual variations with which each infant expresses a given emotion.

However, even in these experiments, the judges could always distinguish between joy (or delight) and distress. It is also possible to recognize laughter and scorn from pictures of adults (Young, 1943, p. 21).

What these studies really show is that emotions cannot be reliably recognized in infants by observers unfamiliar with them; and that even in adults such recognition is difficult if not impossible when only pictures of facial expression are shown, particularly when these pictures are posed. Even under these circumstances, pleasant emotions can always be distinguished from unpleasant emotions, and laughter and scorn are accurately recognized. These studies do not prove that we cannot recognize the emotions of adults whom we know, whose actions we can watch, and who do not deliberately restrain their emotional expressions. When we know a person we may even recognize emotions he wants to hide. In the same way, we can reliably distinguish infant emotions if we know the infant, and particularly if we are familiar with infant behavior.

Clinical evidence. That such recognition of emotion is possible even for infants is borne out by recent clinical studies. Sullivan (1953) insists that the infant recognizes the emotional disturbance of his mother and is in turn disturbed by it. Spitz and Wolf (1946) report in an important study that infants between three and five months can become seriously disturbed when their mother is upset or worried.

Infant emotion not imitation. According to Sullivan (1953), the infant "participates" in the mother's emotion. But the infant's emotion is not necessarily like the mother's emotion. The mother may be irritable, impatient, angry, or worried; but the infant will respond to all these emotions by a generalized disturbance (in the young infant) or by fear (in the infant of a few months). If the year-old baby is scolded by his angry mother, the corners of his mouth will droop and he will begin to wail disconsolately—a very different reaction from the lusty howl of an angry baby. Since the infant's emotion is different from the mother's emotion, he can hardly have become emotional by participating in his mother's emotion. Rather, he must have recognized his mother's state of mind in some way. The infant cannot reflect on his mother's emotion, but neither does he imitate it.

Dumas (1932) has pointed out that people born blind have the same facial expression as their seeing fellows when they experience fear, anger, or other emotions. They have never seen these expressions in others and thus cannot mimic them, nor can they be aware of their own facial expressions. It is unlikely that we who have our eyesight judge the emotions of others by comparing their expression with our own, or that we acquire emotional expressions by imitating those of others. Dumas rightly concludes that emotional expression is native rather than acquired and is recognized intuitively rather than by comparison with the observer's own expression.

Basis of recognition. There is no doubt that we recognize emotion by the same intuitive appraisal with which we respond to all situations that affect us in some way. We appraise another person as he affects us, and he has one effect on us when he is friendly, another when he is indifferent, and still another when he is angry. When father is playful and romps or wrestles with the child, he may be quite rough, and yet the child squeals with delight. If he shakes the child in anger, the actual physical behavior may be the same, and yet the child will be stiff with fear. Somehow the child must know what the father expresses, even without words.

It is not true, as some theorists say, that another person is given only as a sensation complex. He is given first as an object, for we experience objects and not sensation complexes. He is also given as a living being and a human being, who acts toward us in a way we appraise as desirable or undesirable. The emotion he experiences and expresses is part of his approach toward us. Scheler points out that this is a primary perception, not an inference:

That there are "experiences" which are given in expressive phenomena is known immediately in primary perception and not by inference. We perceive shame in blushing, joy in laughter. The saying that "only a body is given primarily" is completely mistaken. Such is the case only for the physician or the natural scientist, someone who artificially abstracts from the immediately perceived expressive phenomena. (Scheler, 1923, p. 6; my translation *)

* Scheler's original: "Dass aber 'Erlebnisse' da sind, das ist uns in den Ausrucksphänomenen—wiederum nicht durch Schluss—, sondern 'unmittelbar' gegeben im Sinne originären 'Wahrnehmens'. Wir nehmen die Scham im Erröten

Spitz and Wolf (1946) have shown that the infant of three to five months smiles in response to any human face as long as that face is smiling or talking, or showing some kind of movement (even a grimace). There is no smile in response to the nursing bottle, a toy, a face painted on a toy or a doll, nor a human face in profile. A human being facing a baby, talking or nodding, surely means a direct friendly approach; when the face is turned away, it means that the person is looking at something else. Hence the infant responds to another person's approach, his looking at the infant. This is shown also by the fact that the infant always looks at a person's eyes, often with a concentrated unwinking gaze (for instance, the nursling at the mother's breast).

When Spitz and Wolf found that the infant greets a grimace (the *rictus sardonicus*) with the same cooing and smiling as a genuine smile, they concluded, curiously enough, that the infant does not react to the emotional expression of the human face. Of course, the infant cannot distinguish expressions accurately, for he smiles at a nodding stuffed head or mask and a smiling human face with equal abandon. But he does distinguish between a motionless human face (which means indifference rather than friendliness) and a face in motion; and he does discriminate between a frowning, scolding face and a smiling, talking face—a distinction which many of us can vouch for from personal observation, though the authors do not seem to have investigated it.

According to Spitz and Wolf, the infant's smile is a response not to the human quality and emotional expression of the face but to a "configuration consisting of certain elements *within the human face,* combined with motion." Surely this ascribes to the baby a subtlety of discrimination that is far beyond his years. His direct experience is with human beings who have human faces that are friendly, withdrawn, or angry. The baby's smile is a response to friendliness, even if he can be deceived by mock smiles or mock human beings.

That the infant's smile is a response to a friendly human approach is shown impressively by one infant in the series of Spitz and Wolf. This baby girl had become very upset when her mother repeatedly quarreled with another woman in her presence. As a result, the baby would scream

wahr, im Lachen die Freude. Die Rede, als sei uns 'zunächst nur ein Körper gegeben,' ist völlig irrig. Nur dem Arzt oder dem Naturforscher ist so etwas gegeben, d. h. dem Menschen, soweit er künstlich von den ganz primär gegebenen Ausdrucksphänomenen abstrahiert."

instead of smiling when the woman examiner approached her, though the male examiner could still win a smile. Surely there is no doubt that the infant could distinguish between a woman and a man, and that her painful experience with the other woman prevented her from appraising the woman examiner's smile as a friendly approach.

These authors also found that the nursing bottle was not greeted with a smile. This surely means that the infant's emotional response to his mother is not, as Freud claims, the result of associating the mother with food. On the other hand, the smile does not mean that the baby can differentiate "I" from "you," as Spitz and Wolf suggested. That requires a degree of reflection not possible until much later, as Piaget (1926) has shown. The infant can distinguish one object from another, and a human being from anything that is not made to look like a human being; he will smile at a stuffed head that moves toward him, but not at a doll. By and large, the infant can also distinguish between a friendly approach and hostile or indifferent treatment. At about six months of age, when the baby will no longer smile at every human face, he has also learned to discriminate between friend and stranger.

Such intuitive, "irritational" recognition of emotion is also reported by Halstead, who showed a series of schematic drawings of faces both to normal people and to psychiatric patients or those with brain injuries. There was overwhelming agreement in judging the faces gay or sad, attractive or unattractive, old or young. Halstead remarks:

It is difficult to see that such ordering behavior is on other than a blind basis. It seems quite unlikely that the child is born with an a priori notion that the distance between the eyes, the height of the forehead, the length of the nose, and the location of the mouth, the four varying elements in this series of faces, are invariable attributes of gayness . . . etc. (Halstead, 1951, p. 262)

Our groups of subjects are sufficiently heterogeneous to suggest that these irrationals are universals, at least so far as the western world is concerned. (p. 263)

While we are not born with a priori notions of what the various proportions of the face signify, we are born with the capacity to judge people and things around us, to estimate what is good for us and what harmful. Other people are appraised in their approach to us, as to whether they are friendly or hostile, whether they mean well or ill. We soon learn that they mean well when they smile and that they bear ill will when they frown. A smiling face gains in breadth; eyes and mouth appear wider. A brooding or frowning face gains in length: "a long face" is the sign of a person who is displeased. Thus we come to interpret faces as showing one or the other emotion even when no more than the bare proportions are sketched.

It speaks for the immediate and intuitive nature of this appraisal that it is not disturbed either by brain injury or by psychiatric illness. As Halstead says, even a four-year-old child was successful in his judgments. Hence the recognition of emotion is a true constant, not dependent on intelligence or age level, at least for the basic distinctions. As soon as perception has developed to the point where the baby can recognize familiar faces, he can also appraise them as friendly or hostile, and know whether he can expect weal or woe.

Recognition of animal emotions. There have also been attempts at judging animal emotions from photographs, with the usual lack of success. Young (1943), for instance, pointed out that a chimpanzee's grimace is interpreted as laughter by a movie audience though it was produced by pinching the animal's hand, out of range of the camera. It is obvious from our discussion that anyone judging the emotional expression of animals would need to know how they act when they are angry or afraid or playful, before his judgment could be accurate.

More recently, Hebb studied the behavior of chimpanzees and reported that their emotions could be recognized and their behavior predicted successfully. To isolate the emotional behavior patterns, he tried at first to list specific movements and activities during emotion, only to find that such a record included an "almost endless series of specific acts in which no order or meaning could be found" (Hebb, 1946, p. 88). When terms familiar to the observer from his own emotional experience were used for description, prediction became possible. Surely this means that there are at least some basic emotional reactions that are recognizable as emotions and commonly so recognized by the same intuitive appraisal by which we react to human emotions. For this reason, it is entirely appropriate to speak of animal emotions and to imply that the animal experiences the emotion and shows it in his behavior. True, the animal's appraisal and emotion are not identical with the corresponding experiences of its human counterpart, but they are analogous and hence can be recognized with equal facility.

If there is a behavior pattern that varies for different individuals and in different situations, though it can be recognized as belonging to the same emotion, the variation must be around a common constant core. This common core is the actual experience of a given emotion. The variation depends on the appraisal that will vary from one fear or anger situation to another, and from one individual to another. We recognize the common core and allow for individual variations. Everybody has a different way of laughing; the laughter of some people is pleasant, that of others may be unpleasant, but we recognize both as a sign of mirth. The recognition of an emotion is immediate and intuitive and depends on the appraisal how a man or animal with this particular expression will affect us, whether he will be friendly or hostile. This appraisal is formed by actual experience with others, whether men or animals. Hence it can be improved by thorough acquaintance with men and animals and particularly with the individuals whose emotions are to be judged.

THE GENETIC DEVELOPMENT OF EMOTION

Emotional reactions require a sufficient development of perception so that an object can be distinguished from other similar things, and can be recognized before it is appraised. Emotions also require a motor organization that has sufficiently matured for emotional expression and action.

Infant emotions. Even at birth the infant experiences his state of functioning and reacts to it. He is at ease when he is sated, warm, and comfortable. He cries when he is hungry, in pain, or uncomfortable. The infant can also experience and appraise touch and will show pleasure when he is cuddled and anger when he is restrained or handled roughly. Such pleasure or distress should be considered feelings rather than emotions because they are reactions to smooth or difficult functioning (see Ch. 4). The pleasure from unhindered motion, which the infant shows very early when he is rocked or allowed to kick freely, also is a feeling.

The infant has wants, too: he actively seeks for food with his mouth, and wants to move freely. He shows anger not only when he is restrained but also when he is disturbed during feeding. When he hears a sudden loud sound or is being dropped, the young infant will show alarm or startle by suddenly throwing out his arms. This is the "Moro reflex," which later disappears and is replaced by the startle reflex.

The infant seems to have four genuine emotions: he *wants* food, *enjoys* it, is *angry* when restrained or disturbed, and can be *startled* or *alarmed*. Watson lists three "innate" emotions as present at birth or soon afterwards: love, fear, and anger. What he calls "love" is the infant's reaction to light stroking. We have identified this as feeling because it is a pleasurable reaction to sensation. What Watson calls "fear" is the startle reaction to loud sound or loss of support, which could be called alarm or fright, to distinguish it from the emotional reaction to danger that does not have this element of surprise.

Fear cannot develop from the startle pattern, as is sometimes believed, for the startle pattern is well developed in early childhood and remains essentially the same during life. It is specific, almost reflex in nature, and appears in response to a sudden intense stimulus (particularly a loud sound or a drop of ice water on the neck, according to Landis and Hunt, 1939). The stimulus interrupts normal activity and is reacted to long before it can be appraised as either dangerous or harmless. The infant can experience such an interruption only when it is drastic (a sudden loud sound or the loss of support), while the adult may be startled when a mouse runs across his path.

Genuine fear develops only when the child is old enough to estimate the possibility of harm. Between three and five months of age, the infant smiles at everyone, because he cannot as yet distinguish friend from stranger. By the age of six months or so, he can distinguish between his mother (or a person mothering him) and a stranger, and will smile at his mother but draw away from a stranger.

The development of appraisal. Since the experience of emotion follows upon appraisal, it will partake of the developing improvement in the child's estimate. What is dangerous for the child may be so no longer for the adult. What may arouse tempestuous joy in the ten-year-old may leave the adult unmoved. Gradually, the child learns to know and appraise ever varying aspects of an object or situation. His emotions will become more complex; rarely will there be anger unmixed with fear, or courage unmixed with doubt. Also, he will gradually come to know things and people in a different way. They will come to appeal to his long-term human desires rather than to the whim of the hour. Episodic emotions will develop into sentiments, and fleeting impressions will develop into organized interests. As appraisal becomes more subtle and more complex, so the massive emotional experience of the child will develop into the subtly shaded emotions of the adult. Emotional expression also changes with appraisal and becomes similarly diversified.

The development of emotional expression. The emotional expression of very young infants is restricted to a general excited reaction that soon develops into recognizable distress on the one hand, and joy and delight on the other. Bridges, still the authority on the infant's expressions of emotion, says:

A strong stimulus or a sudden call to action creates general disturbance or excitement. It is difficult to tell whether a baby is frightened, angry, or even pleasantly excited. . . . This general excitement within a very short time, perhaps days and perhaps only hours, becomes somewhat differentiated into two general types of emotion as a result of experience. . . . There results an emotion somewhat different from general excitement, which may be called distress. This is the concomitant of unsatisfying experience, and is probably what Watson has described as fear and rage. The emotion aroused by progressively satisfying stimuli, such as to and fro movements, stroking and tickling, the contact of the nipple or the appearance of food during moments of hunger, is more akin to the joyous excitement of older children and may be termed *delight*. The infant ceases to cry and smiles, coos and waves his arms. (1931, p. 201)

Probably this development which starts within hours or days of birth is the result of the beginning ability to distinguish between harmful things and pleasant things. What before was merely a response to interruption now becomes a response to something pleasant or something harmful. Bridges also notes that anger can be reliably distinguished from distress and delight in the three-month-old infant, while at six months fear and disgust are added to this repertoire.

When action is added to emotional expression, there is still less chance of isolating a rigidly defined pattern for each emotion. If emotion depends on appraisal, action depends not only on the emotion but also on the individual's estimate of his emotion and the way it will affect others. Such an estimate changes remarkably from infancy to adulthood and differs between individuals and situations.

If the tiny infant encounters an obstacle, there is very little he can do but cry. In fact, crying seems to be his response to danger, frustration, pain, and hunger. Soon enough he will find that crying brings mother, and may use it for this purpose. The two-year-old may still not be able to cope with an obstacle, but he can stamp, scream, and throw himself on the ground. Still later, he may try to remove the obstacle and, failing that, may turn against his parents and angrily accuse them. As he grows toward adulthood, he may have discovered effective ways of coping with obstacles, but if he is pressed for time, impatient or incompetent, there are still grounds for becoming violently angry. As an adult, he will have learned to gauge the expression of his anger according to the situation. He may give in to his temper within the family circle, but be suave and tolerant outside.

Emotional expression and action will be further modified by the person's estimate of what is accepted as reasonable in the community or in his national group. There are accepted ways of appraisal, different in different cultures. For Latin men, seeing a friend after long absence may be an occasion for hugging and kissing, while Anglo-Saxons are satisfied with a firm handshake. Emotional expression and action are not fixed but are modified according to the individual's appraisal of what is fitting, and depend on circumstances, custom, and individual attitudes; hence there is little point in trying to classify or describe the patterns in which anger, fear, love, or joy are typically expressed.

THE DEVELOPMENT OF LOVE

The gradual development from episodic emotion to a stable sentiment can best be traced in observing the development of love from casual liking of things and people to enduring love and interest.

The infant's world. From birth on, the infant sees things and is attracted to them. At first he wants he knows not what: he simply cries because he is hungry or wet or in pain. But very soon he wants something definite. At this point, his mother can recognize whether he is hungry, wet, or in pain. As soon as his mother picks him up, his crying stops, indicating that he expects his want to be satisfied. At first the infant likes what gives him sensory gratification: food, being held or dandled. But very soon the person who nurses him and handles him is liked in her own right and the infant smiles at her even when she neither feeds nor holds him.

Similarly, the infant will like anything that arouses his attention. At first he follows a bright ball with his eyes; later he reaches for it. Whatever brings him into pleasant contact with the world around him, whatever gives him a chance to reach for, play with, or master things, is eagerly welcomed. Gradually, his attention is not only attracted but held: he becomes capable of developing an interest in things and love for people. To develop any, even the most rudimentary, interest, the child must be persistent; he must return again and again to what has attracted his attention. To continue looking and return to exploration means sustaining such attention and developing a habit of concentration.

The earliest and most rewarding object of attention for the nursling seems to be his mother. Gradually he comes to concentrate his attention on her, he comes to know her and learns to love her. If a baby has no mothering adult whom he can come to know and love, his development of interests will be seriously impaired. Interest in things is bound up with interest in and love for other human beings. There is no other object in the child's universe than can attract and hold his attention the way a mothering adult can. If attention has not been trained by interest in such a person, other objects have little chance.

When many adults take care of a child, such interest cannot develop because the infant is incapable of coming to know and recognize (let alone love) several people in succession. Hence clinicians report that infants reared in orphanages where no one adult had the care of a child remain withdrawn and apathetic, without any interest in their surroundings. Their later development is seriously delayed if they cannot form a loving relationship with a mothering adult during the first two or three years of life. In extreme cases there is seriously arrested growth and even death in spite of the best medical care (Spitz, 1946; Bender, 1950).*

The infant's love for his mother is not a disguised love for food or comfort, as some theorists claim, for the babies Spitz describes had all the nourishment they could take and were carefully tended by a rotating nursing staff. That the attention aroused by a mothering adult can become extraordinarily intense and concentrated and arouse great devotion is shown by an interesting study of twins.

Wayne Dennis's studies of twins. Dennis (1941) reported a carefully devised developmental study of twin girls brought up in isolation, for the purpose of observing "native" responses. The two experimenters alternated in caring for the babies, so that each twin was cared for by each experimenter on alternate days. One of the twins gave signs of distinguishing between them and a stranger at less than four months of age. Their interest in the experimenters appeared very early, even though they were bottlefed (the infants stared at the experimenter's face at six weeks), and that interest meant affection because it was accompanied by a smile.

Dennis's study also shows that the infant needs to love rather than to be loved (in the sense of being fondled or dandled). The Dennises carefully refrained (for experimental purposes) from showing any affection

* This interpretation goes a step further than do Spitz and Bender. These authors recognize that a child wants to *be loved* but they do not see what their facts so clearly show: that a child needs *to love,* to reach out to another person, before he can want to be loved in return.

whatever for the first eight months. They neither talked nor smiled at the twins. Yet the babies showed none of the unfortunate effects that occur, according to Spitz, when a succession of adults cares for infants. Here as in Spitz's cases, the children were cared for scrupulously but without any show of affection. In orphanage infants this led to retardation and in severe cases to death. In Dennis's twins it led to seemingly normal growth, except for a delay in motor development. Infants need love and care, but evidently they need an opportunity to love even more than they need to be loved.

It is also of interest that Dennis found no signs of that "primitive aggression" of which Freud speaks, or of the rage reaction to restraint, held by Watson to be one of the three native emotions. Dennis pointed out that general moderate restraint quiets the infant. This is confirmed by Greenacre (1948), who mentioned the fact that swaddling as practiced in many parts of the world has the same effect. According to Dennis, anger appeared only when restraint was severe or sudden. Moreover, with the completely unemotional handling reported by Dennis, there was little show of anger at any time. But the infants did show disappointment whenever the two adults left the infants' room. In spite of the deliberately unemotional handling, the twins developed such a strong attachment to the Dennises (the only adults they knew) that even general restraint (holding the infants' heads and arms motionless by firm pressure) provoked only smiling and cooing. In fact, the experimenters found it impossible to take pictures of distress emotions because their mere presence would quiet the babies and make them smile. In the face of such evidence, it is difficult to take seriously Freud's dictum that "love originates in the capacity of the ego to satisfy some of its instincts auto-erotically through the obtaining of organ pleasure," or that "the relation of hate to objects is older than that of love. It is derived from the primal repudiation by the narcissistic ego of the external world whence flows the stream of stimuli" (Freud, 1915, pp. 81–82).

It is heartening and reassuring that the infants' single-minded devotion finally broke through the Dennises' armor of scientific objectivity. The twins, when they were about eight months old, achieved a genuine human relationship with their foster parents. It seems likely that they might otherwise have recognized the rejection implied in such adult "objectivity" and might have suffered from it.

From infancy to adulthood. At first the affection of the infant for his mother is little more than the pleasure of being with someone whom he knows and who tends him and responds to him, even though it is a genuine human relationship. For the toddler, his mother is a source of comfort as well as of protection and affectionate response. Mother has an answer for his questions; she solves his difficulties, is there when he needs her. For the growing child, playmates become increasingly important. They share the activities of the day, are companions-at-arms with whom to play, to explore, fight, and make up. The adolescent begins to appreciate others as persons and admires them for qualities which a few years before he could not see at all.

As the adolescent matures and the breadth and depth of his knowledge of others increase, his love for them will strengthen and deepen, provided he finds in them what he can love and admire as an adult. There is no joy that can be compared to that of a child who comes to realize that the father and mother he has loved from childhood are also the kind of people who deserve a man's admiration and respect.

As the basis for appraisal widens from adolescence to adulthood, so the object of love will change as well. While the teen-ager is aflutter with adoration of a crooner, rock 'n' roll artist, or film star, at a time when glamor and romance are the highest ideals that can be imagined, the young woman will be attracted by a man whom she can admire and on whom she can depend, even though he is neither a matinee idol nor an Adonis. With increasing maturity, qualities of mind and heart will become more attractive than romantic looks or a dashing manner. With increasing maturity, what is desired is not the merely pleasant, still less the glamorous, but that which shows solid goodness and enduring value.

Not only the basic affectionate relationship between the person and the world around him will change from childhood to maturity with his gradual change of appraisal; every other emotion will show a similar development.

II. EMOTION AND MOTIVATION

We have seen that emotions tend toward or away from an object and urge to action. This raises the question: Are emotions motivating?

The connection of emotion and motivation dates far back in the history of psychology. For James the physiological changes that go with action are experienced as emotion; for Dewey action constitutes both object and emotion; McDougall and Freud connected emotion with instinct, the driving force behind all action. More recently Leeper (1948) insisted that emotions operate as motives because they arouse, sustain, and direct activity. Young (1943), however, claimed that emotion is not a motive but merely a sign that some motive is aroused, thwarted, or satisfied; only when emotions develop into stabilized attitudes do they motivate.

In all these theories motive is understood as some factor that arouses, sustains, and directs activity, all activity, not merely a specific action. This definition of motive is so wide that it includes factors that cannot be motives. Men and animals, for instance, are aroused to hyperactivity by a lesion in the orbital area of the frontal lobes. The same effect can be achieved by giving certain drugs or stimulating certain regions of the brain. Yet lesion, drug, or stimulation can hardly be called a motive in the accepted sense of the word. When the Balinese teach their children to dance by guiding their movements manually, they certainly direct their children's activity, yet their guidance can hardly be called a motive.

Funk and Wagnall's Standard Dictionary (1946) gives this definition of *motive* (when applied to human action):

That which acts as an inducement to preference or choice; that which, speaking figuratively, tends to move the will; a strong or impelling influence toward some particular object to be obtained or end to be secured. *In this meaning of the word reference is always had to some subjective precondition or tendency and never to an external force or cause.* (italics added)

It will be noticed that the usage of the term excludes an "external force or cause." Harriman's definition (1947) has the same import: "a goad to action; usually restricted to a more or less well-verbalized drive to behavior." Hence external guidance, drugs, or electrical stimulation of the brain are not motives according to current usage unless the meaning of the term is extended to the point where there can be no more distinction between motive, impulsion, and brute force.

SPECIAL FORCES MOTIVATING ACTIVITY

The definition of motive as "arousing, sustaining, and initiating activity" really implies that the living being is inert, passive, to be roused to activity by special driving forces. The basic questions: Why does a living being act at all? and Why does he act as he does? are usually answered by analogy with physical objects. Here as there a force must be applied to move a body from one place to another. Hence theorists have assumed that an action can be explained when the forces that act upon the organism or have acted upon it in the past can be isolated and described.

If inertia is basic in the living being, motivation theory must specify the forces that set an individual going and propel him in this direction rather than that. Such forces may be internal, on the analogy of a vehicle moved by an internal combustion engine, or external, on the analogy of a wagon drawn by horses. The organism may be either pushed from within or pulled from without.

Instincts and drives. The older instinct theorists had conceived of instinct as a force that makes the animal act and makes it act in a definite way. Since instinct is a special force, what more natural than to assume a rigidly determined pattern activated by that force? Hence instinct became a fixed action pattern as well as a driving force. Insects conform to this conception without difficulty. Their sequence of instinctual actions is so rigid as to seem mechanical. It was soon found, however, that the instinctual action in mammals is never mechanically rigid, that there is always room for learning and adaptation to special conditions.* Eventually, it was held that the *driving force* is innate, instinctive, while the *action pattern* is flexible and probably largely acquired. Now if only the

* See Linton (1955, p. 8) on instinct in higher primates.

driving force is innate, why not choose a term that would indicate a force without an action pattern? So the term *drive* was finally substituted for instinct, and the action pattern informed by the drive was held to be learned by the individual rather than native to the species.

Both instinct and drive theorists explain why men and animals act by postulating a special set of biological engines, the drives. These have their source in special organs or organ systems and account for the activities that are naturally determined: searching for food, a mate, or shelter; avoiding pain. What is more difficult to explain is the way in which these basic urges can activate the highly specialized pursuits of a civilized adult who wants not only food but a gourmet's table; who not only wants money to buy food but chooses to earn it by painting or writing rather than by raising vegetables or digging ditches.

There is a wide gap between basic drives and adult human motives, and neither drive nor instinct theories have spanned it successfully. If instincts are taken as driving forces, just how do they drive to activities that do not aim at a biological goal? Additional instincts must be added to provide for social, cultural, or religious motivation (e.g., in McDougall's system); or a secondary organization must be assumed that converts the driving force of instinct into ego motives (e.g., Freud's ego-function). If drive is the concept of choice, "secondary" drives must be postulated which somehow stem from primary drives and use their impulsion.

Both alternatives are poor makeshifts. Social and cultural "instincts" cannot have a biological source; yet instincts were postulated to begin with because some biological impulsion seemed necessary to explain action. Without a definite physiological state as the source of instinctual energy, whence comes the impulsion for action in such a system? Similarly, secondary drives are supposed to draw their energy from primary drives; yet the way in which that energy transformation is accomplished and the way in which secondary drives develop "out of" primary drives has never been explained. Both notions, that of social instincts and that of secondary drives, are *ad hoc* hypotheses made necessary by the inadequacy of instinct and drive theories to explain the bewildering variety of human actions.

Stimuli and stimulus situations. The living being can be pulled as well as driven. Since instinct and drive psychology had failed to account for adult human actions, should it not be possible to explain such actions simply, behavioristically, as responses to conditioned stimuli?

On the face of it, this seems an attractive alternative. The most diverse actions of the civilized adult could be explained as a chain of conditioned responses. Once it is accepted that an unconditioned stimulus could be linked to any number of conditioned stimuli, the greatest variety of responses can be explained with equal ease. The difficulty here is how to make such indiscriminate linkages credible.

We have seen before (Ch. 9) that the conditioned response is always a response to the *un*conditioned stimulus, both in classical and instrumental conditioning, because the conditioned stimulus is appraised as announcing or belonging to the unconditioned stimulus. But in acquiring a new motive, the new conditioned stimulus (the behaviorist's "motive") is never actually paired with the unconditioned stimulus. A man may decide to become a painter or a poet in spite of the fact that his paintings or poems have never brought him money or food; in fact, he often has to have a job that pays to be able to spend all his spare time, effort, and money on his avocation. How can conditioning explain, for instance, the case of Heinrich Schliemann, the famous merchant turned archaeologist, who on reading Homer was struck by the thought that Troy must actually have existed! To find it became his dominant motive from that time on. He did not discover the site of Troy until six years after he retired from his business career, but his determination never wavered.

While drive theories cannot explain how secondary drives can develop from primary drives, stimulus-response theories cannot account for the linkage between the unconditioned stimulus and the stimuli (motives) that call out adult responses.

Needs. In the last twenty years the term "need" has been used increasingly as a substitute for drive, because it seemingly relieves the theorist from postulating a biological source of the driving force and makes it possible to extend the meaning of "need" to anything an individual deems necessary. Hence psychological and social needs can be postulated as easily as biological needs.

However, if the need is biological, it is much easier to account for the organismic action that satisfies the need. If food is needed, there is an organismic reaction that leads to getting food and eating it. Now that reaction may be called a drive, an appetite, or an instinct, but in every case it has its source in some kind of biological deficit that must be supplied if life is to continue. Hence biological needs imply some *reaction, inherent in the organism,* that leads toward the needed object. When we go from biological to psychological and social needs, however, there is no inherent organismic reaction toward the needed object and some explanation is required of how any given action toward it is initiated. Maslow's (1954) "need for love" or "need for esteem," for instance, can be fulfilled in the most varied ways; but because of that, some link from need to specific action is urgently required. Hence need psychology will either have to accept the restrictions that apply to drive psychology and postulate some connection between biological needs and adult actions, from which psychological or social needs may be inferred; or it will have to give some explanation of how needs of any kind initiate action.

It is easy to show that needs, understood as a deficit or a requirement of the organism, do not of themselves move to action. The deficiency must register in some way, must make itself felt by the organism before action can be taken. This is so even with a strict physiological need like oxygen deficiency: oxygen lack in the blood must register in the nervous system before the medullary reflex that leads to a change in the rate of respiration can be initiated. It is not the need that moves, it is the organismic reaction to the deficiency that leads to overt action.

If that is true on the purely physiological level (in cases of oxygen deficiency, lactic acid concentration, etc.), how much more so on the psychological level, where something has to be perceived before it can be acted upon. On this level a need must be consciously felt as want or desire before the individual will act. Lack of food must be felt as hunger before a man will forage for food or even before the infant will cry for it. Need theories of motivation are inadequate because they leave out the necessary link (the felt want or desire) that could explain action even in the case of basic needs. We may infer from the felt want (e.g., hunger) that food is needed, but there is not always a direct relationship between need and want. The *anorexia nervosa* patient needs food but does not want any, and hence does not eat. In bulimia, the patient does not need food but wants it, and hence goes on eating. Thus action is dictated by what is wanted, not by what is actually needed.

Moreover, a need may be a requirement without being a lack of something. Any living organism, man or animal, must exercise its functions to keep well. Men and animals need to sense, move about, consort with others of their kind. Man also needs to think, reason, talk, work, love. These "needs" are naturally determined because they require the exercise of inherent capacities. Such capacities are active functions; they move us to their exercise by their inherent impulsion. Muscles, for instance, need to be exercised. The energy for movement is provided by the ordinary metabolic processes delivering glycogen to the muscles, and so enabling them to contract; the impulsion is inherent in the motor function, in the capacity for movement which urges toward motion when the conditions are favorable. The same is true for sensory functions (see Arnold and Gasson, 1954, pp. 175 ff.).

Such active functions account for all behavior that is not goal-directed. To call such behavior "unmotivated," as is often done (Young, 1943; Maslow, 1954), is a contradiction in terms. Something must have "aroused, sustained, and directed" that particular activity, that is, acted as a motive. According to our view, activities undertaken simply for their own sake (children swinging, humming, walking, running down a hill; a baby's gurgling and cooing) are motivated, they are even based on natural requirements, but they are not reactions to a deficit.

Homeostasis. The effort of other theorists to account for organismic activity by one great equilibrating mechanism is no more successful than are need theories. In Freeman's formulation (1948), for instance, all behavior is an attempt to compensate for an organismic disturbance brought about either by the environment or by internal tensions. When an animal becomes hungry, hunger contractions in the stomach produce general restlessness and random activity, and that eventually leads the animal to food and restores homeostasis.

Such a theory, like drive theory, assumes some organismic mechanism (in this case set off by homeostatic disturbance) that initiates action. But the general statement that any disturbance (internal or external) will result in a compensatory reaction, including goal-directed action, is not an explanation of the cause of a specific action. Only in physiological reflexes (carotid sinus reflex compensating for blood pressure changes and the like) is the compensatory reaction specific. In goal-directed action, there is no such inherent specific compensatory mechanism: here the disturbance must be felt and appraised before action will be taken. The disturbance may occasion a reaction that restores homeostasis, but the disturbance does not directly bring about such action. Hunger contractions may arouse restlessness, but they cannot deliver the energy necessary for sustained hunting that may eventually be rewarded with food. The lion and tiger stalking their prey are not sustained or directed by the random restlessness produced by hunger contractions; still less is the man who runs a grocery store or captains a ship. The theory does not even attempt to explain human motives that may involve not only directed and sustained effort but also biological deprivation or suffering—a chronic homeostatic disturbance which is maintained by activity rather than re-dressed by it.

Functional autonomy of motives. Allport suggested that adult motives may develop from biological needs as the result of incidental interests de-veloped during an activity which originally was aroused by biological mo-tives. He pointed out that

motives are almost infinitely varied among men, not only in form but in substance. Not four wishes, nor eighteen propensities, nor any and all com-binations of these, even with their extensions and variations, seem adequate to account for the endless variety of goals sought by an endless variety of mortals. And paradoxically enough, in certain cases the few simplified needs or instincts alleged to be the common ground for all motivation, turn out to be completely lacking. (1937, p. 193)

For Allport, the child acts under the compulsion of biological drives, but during this activity he discovers new interests that develop into new motives. There is an impetus toward the newly discovered goal that re-mains until the goal is reached, the action perfected. For Allport, "only skills in the process of perfecting (mechanisms-on-the-make) serve as drives" (1937, p. 205).

This formulation can be interpreted either as a mechanical develop-ment of a new habit that becomes autonomous from the biological driv-ing force, or as a gradual change in goals selected from the wealth of new situations encountered during life. The first interpretation is favored by the terminology borrowed from Woodworth that "mechanisms-on-the-make" come to serve as drives. The second interpretation is supported by the whole tenor of Allport's argument that stimuli are *sorted out,* that goals are *selected* by the individual himself, so that there is merely a historical but no causal connection between the child's biological drives and the adult's social, cultural, or religious motives.

If the individual selects stimuli and goals, Allport's explanation falls completely outside the customary scheme of drives, needs, or stimuli that are supposed to arouse, sustain, and direct activity. The principle of functional autonomy, so understood, really assumes that the individual is inherently active and that he can direct his activity by selecting his goals. At the same time, Allport's theory does not spell out how a given motive moves to action.

SPECIFIC ACTIONS INITIATED BY MOTIVES

Whenever motivation is explained as the result of instincts, drives, needs, stimuli, or homeostatic mechanisms, the organism is assumed to be a passive reactive system, energized by these motives.* The analogy of the organism with an inanimate object or a system of forces obviously stems from the conception, dating back to classical physics, that an object is at rest unless a force is applied to move it. Today, since subatomic physics has accustomed us to the ceaseless activity of electrons, neutrons, and protons within the atom, an activity not set in motion by external forces, it should be much easier to concede that living things have intrinsic activity. In fact, the very definition of a living being is that of a self-maintaining, self-repairing, self-moving system.

Since the recent description of the "reticular activating system" in the brain stem of mammals (see Ch. 5, in the following volume), we know that there is actually a nervous mechanism for internally initiated action that regulates the rhythm of sleep and waking, rest and activity. When afferent stimulation is excluded but the reticular activating system is intact, such spontaneous activity will occur almost normally; when the reticular activating system is excluded but the afferent sensory system is intact, stimulation will keep the animal waking and active only for a few minutes (see the discussion in Ch. 5, in the following volume). Hence we may reasonably postulate inherent activity in the living organism as a whole, as well as within the various organ systems, an activity that is not initiated by sensory stimulation and that ceases only with death.

Starting with the assumption of inherent activity rather than passivity (or strict reactivity), we do not have to look for special driving forces, be they instincts, drives, or needs, that spur the living being to action; nor do we have to assume that the environment pulls or lures it. What

---

* Recently several theorists have pointed out that motives are not "energizers," notably Maslow (1954), McClelland *et al.* (1953), and Hebb (1949). They have argued that the organism is already active and that motives merely direct its activity.

we do have to explain is how activity is directed, that is, how a specific action is initiated in any given case. The motives that arouse, sustain, and direct such specific action are not just the motors proposed in drive theories but something over and above internal drives or instincts.

That internal drives are not a sufficient explanation of motivated behavior has been emphasized recently in papers by Klein, Bruner, and others (Bruner and Krech, eds., 1950). It seems that both motivational and cognitional processes are needed to explain motivated action; yet these have been traditionally conceived as strictly separate. According to Krech, "a need or a drive is frequently seen as something which supplies energy for behavior and has *its* functional laws; a cognition is seen as something which directs the energy so supplied into this or that specific channel and has *its* functional laws" (Krech, 1951, p. 115). Hence a belief in some interaction between these two factors has developed among theorists; but such interaction poses its own problems. As Krech says: "If 'interaction' is going to be at all helpful in your work, you must have some notion of what interaction is, of how it operates, and of its mechanisms. Anything less than that, I would suggest, is an appeal to word-magic to get you out of difficulties" (Krech, 1951, p. 118).

Krech's solution is to substitute, for the assumed cognitive and motivational processes, unitary "dynamic systems" in the total brain field which cannot be further analyzed. A given dynamic system is the neural organization that persists from earlier brain activity together with the neural changes that come with stimulation. With apologies to Krech, this seems like an appeal to word-magic, too, for we have no notion how such dynamic systems operate or what is their mechanism. Before we follow him on that road, it is worth considering whether the "interaction" between cognitive and motivational factors cannot be analyzed so that its nature and mode of action becomes clear. First of all, let us see how internal driving forces act. Perhaps their mode of action will indicate some link with cognition or perception.

Instinctive motivation. To discover how internal driving forces act, let us reconsider the explanations that have been given or can be given for the way in which instincts urge us to action. For McDougall instinct is an "innate psycho-physical disposition" to perceive an object as significant and feel an impulse toward it that leads to action. This impulse is accompanied by emotional excitement. For Freud the instinct is "a certain sum of energy forcing its way in a certain direction." It has a source (a state of excitation within the body) and an aim (to remove that excitation) usually reached by means of an external object. For Freud the instinct cathects its goal-object when perception informs the ego of such an object.

For McDougall instincts are propensities, innate dispositions made actual by some present situation. For Freud the instinct is always active, always present, now in the conscious, now in the unconscious. What is a potentiality for McDougall becomes an unconscious actuality for Freud. On the human level these diverse concepts cannot be reconciled. From experiential evidence it might seem that McDougall is closer to fact because we experience an impulse to instinctive activities only at intervals. If the instinct existed at all between these intervals, it would have to be as a predisposition. For Freud, however, this is no argument at all. If the instinct is in the unconscious as an active force, it could not be detected, *ex supposito*.

Perhaps the question can be settled by recourse to the facts of instinctive behavior in animals. We know that animals show inherent unlearned action sequences that can be called instinctive. These recur periodically; but even in the quiescent period such activity can be aroused artificially (insulin injection will arouse hunger and food-hunting; estrin injection will put the female in heat and she will accept the male). There must be a potentiality or disposition for such activities, or these injections could not induce them. But can we assume that the instinct is active in the animal unconscious? According to Freud, the source of the instinct is a physiological state, and that state was certainly *produced* by the injection of insulin or estrin. If the source of the instinct is present after the injection but was not present before, from what source does an unconscious instinct draw? Without the physiological state, in what sense could the instinct exist unless as a potentiality, as McDougall claimed?

The physiological state. Hence we can take it for granted that an instinct is an innate disposition toward a specific, naturally determined set of actions, *periodically activated by a change in the physiological state*. When the instinct is so activated, there will be an urge toward doing something about an object that appears satisfying at this particular time. In the human being hunger is felt periodically much as it is in animals, and its rhythm can be similarly modified by habit. Sexual desire, on the other hand, has no such natural rhythm in man. The seasonal rhythm observed in animals is replaced by a rhythm that depends as much on the individual as on circumstances.* But given favorable conditions, sexual activity is possible at any time. Thus the notion could gain ground that the sexual drive is active at all times even when not experienced as sexual desire.

Granted that an instinct is an innate disposition, physiologically activated, it usually also requires a concrete object or situation that is appraised as suitable before it leads to action. This object will not appear suitable unless there is a hormonal state that sensitizes the animal to it. Before a bird will be attracted by a piece of hay or straw for nest building, there must be a definable physiological state, initiated by the developing eggs in the mother bird's body. As a result, the bird finds the piece of hay or straw desirable at this particular time. Before the mating season the bird may see it but will remain indifferent and refuse to pick it up. Similarly, an animal must experience hunger before it will hunt its prey.

Our discussion has shown that there is no sense perception that does not involve some appraisal of the object as good, bad or indifferent to the perceiver (see Ch. 9). Consequently, there is no perception that cannot culminate in a felt attraction or repulsion, that is, an emotion (or appetitive reaction). Indifferent or useless objects will arouse no impulse to approach; and though they do not positively repel, they are registered as unattractive. As soon as they are recognized as useless, the animal moves on to something else.

What distinguishes instinctive action from any other kind of action (which also involves perception, appraisal, and approach) is the distinctive physiological state that is felt as an urge to a particular action and sensitizes the organism to objects offering satisfaction at this and no other time. So the salmon is content in the ocean for four years until the milt and roe begin to form; and only then both male and female feel the urge to travel back to their birthplace. So the female mammal will not let the male approach unless she is in heat.

In Chapter 6 of the following volume we shall sketch what we believe to be the neurophysiological mechanism which sensitizes the animal so that it now finds desirable what was indifferent before. Tinbergen (1951) has suggested that sex hormones act upon the central nervous system and increase the excitability of the sensorimotor system involved in instinctive activity. Our suggestion is that these hormones excite

* If Alfred Kinsey had considered this point, he would not have been so surprised to find that long-term prisoners have a diminished sexual urge.

hypothalamic receptors and so induce a fantasy image of the instinctive object together with an urge to find and approach such objects.

Now let us examine the psychological factors involved in instinctive action. We have seen that an object or a situation usually indifferent now appears desirable and is approached. The object is desirable because it fulfills a want that was not felt before but is now urgent. Picking up a straw and fitting it into a nest is satisfying for the mother bird at this particular time but will not be so when the eggs have been laid or when the young have hatched and flown. Psychologically, what sustains such serial action until its goal is reached is the satisfaction that comes with each successive act.

Instinctive action will continue as long as the physiological state lasts that has brought it about. This state makes a certain object attractive in much the same way as a changed physiological balance may make some foodstuffs palatable that are not sought ordinarily (salt in sodium deficiency, chalk in calcium deficiency). Such a state can even be artificially produced or aborted (see Young, 1952; see also the discussion of instinctive action patterns in Ch. 6, of the following volume).

Instinctive action stops when the physiological state ceases. In nest building, the instinctive pattern of action is so regulated that the bird normally will continue building its nest until the eggs are ready to be laid. The period from ovulation to the complete formation of the fertilized eggs is just long enough for the bird to finish the nest. Until the eggs are ready to be laid, the activity of nest building satisfies a felt urge. When the eggs are being laid, the need is no longer there, and the nest building stops.

Changed circumstances may change the instinctive pattern. Birds will accept strips of paper or cloth as substitutes for hay and straw to build their nests. They will postpone migration south when warm weather is unusually prolonged. It is quite possible that these changes in the environment affect the physiological state, either directly (biochemically), or indirectly via perception and appraisal. Ovulation can be speeded up under continuous illumination; but some animals when kept isolated from their kind do not ovulate or come in heat (Harris, 1948).

Appetite and emotion. The physiological state induces a felt urge that is focused on the appropriate object, sensitizes appraisal, and so triggers off the wanting that leads to action. The physiological state is dynamic; it induces a felt urge or appetite. But it leads to action only when a concrete object (such as food or mate) is found, appraised, and wanted. What we call appetite is often called "tension": hunger tension, sexual tension, and the like. We prefer the term appetite because it indicates a felt urge toward a particular object. The emotional wanting or desire that follows upon the appetite as soon as there is a concrete object will, like appetite itself, have a special quality depending on the goal toward which it tends (e.g., desire for food and drink versus sexual desire).

Emotions themselves are action tendencies like physiological appetites, but they are not activated by a physiological state, nor do they aim toward a specific naturally determined object. Anger, fear, love, or hate is felt whenever the situation is appraised as annoying, threatening, good, or bad, no matter what the physiological state. A small child can feel love, though the lack of sex hormones makes it impossible for him to feel sexual desire. To call such love "infantile sexuality" is to confuse emotion with instinctual desire, to confuse the emotional tending that merely seeks the presence of the person loved with the emotional tending that is initiated by sexual tension and demands a consummatory response. The love of the small child is not "aim-inhibited," it has a different aim altogether. Not until puberty, when sex hormones bring about a change in the physiological state, is there a true desire for a mate. It is then that a boy's appraisal of girls is sensitized by his changing hormonal condition. Now he begins to pay attention to girls, who before were of little importance. Long before he feels any particular affection for any one girl, he begins to feel attracted and wants to be attractive.

Though there is a physiological state specific for each emotion (see Ch. 7 in the following volume) this state is induced *after* the object is seen and appraised. In fear this appraisal activates the sympathetic nervous system, the adrenal medulla begins to secrete adrenaline, and various physical changes become noticeable. But the racing heart, trembling knees, and dry mouth come *after* appraisal, not before. The same is true for anger and love, though the physiological state is different. Emotion organized into a sentiment may combine with the instinctive tendency toward a mate. So the sentiment of love, the result of coming to know another as a person, may combine with sexual desire; but it need not necessarily do so. Conversely, sexual desire may be aroused without the sentiment of love.

The consummatory response. Tinbergen (1951) makes a distinction between appetitive activity and consummatory response in instinctive behavior. Appetitive activity (by which he means the pursuit of the instinctive object) is for Tinbergen "a true purposive activity, offering all the problems of plasticity adaptiveness and of complex integration that baffle the scientist in his study of behavior as a whole" (1951, p. 106). From the context it would seem that the purposiveness Tinbergen notes in appetitive activity is the tendency toward a perceived *immediate* goal, not the purpose of the total instinctive action sequence (a bird wants and takes the piece of straw or hay, but it does not do so *for the purpose* of building a nest and laying eggs in it—such purpose is a fact but is not the bird's intention).

The consummatory response, on the other hand, is relatively simple and completely stereotyped: eating the food, completing the sexual act, laying eggs, and the like. In fact, what Tinbergen calls the consummatory response seems to be closer to a physiological reflex than to co-ordinated action. Though instinctive actions do include firmly fixed action patterns, not all of these are physiological reflexes, nor are they necessarily tied to a given organ system like reproduction or digestion. They may involve inherent action patterns of the whole body (the bird fitting hay and straw into a nest, the beaver building a dam, migratory birds in flight).

Hence Tinbergen's usage of the term "consummatory response," in the sense of a stereotyped physiological reflex, applies only to some instinctive actions and not to others. In our scheme, we can use this term for the activity that brings instinctual satisfaction, is unlearned, but is not necessarily a physiological reflex. The flexibility of some of the actions in the total instinctive sequence (Tinbergen's "appetitive activity") can be explained as the result of the animal's appraisal of the situation. The more adequate an animal's perceptual system, the more flexible will be its appraisal and approach.

The nature of instinct. Thus far, we have described what amounts to the mechanism of instinctive action. The physiological appetite focusing upon the appropriate object, the emotional wanting, the more or less stereotyped action that reaches the instinctual goal and brings satisfaction: these are the ways in which an instinct is activated and consummated. Clearly, an instinct cannot be a source of energy, that is, it cannot deliver the energy that is used by nerves and muscles. Rather, the physiological state must somehow initiate nerve impulses that start muscle action. We shall see later (Instinctive Patterns, Ch. 6, in the following volume) how such a circuit can be conceived.

The animal does not act blindly as does a machine. It feels hungry, sees food, eats, and is satisfied. But neither does the animal act purposefully: the bird does not know that it is going to build a nest, lay eggs, and hatch them, nor does it know that it will migrate to warmer climes. The salmon does not know that it will fight its way home to the spawning grounds. Nor does any animal know that eating will sate its hunger and keep it alive. All these action sequences are naturally determined and seem to work toward a purpose that becomes clear to the observer as the action sequence unfolds and reaches its term. But that purpose is not of the animal's own choosing.

Hence animal instinct can be defined as *a naturally determined disposition to a sequence of actions the purpose of which is unknown to the animal, but is aimed at the maintenance and well-being of individual or species*. The instinct is a disposition to a given sequence of actions rather than felt urge (the physiological appetite) because that urge is focused by appraisal toward *the object wanted at each step* in the sequence, not toward the final aim of the sequence. When the instinct is so conceived, it becomes apparent that there is really only one instinct, absolutely universal among all animals: the instinct of maintaining the individual and the species in the best possible way.

To maintain the individual does not mean preservation from death, which is impossible for organic life; hence we hesitate to call it an instinct of self-preservation. Self-*maintenance,* however, does include all food-getting activity, as well as the actions that help in food-getting in a given species: the spider spinning its web, the beaver building a dam, the bee constructing hive and honeycombs. It includes also the banding together of animals, either in couples for rearing their young, or in herds for mutual protection *and* the rearing of young. Because some activities thus serve both the individual and the species, it seems better to speak of one instinct rather than two.

It would be more appropriate to speak of *instinctive activities* serving the maintenance of individual or species, rather than of separate instincts of migration, nest building, homing, the rearing of young, and the like. A given instinctive action includes many if not all functions of the animal: physiological appetite, perception, appraisal, emotion, co-

ordinated motor action, and often a consummatory reflex. Any one of
these functions may be activated singly, as well as combined into the actions of an instinctive sequence. An animal may see and explore a
building or a maze; it may run when frightened by a man shooing it
away. In these cases there is perception, appraisal, emotion, but no
instinctive action sequence. Even the consummatory reflex may be elicited
(e.g., in forced feeding, or stimulation of the genitals) without being
included in the natural instinctive sequence.

Instinct, then, seems to be a term that is more properly applied to
some attribute of the organism that insures the *organization* and *coordination* of the actions in a serial sequence to achieve a useful result,
rather than to some specific disposition or energy, either physiological
or psychological. It is not an entity distinguishable from the action sequence as a whole and bears about the same relation to a directed (useful,
goal-achieving) action sequence as randomness bears to a random series.
We must keep in mind, however, that every step of the action sequence
called "instinctive" includes some kind of knowing and wanting.

Instinct and intelligence. In the human being instinct is supplemented
by reflection, understanding, and deliberate choice. The human being
knows the purpose to which he is urged by physiological appetites and
either carries it out or refuses to do so. Like instinct, intelligence is not a
single function but a combination of functions set in action toward a
particular goal; but unlike instinct, that goal is determined by a reflective appraisal. The degree of intelligence determines the effectiveness
with which every function is used toward an individual's purpose. Like
instinct, intelligence may serve to grasp together a whole sequence of
acts that are used for a long-range purpose. But man, unlike the animal,
knows the purpose toward which he aims.

We may use the term intelligence analogously in speaking of the way
in which an animal carries out an action. But in the animal intelligence
will mean the effectiveness with which it uses its functions toward its
instinctive goal. When the experimenter or animal trainer introduces
complications in the way to the goal, he merely forces the animal to
learn new ways of coordinated action in reaching an instinctive goal; he
does not introduce a new goal. The animal's functions are used in the
service of instinct; man's functions are used in the service of his intended
purpose.

There are differences in the degree of intelligence in individual animals just as there are in individual human beings. But the human being has at his disposal functions the animal does not possess, and he uses those functions he has in common with animals in different ways. The human being knows and appraises objects and situations not only *as they affect him here and now,* but also as they affect his long-range goals, and *as they are apart from him;* his reaction is not only appetitive (emotional) but can be reflective and deliberate. Animals know by sensing, and appraise directly and intuitively what they see, hear, or touch. Human beings know not only directly, by sensing; they can also reflect, reason, and understand. Hence they appraise reflectively as well as intuitively, abstractly as well as concretely.

EMOTION AS MOTIVE

When we speak of instinctive action instead of instincts, and understand by instinct the inherent disposition to sequences of actions that serve the well-being of individual or species (an aim of which the animal is not aware), we shall not be tempted to look for instincts or physiological appetites that could provide the energy for human actions. Nor shall we have to look for separate emotions experienced whenever such an instinct or drive is active. All that is required for action is an action tendency that follows upon appraisal and leads to action. Emotion is the only such action tendency in an animal's goal-directed action, whether such action is "instinctive" (i.e., triggered off by a special physiological state and concluded by a stereotyped consummatory response) or not. What is required for emotion is an intuitive estimate of something as beneficial or harmful, whether or not it is also the goal of a physiological appetite.

Inspired by the instinct, there may be single or combined instinctive actions; there may also be actions that serve the animal's well-being but are not part of a specific instinctive sequence. Hence all sense functions are implicated in instinctive activities; so are all intuitive appraisals as well as the emotions they arouse; so also are the movements that flow from emotions. What characterizes an instinctive series is the utility of *the whole pattern* rather than the utility of the individual movements.

Goals, purposes, and motives. Similar as these terms are, they can be distinguished. Such distinction is important if we want to discover how motives are formed. Whatever is appraised as suitable or unsuitable and moves the living being to action becomes the *goal* of action. The *purpose* or aim of action is to reach the goal, and hence the purpose is the end for which an action is undertaken. It is customary to speak of animal goals and human purposes, a distinction that points to a difference in the way in which the aim of action is conceived. The animal is attracted, follows his attraction, and so reaches the goal. A man knows in addition that he wants something and can achieve it by a given action: he has a purpose in acting.

What is a motive? We know that something must be appraised as good or beneficial before we can move toward it. But the appraisal itself is not the motive, nor is it the wanting that follows it. The object appraised as suitable cannot be called a motive; it is the goal of action. *A motive seems to be an action impulse (a want) that is appraised as good for action.* This formulation takes account of the fact that there are many wants that do not lead to action. We may long for a warmer clime or a better job or a happier life; but there is no particular action that is judged suitable to bring it about.

There are many things that are wanted that are not available here and now. To experience an action impulse (a wanting), they must be at least conceived or imagined. What is imagined is then appraised as good for action (e.g., good to eat or drink) before it will be actively searched out. Thus predatory animals hunt for food, they do not merely take what happens to come their way. Newborn mammals (even human infants) seek with the mouth until they find the nipple. They do not move randomly, nor do they move just any part of their bodies. Some psychologists claim that hunger brings an increase in random activity which accidentally brings the animal in contact with food. But random activity would not induce the dog to take up the spoor of the hare, nor would it bring the eagle or falcon within reach of its prey. It is much more likely that hunger induces an image of the object that can satisfy it before this object can be appraised as good for eating, and therefore be pursued. The human being, at any rate, imagines what he wants before he decides to obtain it. But for him such images are not merely those of concrete objects or actions. He can conceive of some ideal and pursue it steadfastly, however unpleasant a given step in the chain of actions may be. A boy may decide to become a doctor, work his way through school, and make any number of sacrifices until his aim is achieved. He has a strong motive, something he is convinced is more desirable than many a passing pleasure.

Lest it be objected that it is anthropomorphic speculation to ascribe imagination to animals, we might point out that imagination and remembering are processes that are no more inferential than sensory experience. We know that animals as well as men have a sensory apparatus; hence we conclude that they have sense experiences. And animals, like men, are able to learn; this implies that they remember earlier situations and their effect, and that they expect similar effects from similar things. To restrict our psychological explanation to what is observed is never possible. To understand (and hence explain) either animal actions or physical phenomena we must go beyond what can be observed. For instance, a man who is puzzled when a door opens to let him enter may make a series of observations on the kind of stimulus that will trip off this particular reaction. But unless he goes beyond the response and tries to investigate what makes the opening of the door possible, he will never find the source of the electronic beam, let alone discover its nature.

To infer that animals have memory and imagination is just as legitimate as to infer that they have sensory experience. And since both man and animal can imagine what is good to have or do before they do it, we might ascribe motives to both of them. But the human being not only imagines what he wants, but also reflects upon what he imagines. Thus human and animal motives are at best analogous. Common usage, which ascribes motives only to man, seems to stress the differences rather than the similarities.

Wants that move to action. If an appraisal has to arouse an action tendency before it can lead to action, as we maintain, some impulse other than emotion is needed to move us to an action that is not itself pleasant and leads to a goal that promises neither emotional gratification nor the satisfaction of a physiological appetite.

In the animal this problem does not arise because the animal can only appraise what is pleasurable, painful, threatening, or annoying in a concrete way. Hence instinct as the activated disposition to certain action sequences, and emotions as the action tendencies leading to each specific action in the sequence, are sufficient to account for all goal-directed animal actions. If an ape grabs a stick to rake in a banana, the action is initiated by his desire for the banana. The same is true when he "works" for counters that may be exchanged for bananas, or even when he hoards such counters. For him the counter is literally interchangeable with the banana and means not "money that will buy food" but "this food," even though some action must be taken before the banana can be eaten. Hoarding these counters is an exact counterpart to the hoarding of nuts or other edibles, common to many animal species. It is the experimenter's anthropomorphic interpretation which claims that the animal perceives symbols and uses them.

The case is different with the human being. What is useful in the human sense may be the means toward a goal that has practical value but is not pleasurable. A man may work overtime so he can pay for a series of laboratory tests that will show whether or not he has a malignant disease. That some impulse is needed to initiate an action that is not pleasant and does not lead to a pleasurable goal is even more obvious when there is a strong desire for a pleasurable goal that has to be sacrificed for the sake of a more important motive, particularly when this desire is rooted in an instinctive tendency. The diabetic may be hungry for sweets; yet he restricts himself to a severely reduced sugar and even food intake. To follow doctor's orders in such a case is anything but easy. Gandhi's hunger strikes required an impulse to action that was not emotional and went counter to a physiological need. A poor boy who works his way through college cannot depend on instinctive or emotional impulses to carry him through.

Since human beings are capable of such self-determined actions even when they feel an emotional pull in the opposite direction, we infer that these actions must be initiated by an appraisal that is specifically human. We make a reflective judgment that this is good or useful even though it may mean hardship or discomfort; and we appraise our impulse towards it as suitable, and therefore to be carried out. Since it is our own concrete impulse to action that we judge as good, this appraisal is a sense judgment as well as a reflective judgment and arouses an emotion together with a volitional tendency.*

* Psychologists, following Kant, have usually assumed that there are three kinds of psychological activities: cognitive, affective, and conative. In our discussion, we have shown that emotions are felt action tendencies; thus emotions are both affective and conative. This reduces psychological activities to two main categories, namely cognitive functions (including knowing and judging) and appetitive functions (combining affective and conative aspects). To postulate two separate functions, one called emotion, the other conation, would make

Unconscious motives. Since all motives depend on an appraisal here and now, there cannot be a wholly unconscious motive. To initiate some specific action, there must be an appraisal of the object to be approached or avoided. Even in phobic and compulsive actions, where the influence of unconscious motives is seemingly strongest, there is a *conscious* appraisal that high places or closed places or open places are dangerous and must be avoided; that hands must be washed, the bed must be remade, the word reread, the lamp posts counted, else a calamity is sure to follow.

It is true that such appraisals are incorrect, and can be understood only as the result of factors of which the person is not aware at the moment. But correct or incorrect, the appraisal is made here and now, arouses the appropriate emotion (appropriate to the estimate, not to the objective situation), and initiates the action designed to avoid the estimated danger. In the neurotic the emotion is so strong that it overrides the rational estimate and forces action.

The appraisal may be incorrect either because we do not have enough information about this particular situation or because past emotional experiences with superficially similar situations have blinded us to its real character. We may be unconscious of the fact that our emotional attitudes prejudge the present situation; or we may be unaware of the extent to which they do so. At the same time, these attitudes do not determine perception exclusively. They become dangerous only when they have been given in to so often that they have become emotional habits. The more a man is beset by emotional difficulties, the more will such emotional habits dominate him, and the more important will it be to make him aware of these "unconscious motives."

"Unconscious motives," so called, are more powerful in the neurotic than in the normal person. Normally, past estimates and expectations are corrected in the course of further experience as long as a man is willing to approach each new situation as *new in some respect,** and so is

---

emotion completely static and conation an action tendency without any emotional coloring. But emotions like fear or anger include an urge to flee or attack; and conative experiences like desire or striving have an affective aspect.

* Cf. the counsel of General Semantics to reappraise each new situation. To remind us that each situation is different, Korzybski recommends using subscripts: Mother$_{1960}$ is clearly different in many respects from Mother$_{1940}$; Smith$_1$ is obviously not his neighbor, Smith$_2$, though he has the same name and may resemble him to some extent (Korzybski, 1933).

willing to appraise it on its own merits. It is no accident that the neurotic suffers from a host of likes and dislikes (food dislikes, unreasonable dislikes of certain kinds of people, articles of dress, occupations, and the like) in addition to his main complaint. These are symptoms of his uncompromising rigidity of approach, his emotional habits that prevent him from correcting his expectation.

The normal person appraises things or people primarily as to their value or usefulness and only secondarily as promising pleasure or threatening harm. His motives are rational rather than emotional. When things and people are approached as if they were potential sources of pleasure or harm, the estimate is primarily affective, though a man may try to find reasons that would reinforce such an appraisal.

Normally, the motive for an action is conscious. It follows an estimate that is both intuitive and reflective. When the intuitive appraisal dominates, it may lead to actions that a man may find difficult to explain. He may not know himself "what made him do it." A normal well-integrated person is aware of his motives and his motives are all of a piece. The neurotic can appraise the situation reasonably, and yet acts on the basis of his emotional estimate, the origin of which he does not know. For this reason the normal person will reveal in projective tests the same motives that he will report when asked. Allport comments: "It is not the well-integrated subject, aware of his motivations, who reveals himself in projective testing. It is rather the neurotic personality, whose façade belies the repressed fears and hostilities within. Such a subject is caught off guard by projective devices; but the well-adjusted subject gives no significantly different responses" (1953, p. 110).

Pleasure and motive. We have seen in Chapters 4 and 10 that we experience pleasure when our functioning is smooth and uninhibited; we feel delight when we have something we like and want. Thus pleasure and delight are always the result of activity or accompany activity; they are not normally the motive for action. Without at least some activity, even sensory pleasure may escape us: an apple must be eaten to be enjoyed; unless we actively direct our attention to the source of sensory stimulation, we may not even feel that it is pleasant. A child that is angry or engrossed in his own pursuits will protest against being fondled or petted. If activity itself were not pleasant, we might start an action for the sake of the goal, but it would soon become so tedious that we would never finish it. If smooth functioning were not pleasant, walking or thinking might become a lost art in one generation. It has been said with good reason that activity is more fundamental than pleasure, though it cannot be brought to term without pleasure.*

For the hedonist, pleasure is the basic motive in all actions. Reflection will show that such a statement makes an exception the general norm. An object or a function gives us pleasure because it suits us in some way. We want it because it is something good to have or to do. Our wanting becomes a motive when we endorse it and let it lead us to action. Wanting, as an emotion, always tends toward its object, an object that has been intuitively appraised as good in some way. To appraise pleasure itself as something good to have or something to aim for, apart from any particular object, requires reflection and even deliberation. To intend pleasure rather than the object that attracts us requires an act of rational choice. The animal is incapable of such abstract deliberations. He acts as his emotions urge him to act, and they follow the intuitive appraisal that some *thing* (whether perceived or imagined) is good to have. Only human beings, who can reflect upon their emotions and actions, and can initiate action even without emotion, can conceive pleasure in the abstract as a motive.

Though the human being can want pleasure rather than the activity or object that will bring pleasure, he does not normally do so. A mother wants to be with her child, whether she enjoys herself or not. A man may make a long journey to be with his friend; he enjoys being with his friend but he made the journey *to be with him,* not merely to enjoy himself. Having something we want always brings joy (or pleasure). But the reason for seeking it may or may not be the pleasure of having it.

When the expected pleasure becomes the motive for human action, the *result* of getting something we want, of having achieved our goal, is made the goal itself. That such a substitution is neither natural nor harmless can be shown from clinical experience. When a man's attention is concentrated on the achievement of sexual pleasure, this pleasure consistently eludes him. As a result of observations made during his clinical practice, Frankl says:

---

* See Thomas Aquinas on pleasure as motive: "Pleasure does not occur without activity, nor on the other hand can activity be brought to completion without pleasure. Pleasure is rest (cessation or satisfaction) of the appetite in the pleasurable object that is acquired by action. Now no one seeks rest in anything except he deems rest suitable for himself. Hence the very activity that pleases because it is something suitable, seems to be fundamentally more desirable than the pleasure." (Lib. Eth. Nicomachum, Bk. 10, lect. 6)

The fact is that the pleasure of orgasm is lost when it is forcibly intended. Sexual pleasure is an effect and can never be a matter of intention. *The more one intends sheer pleasure the more it eludes him. . . . The chase after happiness,* we could say, *chases happiness away—the fight for pleasure destroys pleasure.* (1953, p. 115; Frankl's italics; my translation) *

The pleasure that comes from exercising any of our functions and the joy and delight in having something we want are the reward of doing and having something suitable. Something is suitable when it fulfills one of the potentialities of the living being, even though it may not be truly suitable or beneficial in a long-range view. What is suitable, by and large, gives pleasure. But what gives pleasure is not always suitable for the person as a whole. Hence pleasure is not the basis of suitability, as the hedonist maintains. Rather, suitability explains the existence of pleasure. When pleasure for pleasure's sake is made the direct and deliberate intention, it becomes altogether unattainable. Pleasure as a motive requires reflection and deliberate intention, and such intention defeats its own purpose.

McClelland's theory of motivation. A motivation theory based on modified hedonism has been proposed quite recently by McClelland et al. (1953). For these authors *a motive is the redintegration by a cue of a change in an affective situation.* When some situation has brought pleasure or pain, the individual will later expect similar pleasure or pain on encountering the same situation. Actuality either confirms or disappoints this expectation. If the discrepancy between expectation and actuality (in *either* direction) is mild, it arouses pleasurable (positive) affect, if severe, negative affect. After many repetitions, an "adaptation level" of expectation is built up.

McClelland emphasizes that such redintegration always involves a *change* in affect. Originally, something may have brought *pleasure,* but the expectation of a repetition will change it to *appetite.* Or something may have brought *pain,* but the expectation of a repetition will change it to *anxiety.* Appetite and anxiety are the emotions that lead to action. The effect of such action then either confirms or disappoints expectation.

At first glance, there is a surprising similarity between McClelland's

* Frankl's original: "Nun ist es aber so, dass die Lust des Orgasmus einem *vergeht* gerade dann, wenn sie forciert intendiert wird; denn Lust kann immer nur Sache des Effekts sein, aber niemals Sache der Intention. *Je mehr es einem um die Lust geht—um so mehr vergeht sie einem auch schon. . . . Die Jagd nach dem Glück,* könnten wir sagen, *verscheucht es—der Kampf um die Lust vertreibt sie.*"

theory of motivation and our own view. He speaks of expectation and a gradually built up "adaptation level" of such expectations based on experiences of weal or woe, as we do (see Ch. 9). For him, also, emotion is aroused by expectation. But from here on, our ways part. For McClelland, what is wanted or avoided is not the object but the pleasure or pain resulting from it. McClelland admits that the emotional state (both pleasure and pain) aroused by the object on first encountering it is innate. But after another encounter evidently the pleasure or pain is no longer aroused by the object but by the discrepancy between actuality and expectation.

But surely the object must have some effect the second time as well as the first time, else how could it either confirm or disappoint expectations? If the object does not bring either pleasure or pain and these feelings are the result solely of the discrepancy between actuality and expectation, just what effect can the object have had? If it confirms an expectation of pleasure, there must be pleasure before we can judge that the expectation has been confirmed. If the object disappoints our expectation, it must bring less pleasure than we expect and may even bring pain. In both cases it must arouse an affective state *before* we can compare this state with our expectation.

Emotion as the result of discrepancy between actuality and expectation is a notion even more precarious than Hebb's concept of emotion as disturbed or facilitated phase sequences (see Ch. 1, in the following volume) which served as model for McClelland's theory. Small discrepancies do not always arouse positive emotions as required by this hypothesis; and large discrepancies are not always unpleasant. A real danger does not become pleasant when it is slighty less or slightly greater than anticipated. The student who expected to stand first in a class of a hundred and turns out to be second is not pleased but very disappointed indeed, while the student who expected to fail and gets a good grade instead is not displeased but most pleasantly surprised; and the girl who expected merely a dinner in the company of the man of her choice and is given an engagement ring after the dinner is joyful, not sad.

For McClelland, a motive is really an emotional tendency toward something experienced as beneficial; hence it should always lead to action when it is strong enough. But we are often strongly attracted to something we do not permit ourselves to do or to have. We may even have to fight against the emotion to regain our equanimity. McClelland's theory does not allow him to distinguish between a wanting that is emotional in nature and a wanting that comes from the reflective estimate that a particular attraction is contrary to our best interests. With the second kind of wanting there will be an action that is not dictated by emotion, a state of affairs that is completely inexplicable on McClelland's premises.

THE DEVELOPMENT OF MOTIVATIONAL SYSTEMS

We have seen that action is brought about by various action tendencies that are the result of perception and appraisal. These action tendencies can lead to action singly or in combination. In the infant and small child single action tendencies gradually lead to more or less isolated actions. In the older child single actions combine into action sequences, for instance, in playing house or a game of cops and robbers. In the adult, finally, they combine into a connected motivational system.

Inherent action tendencies. Every organismic function has an inherent tendency to go into action whenever the proper conditions are given. This is true not only for organic functions like eating or digestion but for psychological functions as well. The infant sees, hears, feels whenever there is something to see or hear or feel, although it takes some time before he can direct his attention to any given object. It takes him even longer to recognize things and to find out whether they are beneficial or harmful. Smooth functioning is pleasurable, even for the tiny infant. When he is fed and comfortable, he smiles and coos. Liking what he sees, he begins reaching for it and thus begins to relate himself to the world around him.

Coordinated motor activity. A healthy infant wants to move whenever he is awake. Sheer motion is pleasant, as can be judged from the infant's blissful expression when he can wave and kick without hindrance. Later, he uses the control over his limbs gained in this way to explore and manipulate the things around him. Thus motion brings the added satisfaction of getting to know his environment and being able to handle things skillfully. No special "exploratory drive" or "instinct of curiosity" need be postulated to explain the fact that both children and animals want to investigate their environment. Thus monkeys as well as children will solve mechanical puzzles even without an external incentive (cf. Harlow, 1953). As soon as the infant can focus on something, he not only sees, he also looks and knows. When he can reach for a thing and handle it, he comes to know more and more about it. Solving a mechanical puzzle is simply a further step dictated by the desire to know how things fit together. Thus the active sensory functions lead to an appraisal of what is sensed, and the estimate that this is good to know leads to action and manipulation. The child finds his delight in being able to handle things, even if he can do no more than bang, throw, or break them. In this way he is led along the way to mastery until he is able to make and build things rather than to break them.

Physiological appetites. While sensory and motor functions are ready for action at birth, only a few appetites are active at that time. Only those instinctive actions can be carried out that can be initiated by a physiological state and do not demand complicated motor patterns. The infant can and does feel hunger and thirst, and seeks with his mouth until he finds something to suck. Both sucking and swallowing reflexes are part of the infant's equipment at birth. His appetitive activity (to use Tinbergen's term) soon develops to the point where he no longer blindly seeks for the nipple but watches for mother and stops crying as soon as she picks him up. At every stage, he wants what will satisfy him, but refuses what he cannot eat.

As the child grows and begins to investigate the world around him, the automatic gesture of bringing an object to his mouth (developed about the time the infant is ready for solid food) becomes the nucleus of later manipulation. His first interest in investigating anything at all is to find out whether it is good to eat. While eating or sucking has the primacy as the infant's first goal, it is by no means the only pleasurable activity, nor is evacuation.

There is no doubt that the infant will feel the pleasure of touch more acutely in regions where touch receptors are most plentiful, particularly in the mouth and genital regions. Nevertheless, this pleasure is as yet prelibidinal, it is the pleasure of touch or of sucking, not of sexual activity. At puberty, as soon as the production of sex hormones sensitizes the boy or girl to the presence of members of the opposite sex, the sensory pleasure of touching and being touched will combine with the pleasure that comes from activation of the sexual appetite. It is true that direct stimulation of the genitals can produce the consummatory response even before that time; in the same way, the premature infant can be fed with an eyedropper though it cannot seek for the nipple and suckle. This proves merely that one part of the total instinctive pattern may mature before others do. But the infant does need food, while the pre-adolescent does not need a mate. In his case, the artificial arousal of the consummatory response is no indication that the sexual instinct is active.

Either before or after puberty, the young boy or girl may be introduced to the pleasure-giving potentialities of his body by others or may discover them accidentally, and may become addicted to such pleasures. Masturbation is not an instinctual action but is merely the deliberate use of the consummatory mechanism for pleasure. It is an addiction in the strict sense of the term and can be formed as easily as an addiction to anything else that is pleasurable (see Ch. 9). Because modern clinicians often consider it the outlet of an instinctive drive, they find it harmless. If it were recognized as the addiction it is, it would be judged quite as undesirable as any other addiction; and more so, for it represents the abuse of an instinctual response. Instead of tending toward another person as the sexual instinct urges, masturbation is intent upon solitary pleasure. Sexual desire aims for the greatest possible intimacy in mutual confidence; masturbation, urged by the craving for pleasure, leads to isolation and distrust.

Emotions. While instinctive action requires a specific physiological state, emotional tendencies merely require a certain degree of perceptual development, different for different emotions, so that objects can be effectively distinguished and appraised.

Our discussion seems to show that love for another person (mother or mother-substitute), as demonstrated first by the infant's smile, is present before the changed hormonal state indicates the maturation of the sex instinct. Of course, the love of a child toward adults and later the casual camaraderie of one child for another, depend on the way another person is appraised. The small child sees an adult he likes as a benevolent and almost omnipotent provider and as a person but not one of his own world. He sees another child as a fellow citizen of his own small universe. As he grows and develops he responds to more and more personal aspects of other people.

The adolescent is beginning to appreciate personal value—whether he finds it in the matinee idol, the film star, the football hero, or the admired teacher. Boundless admiration, crushes, and hero worship are offered to adults of the same as well as the opposite sex; they indicate a stage in the development of love, not the first expression of the sexual instinct. The "Sturm and Drang" so typical of adolescence is the result of this developing appreciation of the intrinsic value of another person while at the same time the maturing sexual instinct begins to seek expression. Today we see another phenomenon, unknown a generation ago—that of boys and girls of high school or even elementary school age "going steady," though they may change their partner from time to time. Here again, the motive is a developing human relationship, even though this is bound to be a hothouse plant produced by the pressure to have as early as possible what is appropriate to the late teens or early twenties. There is a danger in this forcing. Youngsters who are not ready for a person-to-person relationship may grasp at the budding sexual attraction and so miss the opportunity to combine love and sex in a satisfying and responsible way.

Viktor Frankl (1948) has pointed out that the sexual urge of adolescence loses its hectic insistence as soon as a genuine love relationship is established. In fact, young love has many of the qualities of adolescent hero worship in its tender idealization of the beloved, which for a time disregards and even suppresses all purely sexual attraction. In this way the love relationship between two human persons can mature until sexual expression deepens and completes it. Only when love is dominant will sexual expression be truly satisfying. The emotion of love and sexual desire are both urges to action and may act singly or in combination. It is possible to love (even a member of the opposite sex) without sexual desire or sexual expression, and it is possible to have a sexual relationship without any love at all.

In the animal, as well as in man, emotion and instinct continue side by side, singly and in combination, throughout life. Dogs are devoted to their master, have a tolerant affection for their master's children, and make friends with all kinds of animal pets. When a bitch in heat is anywhere near, they may neglect their friends for a time, but they do not forget them. In some species, the two types of affection, emotional and instinctual attraction, are directed toward the same individual, for instance, in the species where a pair stays together even after their young are reared.

In the human being, a sexual relationship without love will satisfy the sexual appetite but not the person. When the other person is both loved and desired the attraction may be overwhelming, but the future course of the relationship depends on a deliberate decision for reasonable action.

Self-determination. Functions (whether sensory or motor), physiological appetites, and emotions have an inherent tendency to go into action, though the method of activation differs. Sensory and motor functions merely need an opportunity to act and an object to which they are directed by attention; physiological appetites are aroused by metabolic processes; emotions are aroused as soon as there is an intuitive appraisal that something is pleasurable or harmful. But self-determination needs an act of choice which is based on the appraisal that an object is not only pleasurable but also suitable for this person at this time; or that it is not suitable or valuable, though it may be pleasurable.

Rational motives develop when the various uses of a thing can be understood and the value of an object can be grasped. While the inherent action tendencies of psychological functions, physiological appetites, and emotions take us into action without effort, as it were, a rational motive (something conceived as useful or valuable) requires a decision to act, and sustained determination to carry out the action. We have the ability to make a choice on the basis of what is useful or valuable. The act of choice (the will impulse) is an inherent action tendency like any other; it is set in motion by intuitive appraisal, like emotion, but requires a deliberate decision before it will lead to action. When the choice goes against the natural tendency of a function (e.g., the vow of silence), a physical appetite (e.g., the vow of celibacy), or an emotion (e.g., the virtue of long-suffering), the decision is difficult to make and still more difficult to carry out.

Self-determination develops slowly as the child begins to understand how something he wants or does not want affects more important, more valuable goals. While the two-year-old may leave the jam alone after he has been repeatedly punished, the eight-year-old may do without it if he understands that eating between meals takes away his appetite, or that too much sugar will make him fat. This is not a simple "internalizing" of earlier external punishment. The child does not threaten to punish himself for eating between meals. He realizes that gorging himself on jam and developing muscle so that he can make the ball team do not agree. He can have one but must forego the other. Hence he chooses; and if he chooses against his liking for jam, he will have to renew his decision many a time until the craving for sweets subsides. In the meantime, he will suffer considerable discomfort. What used to be called "a strong will" is the readiness to reaffirm a rational decision time and again, instead of giving in when the pangs of unfulfilled desire make us forget the original motive.

Rational motives do not develop "out of" instinctive or emotional motives, nor do physiological appetites or emotions develop "out of" sensory or motor functions. The individual functions tend to action as soon as the opportunity is given, but they can be combined and ordered, for instance, in examining or handling an object. Knowing the object leads to appraising and wanting it, and wanting leads eventually to obtaining it. When wanting a thing leads to attaining it, it is enjoyed whether or not it also satisfies a physiological appetite. The action that leads to possession may be initiated by physiological appetite and desire, by an emotion that has no direct instinctual tie, or by a wanting that is deliberate rather than emotional in nature. In the nature of things, some appetites (e.g., hunger) will function long before emotion or reflection can lead to action; but this does not mean that every other action tendency develops from hunger.

The instinctive action sequence is guided by natural impulsion, though each action in the sequence is initiated by knowing and wanting something. Sensory, motor, and appetitive functions are ordered and combined into an instinctive sequence. This combination is functional, but once initiated it is a coherent unit. Even then, part responses are always possible. The individual functions can still be used singly: we can see without appraising or approaching; we can wiggle our big toe, scratch behind the ear, or run down a hill without any particular purpose, just for the sake of doing it. Perceptions and movements are not only part of instinctive sequences; they also function in their own right and bring their own satisfaction.

The point to be remembered is that instinct as we understand it is an impulse and urge *to ordered activity,* achieving a naturally determined goal. It is not an impulse and urge *to action*—that, we have shown, is the felt action tendency of emotion and, in human beings, of choosing. Instinct directs the *ordering* of action sequences, which in human beings has to be implemented by reflective choice and deliberation. Obviously, there are some actions and action sequences even in human beings that are ordered exclusively by such inherent impulsion: for instance, the whole complicated sequence of physiological activities that make up the total bodily economy. There are other actions that are ordered in every detail primarily by reflective decisions, like the choice of a particular vocation and the planning of the intricate steps that lead to it.

When the emotional goal is at the same time an instinctual goal and a rational motive (a young man wanting to marry the girl of his choice), emotion and sexual desire are included in the rational motive, but the motive is no less rational for all that. Only when emotion and sexual desire pull in one direction and the reasonable course points in the other (when the girl is already married, for instance) is there a conflict that requires a difficult choice. The decision itself is the result of reflection and deliberation, no matter which course is taken. The decision to give in to emotion is still self-determined, willed. For adults and older children, simple acting from instinct and emotion is impossible, unless the emotion is sudden and overwhelming, and action occurs on the first intuitive appraisal.

Such a view of motivation assumes that the sheer muscular energy for every action stems from the normal physiological processes that maintain the organism as a living system, rather than from some specific biological "drives." Hence there is no need to derive adult human motives from a few basic (because biological) energy sources. The bodily economy provides muscles with nourishment so that they can contract in ordered sequence. Action is initiated by knowing, appraising, and wanting something. Such wanting (whether emotional or deliberate) is an action tendency mediated by neural pathways that carry motor impulses to the appropriate muscles (see Chapters 2–6, in the following volume). Neither emotions nor will impulses are energies or energy sources, they are action tendencies that lead to motor performance. Other motivation theories assume that a special motor must deliver the energy for all actions; hence they have to derive all motives from basic biological drives. Yet they have never described in detail how action is initiated, or just what are the psychological antecedents and what the neurological connections. We hope to show in Sections I and II of the following volume that the available evidence does indeed allow us to give such a description.

The function of motivational systems. We have seen how functions are ordered by appetites and emotions and combined into actions; and how these emotions become factors in rational motivation. Motivational systems do not grow naturally. They are formed by every individual as he exercises his functions, uses them to deal with things and people around him, and appraises the world in relation to himself.

A motivational system may develop with little self-direction, almost randomly, when a man's choices are dictated by the opportunities of the moment, by prevailing opinion, or by the dominant cultural and intellectual climate. Or a man may come to value a good table and a comfortable life above everything else he could achieve; his life will be directed more and more toward sensory satisfaction. A man may also choose by careful search and deliberation the values that will govern his life, and may then organize his conduct accordingly. In every case, a motivational system will develop that is of his own making; but only in the last case will it be based on conscious deliberation. Even when it is, one man may act reasonably, by and large, in accord with his ideals. Another may be led astray over and over by his emotions.

There will be wide individual differences in the motivational system developed by each individual, in his self-ideal. There will also be wide individual differences in the degree to which he implements his values, whatever they may be, in each individual situation. One man may pursue his goals in life in such a way that every important action will harmonize with them. Another may have purposes but follow them by fits and starts; he may be a hero in a pinch but a slacker most of the time. One man's values may shift rapidly; another's may be so rigid that he can adapt to the changes brought about by new discoveries or inventions only with the greatest difficulty.

In this way, wittingly or unwittingly, every man establishes in the course of his life a hierarchy of values for himself that guides his actions. This may lead him to his development and perfection as a human being or far away from it. Later we shall examine the role of emotion in this quest (see Chapters 10 and 11, in the following volume).

12. BASIC EMOTIONS IN PSYCHOLOGICAL THEORY

Some of the basic emotions have early come to the psychologist's attention because they are so noticeable and their long-term effects are so devastating. Chronic fear (anxiety) is a prominent symptom in neurosis. Among acute emotional episodes, anger is particularly spectacular. The number of temper tantrums has often been recorded faithfully for research in the development of emotion, while the far more ubiquitous likes and dislikes (of food, clothes, people, etc.) have gone unnoticed. At best, specific refusals (dislikes) of numerous things have been included under the vague term of "negativism" and held to be a characteristic of the toddler. Thus an invaluable opportunity was missed to watch the growth of such dislikes and correct them before they become a firm attitude.

Fear and anger are the emotions with which the psychologist has felt most familiar. Their origin in conflict seemed so plausible, the physiological upset they create so extreme. What wonder that conflict theories of emotion have flourished, and fear and anger have become the prototypes for all emotions. With the advent of psychotherapy, the attention of clinicians was directed toward those emotional attitudes and habits that were the most obvious obstacles to recovery: anxiety and hostility. As clinical interests spread, theorists began working out special theories of anxiety or aggression. The positive emotions, love, joy, hope, courage, were either entirely ignored by theorists or, in the case of love, treated as the expression of the sexual instinct, Eros precariously counterbalancing Thanatos. As a result, the *sentiment* of human love has been practically unexplored, though in recent years there seems to be an encouraging upsurge of interest.*

* See Sorokin (1950), Guitton (1951), Montagu (1950), Suttie (1952).

In Freud's system, the phenomenon most closely resembling human love is "identification," which will be discussed in Chapter 10, in the following volume. Here we will attempt only to discuss some of the theories that have grown out of this preoccupation of psychologists with anxiety and aggression, and see how they fit into a general theory of emotion. In the last analysis, every special theory must find its place within a general framework if a science is to become comprehensive and comprehensible.

ANGER AND AGGRESSION

The term aggression, stemming from Freud's hypothesis of an aggressive instinct (death instinct), is a concept that includes at the very least the basic emotions of anger (in the acute form) and of hatred (in the chronic form). But it includes more than emotion: it contains overt action, whether hostile or assertive, both supposedly the expression of an "aggressive drive." Theories of aggression, dealing with this concept in its psychoanalytic meaning, find it notoriously unwieldy.

Aggression as seen by Freud. To sort out the different factors contained in the psychoanalytic concept of aggression, let us examine the position of Freud. As we have seen before, Freud considers affect as the consciously experienced discharge of an instinct or drive. Now aggression is the instinct, aggressive action is the outward expression of that instinct, and hostility presumably is the felt emotion. However, we have seen also that Freud later suggested that emotion is an alternative expression of the drive, acting as a safety valve when the drive itself is blocked. Hence he is led to a further postulate, namely, that sexual and aggressive instincts always act together: "In biological functions the two basic instincts work against each other or combine with each other. Thus, the act of eating is a destruction of an object with the final aim of incorporating it, and the sexual act is an act of aggression having as its purpose the most intimate union" (Freud, 1949, p. 21).

Now in eating there is no felt emotion of hostility; yet for Freud the aggressive instinct is at the root of it. If aggression can be expressed in action even though there is no corresponding felt emotion, it becomes plausible that any action whatever may contain a component of "aggression." It is less plausible that enjoyment should be the emotion felt during eating, or pleasure during the sexual act, if emotion is an *alternative* to action. But most psychoanalysts would contend that emotion may be both a safety valve and the experience of the drive in action (see Ch. 7), though such a solution does not make for scientific clarity and consistency. At any rate, it is clear that aggression in psychoanalytic usage includes not only hostile attack but every kind of constructive action. Carving a statue, painting a picture, making a cake, engaging in competitive sports, all are manifestations of aggression. Only on Freud's dogmatic assertion that libidinal-aggressive drives supply the energy for *all* goal-directed action can such usage be defended.

As indicated in Chapter 11, Freud seems to have chosen to interpret aggression as an instinct because he assumed (with most of his contemporaries) that the living being is inert and must be driven to action by special motors. On this assumption, actions without a sexual goal require a nonsexual motive force. Later, as the above quotation shows, Freud assumed that even sexual actions must draw on such a force. Whatever Freud's reason for this interpretation, it obliterates the distinction between hostile attack and constructive action, a distinction all of us make in everyday life. It is true that we often speak of "attacking a problem" when we mean no hostility. But in so doing we are using a metaphor and know that we are using it. Unless forced by factual evidence to declare experience wrong, we hate to elevate a metaphor to the dignity of a scientific concept.

Recently, some evidence has been quoted as supporting the psychoanalytic definition of aggression. Else Frenkel-Brunswik, for instance, referred to a study that "corroborated the hunch that two phenotypically unrelated, or even diverse, types of manifestations can be related to one and the same set of dynamic factors" (1951, p. 361). As an example, she mentioned the traits of exuberance and irritability that were negatively correlated with each other in 95 subjects (r—.52) but were positively correlated with aggression (+.30 and +.41). The multiple correlation between exuberance, irritability, and aggression was +.73.

At first glance, this looks like convincing proof that spontaneous activity and irritability flow from the same root, namely, the drive of aggression. On the psychoanalytic hypothesis, we would have to say that this drive can express itself in either exuberance or irritability, or both. But when we look at the way in which these traits were measured, the facts tell a different story.

Adult raters who had known the children over a period of eight years rated them on various traits (e.g., exuberance, irritability) by observing their behavior in social situations. Then the raters were asked "to forget about the manifest behavior of the children" and to rate them according to nine underlying basic drives, amongst them aggression, abasement, succorance, and the like. The correlations were based on the relationship of *behavior ratings* (exuberance, irritability) with *drive ratings* (aggression, etc.). In drive ratings, the judges had to attach some definite meaning to the terms used for drives. Obviously, the meaning of "aggression" was the psychoanalytic definition, which would allow the raters to judge exuberant as well as irritable behavior as the expression of an aggressive drive. The instruction to forget about the manifest behavior of the children can only mean that the judges were not to rate the actions themselves but rather what they thought these actions indicated. To do this, the raters must have made an inference from some evidence. And what could that evidence be except the impression they gained from the way the children acted? What the correlation really indicates is that aggression can be inferred (in the opinion of the raters) from behavior that can be called exuberant as well as from behavior that can be called irritable. The correlation was between raters' inferences, and does not show that there is a drive of aggression which includes these alternative expressions.

Unless we are constrained by common usage, we could easily tabulate both boys and puppies as "children," just as we can rate both exuberant and irritable children as "aggressive." If we do so, our statistical analysis will not prove that the term children is properly applied to both human and animal young, nor that aggression actually includes both exuberance and anger. There is a specific distinction between human and animal young, which is obliterated by using the term "children" for both. Such usage would become downright wrong if we were to conclude that puppies must be boys because they are called "children." If aggressive behavior stems from an aggressive drive, there is at least a presumption that exuberant behavior stemming from the same root includes a hostile element. The term *aggression* as well as the term *children* is loaded by its common usage. In addition, aggression carries the meaning of destructiveness in virtue of its association with the death instinct which is its ultimate source. If the death instinct is active in the drive of aggression, all behavior that flows from it will perforce have the connotation of destructive hostility; even exuberant, outgoing, constructive actions.

Freud's concession to common sense is to assume that the aggressive drive is "bound" by the erotic instinct in nonhostile actions. On the other hand, the libidinal drive seems to need some admixture of aggression, according to Freud, to achieve its ends. This makes the death instinct serve the ends of life and puts the life instinct at the mercy of the death instinct—surely a peculiar antinomy. Freud's expedient of explaining human action as the outcome of two opposing instincts instead of considering it the result of interlocking human functions leads always to the same impasse (see Ch. 7).

Aggression and contending emotion. That aggression cannot be an instinct has emerged from our analysis of instinctive motivation (Ch. 11). It cannot be an instinct because it is not triggered off by a periodically recurring physiological appetite that leads to an instinctive goal, nor is it followed by an ordered series of actions ending in a consummatory response. For Freud, the concept of an "aggressive instinct" was necessary to account for the energy spent in nonlibidinal actions. But we have shown that the energy for action is never supplied by instincts. The physiological need triggers off an impulse to action directed by the image of what is needed; the energy for the action itself comes from metabolic processes.

The impetus to a given action comes from the emotional tendency toward a particular object, whether that can give instinctual satisfaction or not. Under some circumstances a special impetus is needed, for instance, when the action intended is arduous or has to contend against obstacles. This impetus is provided by the contending emotions. If the goal is attractive but difficult to reach, the emotion of hope or of striving will urge us to keep after it. If something threatens that can be overcome, audacity will urge us to victory. If something obstructive is actually upon us, anger urges us to attack and remove it. If there is something we have decided on doing or attaining though there is no emotional attraction, a deliberate effort provides the additional impetus if reaching our goal proves unexpectedly laborious. Hence our scheme does provide active tendencies initiating overt action, impulse emotions coupled with a simple will impulse when the goal is within easy reach, contending emotions implemented by deliberate effort when it can be reached only with difficulty. There is an increased impulsion behind such contending emotions which may lead to a clash with any obstacles that stand in the way, but there is not necessarily a hostile intent. Maslow (1954), for instance, has pointed out that a child does not intend destruction when he pulls a clock apart; he merely wants to examine it. Nor has he any hostile intent when he takes a toy over the resistance of another child; rather, he acts as if he were wresting it from a tight container.*

Hostile aggression flows from hate rather than from anger, and is comparatively independent of provocation from another. When hatred has developed into a sentiment, it does seem to act almost like a constant force, close to the Freudian conception of aggression. Since the term "aggression" implies hostile intent in common usage, it seems safer to use it only for an actual hostile attack and not for the postulated driving force initiating such attack. While anger is the emotion that urges to violent attack upon something appraised as an obstacle that can be overcome, it is not the only contending emotion, nor is it the only urge that will lead to forceful action (see Gasson's discussion of impulse and urge, in: Arnold and Gasson, 1954, Ch. 6).

In recent years several writers have insisted on the fact that aggression is primarily a reaction to provocation or frustration of some kind. Among modern analysts, for instance, Bergler (1949) considers "normal reactive aggression" as a response to frustration. For him, normal aggression is used in self-defense or defense of others, is directed against the true source of the frustration, is judged as justified (hence not accompanied by guilt), is proportional to the frustration and used appropriately, is provoked only by a great offense, and is not a remnant of childhood frustrations (Bergler, 1949, p. 78). Allport also insists that aggression is not an instinct demanding an outlet, but is rather a reaction to some provocation. Hence aggression does not require "drainage," nor can it be "channeled" into constructive outlets:

To say that free-floating aggression may be channeled into creative work in literature, art, public works, is too far-fetched. Normally there is no aggression in painting a picture or drafting a blueprint. This [notion] seems to return full force to the Freudian view that a certain quantum of aggression exists. It may "float" anywhere. It may even be sublimated into non-aggression (peaceful pursuits). In other words, it may exist even when it doesn't exist. (1954, p. 358)

The conception of aggression as energy that can be drained or channeled is another instance of a metaphor that is developed without regard to the actual manner in which a biological instinct or an emotion can

---

* In habitual irritability, there may be a similar attempt to remove annoyances, yet with no true hostile intent. Such irritability is the remnant of many earlier anger reactions, congealed into an attitude and acted out habitually.

operate. Fortunately, an increasing number of psychologists are beginning to advocate operational definitions. These are restrictive because they do not examine by a careful phenomenological analysis what really happens but merely assume that the way in which a phenomenon is measured must be the way in which it acts. At the same time, an operational definition at least attempts to eschew metaphors and keep close to facts.

The frustration-aggression hypothesis. Dollard and his associates (1939), for whom aggression is the reaction to a frustration of goal-directed behavior, apparently also adopted the view that aggression is reactive. They define aggression as "an act whose goal-response is injury to an organism (or organism-surrogate)." In later publications (Miller *et al.*, 1941; Sears, 1941) the Yale group have indicated that frustration is not invariably followed by aggression. Rather, frustration instigates a hierarchy of response tendencies, one of which is aggression; but the tendency to aggression must be dominant in the hierarchy before an overt aggressive act will occur. When frustration is continued, the tendencies leading to nonaggressive behavior will be extinguished so that actual aggression may eventually occur. If aggression is punished, as happens from childhood on, the punishment is said to be another frustration that will produce renewed aggression. Hence "the expression of any act of aggression is a catharsis that reduces the instigation to all other acts of aggression" (Dollard *et al.*, 1939, p. 53).

Criticizing the frustration-aggression hypothesis, Sargent (1948) points out that aggression does not follow immediately upon frustration: a "pronounced emotional reaction" intervenes. This emotion, he says, may be a generalized anger or fear reaction, but it may also be a specialized emotion like hostility, jealousy, inferiority, or shame. If the emotional reaction is anger, it is more likely to lead to aggressive action than is anxiety or shame. After the emotional reaction comes "habit or mechanism," by which Sargent means the way in which the individual expresses or controls his anger (for instance, by overt expression, displacement, regression, rationalization, repression, etc.). Since it is the individual who uses these mechanisms, Sargent insists that the crucial factor that determines the final action is not the objective frustration but the person's definition or interpretation of the situation.

This was also emphasized by Pastore (1950), who showed that overt aggression is not likely to follow if the frustration is appraised as reasonable instead of being considered arbitrary, unjust, or malicious. We might add that this is as true of anger as it is of aggressive action. If a group of hungry men are promised food, and food is available but is not given them, they will be angry and may act aggressively. If they cannot have food because none can be obtained *and they know it,* they will be dejected rather than angry or aggressive.

Sargent has made clear that neither anger nor aggression follows automatically upon frustration. The emotional reaction to frustration depends on the individual's appraisal of the situation; the action which follows depends on the emotion as well as on his habits of action and, we would add, on his purpose of the moment. Though anger is a response to anything appraised as frustrating, not every frustration is appraised as such, and hence not every frustration arouses either anger or aggressive action.

Moreover, Morlan (1949) has pointed out that unhindered expression of hostility does not always act as catharsis. Expression of anger or hostility may sometimes intensify it, as William James pointed out long ago. Morlan quoted some recent evidence which at first glance seems to confirm Dollard's hypothesis that expression acts as catharsis: Appel (1942) found that the most quarrelsome children had fewer quarrels the following year; Jones (1926) found that babies who cried readily showed less "tension," as measured by the psychogalvanic reflex; Allport (1954) found that expressions of hostility against the teacher in a course on race relations, when permitted, promoted understanding and constructive changes in attitude. Morlan suggested that all these instances may have another explanation, namely, that expression of emotion permits the development of techniques of dealing with others.

At the same time, it is a fact that frustration *does* arouse anger and aggression, though it may not do so every time; and it is a fact that emotional expression brings relief, though it may not do so under all circumstances. Let us see under what conditions anger or any other emotion will be aroused, and when emotional expression will act as catharsis.

Frustration and anger. In our earlier discussion (Ch. 10, p. 196) we have found that anger is a positive reaction to something that does us harm *here and now,* in contrast to courage, which is a positive reaction to something that is merely *threatening* harm. Courage urges us to go out and meet the threat; anger, to combat harm when it is already upon us. If a man is frustrated in reaching some goal, what frustrates him is certainly present and will be appraised as harmful. Hence his first impulse will be anger, a rising up against the obstacle. If the obstacle cannot be overcome, dejection or despair will take over. But as long as there is any hope of removing the interference, there will be a contending emotion urging action against the obstacle and against anyone who might have put it there. Anger and courage overlap to some extent as the threat is gradually actualized; hence anger and courage, both positive reactions to something harmful, often seem to merge and act in combination.

Anger itself may be appraised in turn. If the interference with our goal is the doing of someone in authority, we may be afraid that our anger might be met with anger and possibly with retaliation. When our anger is directed toward someone we love, we may be afraid that our anger might hurt him, and we cannot bear to give him pain. Hence anger will arouse fear whenever we are afraid of the consequences of such anger, whether these may be retaliation or the pain of hurting someone we love. In either case, we are not afraid of our own anger but of its foreseen results.

As soon as anger arouses fear, it will give way to fear, because an appraisal leading to a positive emotion has given way to another leading to a negative emotion. While anger and courage may act in combination, anger and fear cannot. We cannot attack the obstacle as long as that attack threatens serious harm. Anger is not repressed, it is *replaced* by fear, as soon as this appraisal prevails. And once fear is aroused by anger, fear will increase with every similar frustration. In this way a reaction to frustration may be established that represents an enduring attitude of fear. The son who never contradicts his father has not really "repressed" his resentment, for he is well enough aware that his father annoys him occasionally. What he does not know is that his habitual concern for his father overrides his resentment before it can fully develop. When his fear is reduced (e.g., in psychotherapy) his resentment may finally burst through like a spring flood. This is not necessarily proof of repression, but can be explained by the same constancy of appraisal we have discussed before. Resentment has established a habitual appraisal and a budding attitude which was not fully expressed because it was always followed by another, more urgent appraisal. Now, when the frustration is fully focused on, the son's anger is allowed to develop and can be expressed: immediately, it will take him captive and he will recall innumerable previous occasions for the same resentment.

Not only can anger be replaced by fear; fear sometimes makes place for anger. When flight is unsuccessful and the threatening thing is upon us, we may yet fight it and succeed. Anger born of desperation has saved many a lost cause.

Frustration and catharsis. Now let us see whether we can identify the conditions which determine when the expression of anger and overt aggression will act as catharsis, and when such expression will intensify the emotion. Morlan suggested that the expression of hostility is sometimes rewarded and thus may come to be repeated. This happened, for instance, in Nazi Germany, where hostility against the Jews was encouraged as well as rewarded. During a war, when every propaganda effort is made to arouse hatred toward the enemy nations, such expression is similarly rewarded; it becomes a patriotic duty.

But there are a number of cases on record where open aggression is not rewarded, and yet emotional expression acts as a spur to further aggression rather than a catharsis. Morlan quoted two cases: one of a boy brought up in Nazi Germany, persecuted and imprisoned in a concentration camp, who later came to this country and became the terror of the whole neighborhood. The other was a janitor who had been frustrated and misused by a tenant and one day stopped her in front of the building with a stream of abuse. Even after she had gone, he did not cease to rage, and he was still upset and furious two days later.

"Abreaction" evidently does not exhaust the emotion.* When emotional expression brings relief and improvement there must be another factor responsible for it. Such relief is achieved in therapy. The therapist is not only another person but someone who is not emotionally involved. He "stands by," with the intention of helping the other understand himself. Here the client not only expresses his emotion; he appraises it as well and comes to see that his emotional reaction was neither the only response to the situation confronting him nor the best response. In the two cases quoted by Morlan, there was mere emotional expression but no reflective appraisal: the janitor finally gave vent to the resentment that had accumulated, the refugee boy had developed a hatred toward people that led him to torment them in turn.

Mere expression has value only when the action to which the emotion urges removes the source of the emotion: when an angry attack has removed the obstacle, when flight has brought us to safety, there is a genuine

---

* Clearly it could be supposed to do so only on the Freudian assumption that aggression is an instinctive force that must be discharged either in emotion or in action.

relief. But where the cause remains, other ways must be found to deal with it. Emotional expression will only intensify the emotion. The boy's attacks earned him the dislike of everyone and so increased his vindictiveness; the janitor's resentment was kept alive by the fact that the tenant was still in the house. In neither case could expression of that resentment exhaust the emotion. In fact, expression merely solidified the resentment and made it articulate.

The recent evidence quoted by Morlan can be explained without recourse to the frustration-aggression hypothesis. Appel's children had discovered by quarreling how others would take their aggression, and found that they could deal with the situation without outright attack. Jones's tense babies may have been more fearful than those that cried a great deal: children are tense when they are afraid, and when they are afraid they do not cry.* Emotional expression did not *produce* freedom from tension; it merely indicated such freedom. Allport's students had to express their emotions to be able to assess them and to look at the situation objectively. In every case, it was not the expression of anger per se that brought the improvement.

Displaced aggression. Both psychoanalysis and the frustration-aggression hypothesis lay great emphasis on a displacement of aggression from the source of frustration to innocent bystanders. For psychoanalysts, of course, this is simply a consequence of repressing the instinct of aggression. Miller (1948), on the contrary, insists that displacement is a mechanism employed in reacting to frustration. The difference in the two views, as Allport (1954) points out, lies in the fact that displacement as a reaction to frustration does not imply that aggression is drained off into a different channel or that its "release" through such a channel will make it less likely that aggression will be shown.

Allport himself thought that aggression can lead to displacement. Now there is no doubt that venting one's anger on a scapegoat is a familiar experience; but let us consider for a moment just what happens in "displacement," what kind of a mechanism it could be. A man is severely criticized by his employer and takes it with good grace, but on coming home finds fault with the dinner, his wife, his children, his dog. There is no doubt that he was angry at getting a reprimand, but fear of losing

---

* Children may cry from startle or sudden fright, but not from fear or anxiety. We shall see later that fear and startle have opposite physiological effects (Ch. 7, in the following volume).

his job prevented him from expressing his resentment. Perhaps he also smarted under the realization that he deserved at least some of it. If he were willing to acknowledge that and resolve to do better, all would be well. But his pride is hurt, and he is angry at his employer for having made him look incompetent, at himself for having laid himself open to such an insult, and at everybody and everything because nobody prevented it.

The very fact that his wife, his children, his dog seem to be cheerful and unconcerned, though he has been insulted, is another blow: he has a right to expect their support. Now he is well aware that he cannot blame them, because they do not even know what happened to him—but he cannot easily change his intuitive appraisal which judges only the unconcern, not the reasons for it. Hence his anger continues and will be expressed at the first opportunity. But there must be an opportunity; he does not berate his family the minute he comes in the door, if he is a reasonable man. True, that opportunity might not have been a source of annoyance at any other time, but with the anger still smoldering in him, the slightest occasion will fan it into flame.

In this case, the anger is not really "displaced" from one object to another; it is directed toward something that really annoys him, and everything annoys him at this particular time. In much the same way, a baby screams, kicks, and hits out at everything when he is balked. He is angry not only at the mother who has taken a dangerous toy away from him, but at everybody and everything because he cannot have what he wants. The baby cannot reason as yet that screaming and kicking won't help him get his toy back, nor does he stop to consider what others will think of him. He is simply giving in to the natural impulse to contend for what he wants with all his might. The baby does not displace his anger from mother to everything else; he simply expresses it without restraint. Both baby and adult are angry at the obstruction of their wishes, and their anger, like any violent emotion, spreads over the total situation. While they are angry, they are angry at everything; the only difference between baby and adult is that the baby can soon be interested in something else, while the adult may spend the trip home imagining cutting rejoinders and may smart under the reproof for days to come.

The concept of displacement is often used to explain the scapegoat theory of prejudice. Allport (1954) quotes the case of a student who was continually criticized by his father because his grades in college were not quite as good as his father's had been. He felt utterly frustrated but finally consoled himself by proclaiming that "it was only the Jewish grinds and cheats" who prevented him from heading the class. This boy undoubtedly was angry, not only at his father but at the whole school situation, particularly at his classmates who topped his performance. He did not actually know whether they cheated or whether they were Jews, but gave that as a reason to himself and others to excuse his apparent inferiority. Here again, the anger was not "displaced," but was spread out over many things. It was a reaction to the whole school situation that dictated a pseudo-explanation.

To be free to express anger openly or even to accept his own anger, an adult must have the assurance that the goal toward which he aims is justified, and that whatever obstructs him is not. Anger is either righteous anger or it is malice. For it to be righteous anger, there must be some fault in whatever obstructs a man's goal. Hence our student had to endow his classmates with characteristics he considered undesirable before he could legitimately resent them. By reflection, he discovered that he was angry at his bright classmates. Anger has a cause; hence he proceeded to look for it and found it in his rationalization.

There is still another kind of displacement, which has been explained as a remnant of infantile frustrations: Allport has suggested that aggressiveness may become a character trait that is habitual and compulsive, so that anger may be excessive, displaced, inappropriate. We have seen in our discussion of emotion (Ch. 10) that any emotion leaves a residue that may develop into an emotional attitude when extremely intense or often repeated. When acted out, this attitude may become an emotional habit. There may be individuals who have developed such a habit of anger or irritability or hatred, who are "agin the world," no matter what. But here again the anger is not "displaced" from the original object. Like every other emotional attitude, such aggressiveness, once it has become a habit, spreads over similar situations and is expressed on the slightest provocation.

Such an interpretation is supported by the finding that people who are aggressive in one direction are similarly aggressive in others (Stagner, 1944). Also, an emotional habit can be supported by the customs in a given culture.* Thus Boggs (1947) found that aggression is either present

* R. L. Jenkins's recent report on personality disturbances in children is relevant here. He says: "There is a continuing tendency in some circles to consider children's

and, if so, spreads over a wide variety of situations, or it is relatively lacking in a given culture.

It has been said that Miller's (1948) experiment with rats has proved that aggression can be displaced. But when we examine the experiment, a different picture emerges. Rats in pairs were given an electric shock which was turned off whenever they touched one another in sparring position. Later, the current was turned off whenever they struck at each other. Eventually, a rubber doll was stood up in the cage with the pair of rats. While another rat was in the cage, a rat would never strike the doll. But if a rat was alone with the doll, half the rats did strike the doll. From this experiment Miller concluded that aggression can be displaced from rat to doll.

Is this really a justified inference? Obviously, the rat's normal reaction to electric shock is not attack but attempted escape. Learning to "strike" another rat is not aggression, any more than is pressing a lever in the Skinner box. Touching the other rat means the end of pain to a rat subjected to electric shock, just as lever pressing means food to a hungry rat. And just as a rat will press a lever of any shape, once it has learned that lever pressing brings food, so a rat will strike or touch any object that happens to be in the cage, once it has learned that such an action will stop the shock. The experiment shows merely that a rat can learn to "strike" something to avoid pain; and that this learning may be generalized to other objects. The experiment does not illustrate aggression nor does it prove the displacement of aggression.

From our discussion it appears that the frustration-aggression hypothesis needs qualification. Frustration arouses anger because we are hindered in what we want to do or to have; and what hinders us is appraised as an obstacle to be removed. In animals this appraisal is intuitive; in human beings it is both intuitive and reasoned. Hence animals will always respond with rage in such a situation. Human beings, on the other hand, will always have an impulse to anger, but they will also appraise the situation, as well as their anger, reflectively and will deal with it accordingly. They may find that their anger is justified, or they may justify it by rationalization, and express it freely. But they may also reappraise the situa-

---

aggressiveness toward other children sacrosanct: a refusal to believe it can advantageously be discouraged. There is a failure to recognize that much of aggressive behavior in children does not spring from spontaneous drives but is a learned adaptive pattern sanctioned or required by the mores of the group and may be as unspontaneous as table manners." (In: Reymert, 1950, p. 361)

tion as a problem to be solved, a challenge to be met, and look for possible means of overcoming it. As soon as they direct their attention to a possible solution, their anger will disappear without being either suppressed or repressed. If they focus on the difficulty of overcoming the obstacle or on the fact that it obstructs them, their anger will be prolonged and intensified, whether it is expressed or suppressed.

Maier's "frustration-instigated" behavior. Maier has suggested that the behavior instigated by frustration is essentially different from goal-directed or motivated behavior. He bases his hypothesis on the following observation:

Animals which were placed in an insoluble trial-and-error learning problem and which were not allowed to escape but were forced to continue responding soon developed a specific mode of behavior [jumping toward the door in a discrimination apparatus broadside-on]. . . . Therefore . . . the introduction of frustration causes animals to settle on some form of behavior and to cease expressing the variable behavior usually expressed in a trial-and-error learning situation. Further, if sufficient frustration is introduced, they continue expressing behavior that no longer is adaptable. (1949, p. 78)

Hence frustration results in "fixation." And because such animals do not learn a new discrimination task, while rats which have developed the same position habits (jumping either to left or to right) without frustration do learn it, Maier concludes that there must be two different processes, the one goal-directed learning, the other frustration-instigated behavior. These two processes, he thinks, are touched off by different degrees of punishment. Mild punishment produces learning; excessive punishment results in frustration and therefore in fixation, which prevents learning. According to Maier, frustration-instigated behavior has no goal; it has the character of a compulsion which seizes upon the most easily available response. From the hypothesis of Dollard *et al.* Maier accepts the suggestion that aggression is frustration-instigated behavior, but rejects the notion that aggression is goal-directed. He considers physical aggression merely as the most easily available response, directed at the obstacle merely by accident. Maier also suggests that regression and resignation, as well as fixation and aggression, belong in the category of frustration-instigated activities, and are therefore not goal-directed.

Now let us see what really happens in Maier's frustration situations. The rat first learns to jump to one card in the discrimination apparatus but not to the other. Maier, like other experimenters, found that position responses are more easily learned than object ("symbol") responses; in fact, a position habit is often acquired which makes later object responses difficult to learn. After the rat has learned to solve a discrimination problem, "pressure is applied to force it to solve a problem that it is incapable of solving" (p. 127). Similarly, "a problem situation may become frustrating when the motivation to solve the problem is intense and the obstacles are insurmountable" (p. 128). In these two situations, the rat cannot learn what it has to do to obtain food. Maier reports that many animals starve to death rather than jump. When the rat is forced to jump by an air blast or electric shock, it develops a "fixation," that is, it always jumps to the same door, no matter how often it is forced to jump, and jumps in such a way that it could not clear the door even if it were open.

From the experimenter's point of view, such jumping may not be goal-directed because it does not achieve the goal set by him, namely, food. But is there no goal for the rat? Surely by jumping it evades the air blast or shock, no matter how it jumps. As a result of the earlier frustration the rat has learned that it cannot obtain food by jumping, but will merely hurt its nose by jumping straight at the door. Thus the rat does not jump straight but broadside-on which does not hurt; it avoids the air blast and pain as well—is that not a response well and truly directed, away from harm?

Since the animal is successful in avoiding harm, there is no need to change its response to air blast. It does not expect food in this particular situation, and so relearning is impossible. However, if it finds that food can be obtained again (if, for example, the experimenter guides the animal with his hand to the correct door) the rat learns the new response amazingly quickly, in less than 20 trials—although the earlier "fixation" had remained unchanged for 460 trials! What happened was that the original aim (food) had been abandoned after an interference that consistently disappointed the expectation of food. This is shown by the fact that the rats do not try any more, but rather starve to death. This represents the hopelessness or despair in the face of an obstacle to reaching the goal that cannot be overcome.

When a new goal was supplied (harm was threatened by air blast or shock), the rat learned to avoid pain by jumping. Such avoidance of harm was now the goal aimed for and achieved. The response that successfully avoided punishment persisted and became a "fixation," from the experimenter's point of view. Unless a corrective experience teaches the rat that food is again available, such a "fixation" is bound to persist in that situation; yet it is as goal-directed as every other response.

Maier then explains aggression, fixation, resignation, and regression, as possible alternative responses to frustration. Resignation he calls the refusal to jump in the above frustrating situation. Regression is shown, according to Maier, when a much-wanted toy is taken away from a child and put behind a wire screen where the child can still see it; the child responds by "regression": he ignores all other toys, sucks his thumb, or aimlessly pushes a toy to and fro. Yet the child's attention is obviously still centered on the wanted toy and he gets what comfort he may while he waits for the obstacle to be removed.

If these four responses are alternative reactions to frustrations, how did it come about that aggression was never shown in Maier's experiments? (Nor was regression, but it could be objected that there was no opportunity for this type of behavior.) We agree that these are possible alternatives, though not the only ones. Every one of these responses, moreover, is goal-directed. The different conditions under which either one or the other alternative will be chosen can be specified without difficulty, according to the individual's appraisal of the situation: in aggression, he has estimated that the obstacle can be overcome; in resignation, that it cannot; in fixation, that he can escape punishment; in regression, that the original goal can still be attained by waiting.

Recently, Marquart (1948, 1952) has reported studies with human subjects that bear on Maier's hypothesis. She instructed subjects to find the principle of discrimination for two series of shapes. For the first series, either a painful shock was given or a red light was flashed *at random,* but the subjects were informed that this was a punishment for wrong responses. Immediately following the first series the second series was given; and now a shock or red light really indicated wrong responses to a simple principle of discrimination. Most of her subjects learned the principle (and could report it) in less than 80 trials, which included the random trials. Those who did not learn it during that time needed more than 94 trials, and some did not learn it at all during the experimental sessions. Hence Marquart found that the distribution of learning time was bimodal; one mode indicating motivated learning, the other, the result of frustration and failure. She concluded that motivation and frustration are qualitatively different processes.

This conclusion is open to the same objection as Maier's original hypothesis. Frustration is neither a process nor a motive; what motivates is the person's appraisal of the frustrating situation. Both the fast and the slow learners were motivated, as shown by the fact that they carried on the task. But though the slow learners were motivated by the desire to learn, they were influenced also by the fear that they would not succeed, regardless of whether the fault was the experimenter's or their own. Fear actually and physically impedes mental processes (see Drug Effects, Ch. 5, in the following volume); hence their learning was delayed and sometimes altogether prevented. In addition, their fear made them reluctant to try. Fear motivated them rather to escape or evade the task; hence their motives conflicted or rather alternated in this particular situation.

If Maier were right, emotion would not be an action-tendency toward *or away* from some goal. If Dollard *et al.* were right, aggression would be a reflex automatically aroused by frustration. Maier did not take into account that an action can be directed away from something as easily as toward something and still be motivated. Dollard *et al.* did not consider that frustration must be appraised as such and there must be a hope of overcoming it before anger can be experienced or expressed.

FEAR AND ANXIETY

We have seen in Chapter 10 that a man feels fear whenever he appraises something as threatening, whenever he expects harm of some kind that can be avoided only by strenuous effort. Since fear is one of the basic emotions, the question arises: What is its connection with the fear state that is called anxiety and plays so large a role in neurotic disorders? The term *anxiety* is used with many meanings, but there is always some connection with fear: anxiety is held to be either diffuse fear or chronic fear, though it is sometimes said to be a precursor of fear. To find out what usage we may adopt, let us see how the term is used in various theories of anxiety.

Psychoanalytic theory of anxiety. Freud considered anxiety as a form of fear, both in his earlier and in his later work. The only distinction he made was between normal and neurotic anxiety. In his later work (see Ch. 7) he pointed out that normal anxiety is a reaction to external danger, stemming from the birth trauma. Neurotic fear, however, he conceived as a fear of libidinal impulses, rooted in castration fear. Hence he distinguished between acute fear, which he called "normal anxiety," and a chronic fear of internal impulses which he called "neurotic anxiety" (cf. Freud, 1926).

Freud distinguished between acute and chronic (or developmental) neurosis. The former he called "Aktualneurose" and conceived it as a transformation of dammed-up sexual energy into acute anxiety, caused by sexual frustration. Hence, in this first formulation, anxiety appeared as a form of instinctual energy. In contrast, developmental neurosis seemed to stem from the repression of powerful sexual or aggressive impulses, aroused in a traumatic situation. These impulses, he thought, continue underground and must be controlled by defense mechanisms. If the impulse pressure is increased at any time, symptoms appear, binding the energy about to erupt (e.g., in phobias, compulsions, hysterical symptoms, etc.). Only a small share of this energy will break through as "free-floating anxiety." While Freud at first thought that the repression of libidinal impulses creates anxiety, he later decided that it is the anxiety that causes the repression, and not the repression the anxiety. Apparently, anxiety first forces repression and then maintains it because instinctual drives continue to be dangerous. Since the origin of the anxiety is not recognized (is "unconscious"), it is experienced as "objectless."

It is difficult to discuss psychoanalytic formulations because they employ the language of energetics, yet also use such terms as fear and anxiety, which imply subjective experience. Thus the theory holds that instinctual energy is "dammed up," repressed, and that this repression is forced by anxiety. If we speak in terms of energetics, the dam against instinctual energy should itself be a form of such energy. If anxiety forces repression and is a form of energy, the dam should become stronger as the anxiety increases—which obviously is not the case. But if it is the ego that is forced by felt anxiety to build defenses against instinctual energy, what is the material of the dam in terms of energetics? And what is anxiety, where does it come from, whence does it derive its energy? Moreover, in a system of energetics, it is the dammed-up instinctual energy that should break through and overwhelm the ego when defenses become inadequate. Instead, it is the anxiety that breaks through and constitutes the neurosis, or, at least, its most conspicuous symptom. Libidinal energy seems to be completely submerged in this breakthrough, as shown by the absence of sexual interest, often amounting to complete impotence, during an acute anxiety attack. Even in chronic ("developmental") neuroses, anxiety is the most prominent symptom and seriously impairs sexual activity.

It is probably this fact (that neurosis expresses anxiety and not the repressed impulse) which moved Freud to come back again and again to his first explanation that anxiety is converted sexual energy. But the transformation of sexual energy into anxiety poses even more difficult problems and does not answer the question as to just what engineers the repression. Reluctantly, Freud had to abandon the hypothesis that would have lent consistency to his system of energetics. As it stands, Freud's theory combines concepts that refer to different systems of explanation: instinctual energy is opposed by anxiety, which is a subjective experience. In a system of energetics, anxiety is an orphan. It was Freud's clinical insight that forced the importance of anxiety in neurosis on him, but his mechanistic bias never allowed him to change his theory accordingly.

Anxiety as catastrophic reaction. For Goldstein (1939, 1951), anxiety is a catastrophic reaction. It is not a fear of something but the experience of a "dissolution of the world and a shattering of one's own self." For him, the basic factor in anxiety is the feeling that one is not able to react adequately, a feeling that is particularly frequent in infancy. According to Goldstein, this realization that something does not "fit" into the total situation comes before any perception of the single elements in it, "in the same way as an infant grasps facial expressions before it reacts adequately to other visual elements."

We have tried to show (Ch. 10) that the recognition of facial expressions is based on the same intuitive appraisal that comes before any kind of action. Both in fear and in anxiety the situation must be appraised as it affects the person; and this presupposes sufficient experience to know what may threaten or harm him. Now it is easier to appraise a concrete object as dangerous, once we have had some experience with harmful things, than to grasp the fact that a situation is beyond one's power or skill. We venture to think that the infant experiences neither fear nor anxiety until he can recognize things and people and estimate whether they are friendly or hostile, which does not seem to occur much before six months of age (cf. Spitz and Wolf, 1946).

Sometimes the infant's disturbance when his mother is anxious, or his wailing when left alone, is interpreted as "anxiety" (cf. Sullivan, 1948). But the mother's disturbance makes the infant uncomfortable rather than fearful; and separation from someone loved is met with sadness. When the child is old enough to realize that mother is going out and he will be left alone, he may show considerable apprehension, but that is a specific fear, not general anxiety.

Rollo May's theory of anxiety. May's theory (1950) follows Goldstein's with some interesting variations. His fundamental thesis is that "anxiety is the apprehension cued off by a threat to some value which the individual holds essential to his existence as a personality" (1950, p. 191), and that "an individual experiences various fears on the basis of a security pattern he has developed; *but in anxiety it is this security pattern itself which is threatened*" (p. 191; May's italics). For May, as for Goldstein, anxiety is objectless, threatens from all sides at once, and threatens the individual's existence or development. Anxiety is basic and fears are derived from it because anxiety is simply the formless experience of a threat while fear relates the individual to an object, and enables him to "stand outside" the threat and take steps to meet it. While we are in complete agreement with May and Goldstein (and many others) when they describe the seemingly objectless character of anxiety and its effects on the person, we cannot agree that anxiety is simply a formless *experience of a threat*. A threat cannot be sensed by any sense organ; hence fear or anxiety depends on our intuitive estimate (sense judgment) that there is a threat in what is sensed. It is easier to recognize a barking, snarling dog as dangerous than to fear the dark, until the dark can be imagined as holding dangerous things. That is why children are afraid of many concrete things before they develop a fear of darkness.

May distinguishes normal from neurotic anxiety. Normal anxiety is proportionate to the objective danger and is relieved when the threat is removed, while neurotic anxiety is enduring and disproportionate. Neurotic anxiety involves repression and conflict and leads to the development of defense mechanisms. We completely agree with May's distinction between normal and neurotic anxiety, though we do not agree that either conflict or repression is necessary for neurotic anxiety.

May further suggests that fear and anxiety have different physiological symptoms: that fear is accompanied by sympathetic excitation and anxiety by parasympathetic activity. But in that case, how could a parasympathetic response, accompanying basic anxiety, turn into sympathetic excitation when formless anxiety becomes differentiated into fear? On May's own showing, that is what would have to happen if anxiety were basic and fear derived.

The evidence he presents allows a different interpretation. He cites the case of Tom, a man with a gastric fistula, studied by Wolf and Wolff (1943). During *fear,* his *stomach lining was pale, and gastric activity ceased.* Fear occurred on one occasion when Tom had mislaid some records and saw an irate doctor searching for them, for Tom thought he would lose his job if he were found out. During another emotional upset, which Wolf and Wolff, as well as May, call anxiety, *stomach function and acidity were sharply increased, and the lining was red* and engorged. The occasion for this upset was the aftermath of the episode of the mislaid records, when Tom and his wife discussed the possibility of his losing his job. Both were so upset and concerned about the possible consequences that they talked far into the night and neither of them could sleep.

Anxiety and worry. Now there was nothing diffuse or objectless about Tom's emotion. The threat was implied in the episode of the previous morning which at the time had aroused acute fear. It is easy to conjecture that the sleepless night was spent in thinking and talking about the possibility of his being discharged, the difficulty of finding another job, the means he could use to find a suitable opening, and the like. In short, Tom and his wife worried. In common experience, worry is a state of anxious striving for something made difficult by the dangers involved in it. It is accompanied by increased mental activity rather than by the slowing-up of mental activity experienced during fear.

Psychiatrists have substituted the term *anxiety* for the commonly used term *worry* on the assumption that both are reactions to threat. They are, but there is an important difference in the appraisal of the threat. Worry concentrates not so much on "what will happen when . . ." as on "what will I *do* when. . . ." It is a striving made difficult by apprehension, while anxiety is the fearful expectation of some unknown danger which must be located before escape is possible. Psychiatric and especially psychoanalytic usage of the term *anxiety* covers both worry and objectless fear, just as aggression covers both exuberance and hostility, and depression is used for both agitated and retarded states. The better procedure is to choose different terms for states that lead to decidedly different behavior.

Since worry contains both striving and apprehension, the physiological symptoms will not be those observed in simple fear. In fact, it would seem that worry is an attempt to incite one's self to courage so that the thing feared can be attacked instead of avoided. When something harmful is appraised as a danger to be overcome, there is an emotion akin to anger. Indeed, after that bout of worry Tom's stomach had an appearance very similar to that observed during an episode of anger and resentment: it was red and engorged, with increased activity and acidity (cf. Ch. 7, in the following volume).

When the danger increases and the threat cannot be avoided or overcome, worry ceases and stark fear takes its place, ending in despair or depression. Hence fear, despair, and depression have similar effects, very different from those of worry or anger. Wolff says that there is "a pattern associated with overwhelming catastrophe, with feelings of fear, terror, horror, abject grief, depression and despair, in which practically all gastric function comes to a standstill" (1950, p. 300).

We may reasonably assume that those emotions are related that have a like physiological effect, rather than those whose effects are diametrically opposed. Hence we would expect that fear and anxiety are related. Fear is an emotional episode that may develop into an attitude of anxiety; thus anxiety would be defined as chronic and generalized fear. Both fear and anxiety seem to be related to grief, depression, and despair. On the other hand, worry as defined here would be related to anger rather than to fear, also to longing and striving.

However, to decide this question and to evaluate the physiological effects of various emotions we must examine the evidence neurological and physiological research have provided for us. We shall do so in Chapters 2 to 8, in the following volume, and shall then be able to assess emotion in its effects on the personality as a whole.

In the usage of Freud, Goldstein, and May, "normal anxiety" seems to be an episodic fear reaction, while neurotic anxiety seems to be a chronic state of either fear or worry. In addition, for Goldstein and May normal anxiety seems to be diffuse in early childhood and to become specific only gradually. For May, also, normal anxiety in the adult seems to be the reaction to an overwhelming danger, a "fear for oneself" rather than a "fear of something." Now let us see whether we can find any clear-cut differences between fear and anxiety, and between normal and neurotic anxiety.

Anxiety as fear of the unknown. The dictionary definition of *anxiety* (Oxford and Webster) is "a disturbing uneasiness regarding what is future or uncertain." Another meaning is "solicitous desire." This second meaning can be disregarded for our purposes, because it obviously is not intended by anxiety theorists, nor does such anxious concern fit into the clinical picture of anxiety. Hence we are left with the meaning of anxiety as apprehension or fear ("a disturbing uneasiness") of what is future or uncertain. It is an apprehension that something may happen—we know not what.

Such fear has no particular object or source, but it is "objectless" only in the sense that what is feared is danger in general. But it is doubtful whether the term "anxiety" is an improvement over the term "fear of the unknown." Like any specific fear, it is a reaction to a danger appraised here and now; that the danger is unknown in its exact details is irrelevant. In human life, there are always possibilities of danger: we may have an accident on the road or a heart attack; we may lose our job or be deceived by a friend. Anyone who dwells on these possibilities is bound to feel fear, but it is his imaginative preoccupation that provides the object—his anxiety is not "objectless."

Existential anxiety. Ordinarily, we do not dwell on the possibility of serious illness, accident, or death unless a contemporary event, like the threat of an H bomb explosion, brings it forcibly to our attention. When we do begin to face these threats to which every creature is exposed, we are bound to feel fear and apprehension. Kierkegaard and the modern existentialists are right when they maintain that every human being is exposed to apprehension in the thought of his helplessness against the forces of nature, particularly death. Even this fear, however, has an object. It can become real existential dread; but when that happens, death is not appraised as a definite external threat to a man's personal existence. Rather, it is the logical consequences of dying that arouse dread: if a sentient, reflective, moral being can be snuffed out like a candle or wilt and die like a flower in autumn, our human achievements, our dreams and endeavors mean no more and no less than yesterday's snow.

It is not the threat of death as a single inevitable event, it is the threat of meaninglessness, the threat of being lost in an empty unfeeling universe, that arouses a nameless fear "threatening from all sides at once," as May puts it. This is the existential anxiety Sartre and others * talk about, which has no source outside our own heart that first appraises death as final despite the witness of faith, and then recoils from the consequences of its verdict. It is not a fear inherent in existence; it is the

* Cf. Tillich, 1952; May *et al.*, 1958.

fear of a universe we have created out of our own despair. Hence existential anxiety need not and does not pervade the life of every man but, when it does so, it is a fear like any other except that its object has been created by a man's own unaided thought.

Fear of inadequacy. So far, we have seen that the anxiety felt as seemingly objectless has an object, either the possible (an external threat like the unknown future), or the meaninglessness we have espoused. There may also be a pervading fear reaction to demands we feel ourselves unable to meet. We may be afraid of excessive demands on us, but the demands are excessive only because we feel inadequate. The child is ostensibly afraid of strangers or of school; yet he has never been to school and has never been hurt by a stranger. The fear he feels comes from meeting something that goes beyond the narrow confines of his life of home and family where he feels secure. He knows that the threat does not really come from school or from strangers but is inherent in going to school and in meeting a stranger.

The same kind of pervasive fear occurs again in adolescence. The adolescent often suffers from excruciating shyness and is afraid of many social situations. He is afraid, yet cannot assign any valid reason for his fear, though he may complain that he has no small talk or does not know what is required of him socially. Both adolescent and child are afraid that they will be found wanting, and until they have proved themselves the fear is bound to remain.

On the adult level, similar diffuse anxiety will be experienced when a person meets a situation that challenges his established convictions or his self-ideal. This happened in extreme form to prisoners freed from concentration camps. While in the camp, they lived under conditions of such brutality and privation that their resistance crumbled and their conduct often became hardly human. After their release, when they were again able to take stock of their actions, they suffered intense anxiety and often complete demoralization (Bondy, 1943; Bettelheim, 1943). When that happened, there was no threat from outside. Their picture of themselves had been shattered. They were forced to come to terms with themselves and saw no possibility of escaping their self-condemnation or regaining their self-respect. Most of them had no religious convictions, nor were they threatened by public disapproval. Nobody accused them; yet they stood self-accused, expecting a punishment that ought to come—from where they did not know.

Whenever child, adolescent, or adult is forced to meet a situation that challenges his way of life or makes demands he feels himself unable to fulfill, even when that situation is of his own making, there will be a pervading fear that is akin to genuine anxiety because no definite object can be assigned to it. This fear may be rationalized in many ways but is difficult to overcome because its source cannot be isolated, at least by the person himself.

There is another generally unrecognized source of anxiety in the prevailing temper of modern life. We have come to a distrust of reason and logic perhaps unequalled in history. The theory of relativity, that symbol of modern scientific achievement, was transferred from physics, where it does apply, to the sphere of human action, where it does not, and led to a conviction of the relativity of all human values. Next the stronghold of science as a whole was invaded. Except for mathematics, we are told, science cannot come to true conclusions; it must be satisfied with consistent ones. As soon as new facts are discovered, that consistency is disturbed and a new explanation must be found. The old theory is no longer considered an incomplete explanation; it becomes a discarded guess with no truth value at all. Theories now are not disproved but superseded; the value of a theory is not that it is true, or even true in part, but that it is interesting and gives rise to further research. From being a body of knowledge or a method of investigation designed to discover objective facts and relationships, science has become a fascinating game. Modern man, trained for decades to see in the scientist the ultimate arbiter of his beliefs, is left with neither certainty nor faith. No wonder that he is confused and disoriented, now that his last hope of truth and certainty is gone.

Anxiety as an attitude. All fear is a response to estimated danger. As long as we are afraid of something concrete, the threat is localized and there is hope of escape. With escape, the fear disappears. But when we are afraid of something unknown, or when we are afraid that we cannot cope with a new demand, and cannot understand either the world around us, ourselves, or our position in the world, then the threat is general, diffuse, and we try in vain to escape it. As our preoccupation continues, an attitude of fear will develop. At this point, we can speak of "anxiety." Fear of the unknown, existential anxiety, and fear of inadequacy are fears that need some time to develop; but they may become attitudes before their influence is recognized.

An attitude of anxiety can also stem from a harrowing experience (e.g., the feelings of survivors dug out after a bomb had buried them under debris) and give rise to neurotic symptoms. Or an anxious attitude of long standing may suddenly blossom into an acute anxiety attack. Such acute attacks never come out of the blue. The occasion that triggers them off may be out of proportion to the violence of the reaction, but it has merely intensified an already existing emotional attitude to the point where the person is helpless and desperate.

Now an attitude of fear may be met by specific counter measures. A man may try to avoid fear by retreating from the situation that may trigger it off; he may develop a phobia, i.e., a specific avoidance habit. Or he may try to avoid fear by some positive preventive action (e.g., washing his hands), thus developing a compulsion. In either case, the fear remains and is barely held in check by such maneuvers because they serve to rehearse the danger in imagination. In fact, the fear is bound to grow stronger, for the danger is not overcome, nor is the fear proved groundless.

We could define normal anxiety as an *attitude of fear,* and neurotic anxiety as a *habit of avoidance.* When this becomes avoidance of a specific object or situation, we speak of *phobia;* when stereotyped patterns of defense have been developed, of *compulsion.* An *obsession* is the imaginative preoccupation with some specific danger. Neurotic anxiety develops only when a man habitually withdraws from the danger or when he is helpless to cope with it (e.g., as with the bomb blast victim); or, finally, when he copes with the danger by means that prolong his fear (so-called "defense mechanisms").

CONCLUSION

Whether anger and fear are acute or chronic, they, like other emotions, urge to action. Anger impels us to attack what is annoying; fear, to escape from something that threatens harm. The appraisal that something annoying can be overcome or that something dangerous can be escaped may be objectively true. What annoys us may be really frustrating and could be removed by immediate attack. What we fear may be a real danger from which we can escape by instant flight. In that case, anger and fear urge to appropriate action. Anger makes it easy to attack the obstacle and sudden fear facilitates escape. But if an attitude of irritability or anxiety biases a man's appraisal so that he finds annoying what others would see as a challenge, or sees dangers where others would detect opportunities, anger and fear will urge to inappropriate action. Even when reflection restrains him from giving in to his emotion, rational choice will be delayed and uncertain, and reasonable action will prove burdensome. The physiological effects of emotion contribute their share to such an interference with deliberate choice. To prevent undesirable emotional attitudes or to correct them if they have developed unchecked, it is important to know how emotion can be controlled.

In the second volume, we plan to trace the physiological effects of emotion. First, we hope to identify the structures and pathways in the brain that mediate emotional experience (Chs. 1–6); and next, to discuss the peripheral changes that stem from such central excitation (Chs. 7–8). Finally (Chs. 9–11), we will sketch the role of emotion in personality organization and explore the manner in which emotion can be controlled and used constructively.

REFERENCES

REFERENCES FOR CHAPTER 1: THE NATURE OF FEELING

Alechsieff, N. 1907. Die Grundformen der Gefühle. Psychol. Stud. 3:156–271.

Beebe-Center, J. G. 1932. The psychology of pleasantness and unpleasantness. New York, Van Nostrand.

Koch, B. 1913. Experimentelle Untersuchungen über die elementaren Gefühlsqualitäten. Heidelberg, Quelle & Meyer.

Scheerer, M. 1954. Cognitive theory. In: Gardner Lindzey, ed. Handbook of social psychology. Cambridge, Mass., Addison-Wesley.

Titchener, E. B. 1908. Lectures on the elementary psychology of feeling and attention. New York, Macmillan.

Wohlgemuth, A. 1925. The coexistence and localization of feeling. Brit. J. Psychol. 16:116–22.

Wundt, W. 1920. Grundriss der Psychologie. 2d ed. Stuttgart, W. Engelmann.

Yokoyama, M. 1921. The nature of affective judgment in the method of paired comparisons. Am. J. Psychol. 32:357–69.

REFERENCES FOR CHAPTER 2: IS FEELING AN EXPERIENCE OR A CONSTRUCT?

Beebe-Center, J. G. 1932. The psychology of pleasantness and unpleasantness. New York, Van Nostrand.

Gibson, J. J. 1951. What is a form? Psych. Rev. 58:403–12.

Hebb, D. O. 1949. Organization of behavior: a neurophysiological theory. New York, Wiley.

Lashley, K. S. 1938. The mechanism of vision. XV. Preliminary studies of the rat's capacity for detail vision. J. Gen. Psychol. 18:123–93.

Nafe, J. P. 1924. An experimental study of the affective qualities. Am. J. Psychol. 35:507–44.

Nafe, J. P. 1927. The psychology of felt experience. Am. J. Psychol. 39:367–89.

Ruckmick, C. A. 1936. The psychology of feeling and emotion. New York, McGraw-Hill.

Titchener, E. B. 1908. Lectures on the elementary psychology of feeling and attention. New York, Macmillan.

Titchener, E. B. 1915. Sensation and system. Am. J. Psychol. 26:258-67.

Titchener, E. B. 1925. Primer of psychology. Rev. ed. New York, Macmillan.

Young, P. T. 1918. The localization of feeling. Am. J. Psychol. 29:420-30.

Young, P. T. 1927. Studies in affective psychology. Am. J. Psychol. 38:157-93.

Young, P. T. 1930. Studies in affective psychology. Am. J. Psychol. 42:17-37.

REFERENCES FOR CHAPTER 3: FEELING AS MEANING, ATTITUDE, JUDGMENT, AND AS SUCCESS OR FAILURE

Beebe-Center, J. G. 1932. The psychology of pleasantness and unpleasantness. New York, Van Nostrand.

Beebe-Center, J. G. 1951. Feeling and emotion. In: H. Helson, ed. Theoretical foundations of psychology. New York, Van Nostrand.

Carr, H. A. 1925. Psychology. New York, Longmans Green.

Conklin, V., and F. L. Dimmick. 1925. An experimental study of fear. Am. J. Psychol. 36:96-101.

Corwin, C. H. 1921. The involuntary response to pleasantness. Am. J. Psychol. 32:563-70.

Flügel, J. C. 1939. Feeling and the hormic theory. Char. & Pers. 7:211-29.

Humphrey, G. 1951. There is no problem of meaning. Brit. J. Psychol. 42:238-45.

Hunt, E. B. 1932. The genetic primacy of hedonic terms. Am. J. Psychol. 44:369-70.

Hunt, W. A. 1933. The meaning of pleasantness and unpleasantness. Am. J. Psychol. 45:345-48.

Hunt, W. A. 1939. A critical review of current approaches to affectivity. Psychol. Bull. 36:807-28.

Koch, B. 1913. Experimentelle Untersuchungen über die elementaren Gefühlsqualitäten. Heidelberg, Quelle & Meyer.

McDougall, W. 1923. Outline of psychology. New York, Scribner.

McDougall, W. 1927. Pleasure, pain and conation. Brit. J. Psychol. (Gen. Sect.) 3:171-80.

McDougall, W. 1933. The energies of men. New York, Scribner.

Maslow, A. H. 1937. The influence of familiarization on preference. J. Exp. Psychol. 21:162-80.

Münsterberg, H. 1892. Die psychophysische Grundlage der Gefühle. Internat. Congr. Exp. Psychol. London, p. 132.

Peters, H. N. 1935. The judgmental theory of pleasantness and unpleasantness. Psych. Rev. 42:354–86.

Peters, H. N. 1938. Experimental studies of the judgmental theory of feeling. I. Learning of positive and negative reactions as a determinant of affective judgments. J. Exp. Psychol. 23:1–25.

Peters, H. N. 1939. Experimental studies of the judgmental theory of feeling. III. The absolute shift in affective value conditioned by learned reactions. J. Exp. Psychol. 24:73–85.

Remmers, H. H., and L. A. Thompson, Jr. 1925. A note on motor activity as conditioned by emotional states. J. Appl. Psychol. 9:417–23.

Young, P. T. 1921. Pleasantness and unpleasantness in relation to organic responses. Am. J. Psychol. 32:38–53.

Young, P. T. 1922. Movements of pursuit and avoidance as expressions of simple feeling. Am. J. Psychol. 33:511–25.

REFERENCES FOR CHAPTER 4: FEELING AS REACTION TO SENSORY EXPERIENCE

Beebe-Center, J. G. 1932. The psychology of pleasantness and unpleasantness. New York, Van Nostrand.

Bishop, G. H. 1949. Relation of pain sensory threshold to form of mechanical stimulation. J. Neurophysiol. 12:51–57.

Dodt, E. 1954. Schmerzimpulse bei Temperaturreizen. Acta physiol. Scand. 31:81–96.

Elsberg, C. A., I. Levy, and E. D. Brewer. 1935. The sense of smell. VI. The trigeminal effects of odorous substances. Bull. Neurol. Inst. N. Y. 4:270–85.

Gasson, J. A. 1954. Personality theory: a formulation of general principles. In: M. B. Arnold and J. A. Gasson, eds. The human person. New York, Ronald.

Gemelli, A. 1949. Orienting concepts in the study of affective states. Part I. J. Nerv. Ment. Dis. 110:198–214.

Gemelli, A. 1949. Orienting concepts in the study of affective states. Part II. J. Nerv. Ment. Dis. 110:299–314.

Gibson, J. J. 1950. The perception of the visual world. Boston, Houghton Mifflin.

Herrick, C. J. 1918. An introduction to neurology. 2d ed. Philadelphia, Saunders.

Koch, B. 1913. Experimentelle Untersuchugen über die elementaren Gefühlsqualitäten. Heidelberg, Quelle & Meyer.

Lehmann, A. 1914. Hauptgesetze des menschlichen Gefühlslebens. 2d ed. Leipzig, O. R. Reisland.

Phelan, G. B. 1925. Feeling experience and its modalities. London, Kegan.

Piéron, H. 1950. Sensory affectivity. In: M. L. Reymert, ed. Feelings and emotions. New York, McGraw-Hill.

Richter, C. P., L. E. Holt, and B. Barelare, Jr. 1938. Nutritional requirements for normal growth and reproduction in rats studied by the self-selection method. Am. J. Physiol. 122:734–44.

Sweet, W. H. 1948. Bulbar trigeminal tractotomy; a new operative technique and results. Presented to the Harvey Cushing Society, Aug. 19, 1948.

Thorndike, E. L., and others. 1927. Measurement of intelligence. New York, Teachers' College.

Troland, L. T. 1928. The fundamentals of human motivation. New York, Van Nostrand.

Young, P. T. 1943. Emotion in man and animal. New York, Wiley.

Young, P. T. 1948. Appetite, palatability and feeding habit: a critical review. Psych. Bull. 45:289–320.

REFERENCES FOR CHAPTER 5: PRESCIENTIFIC THEORIES OF EMOTION

Aristotle's De Anima, in the version of William of Moerbeke, and the Commentary of St. Thomas Aquinas. Trans. by K. Foster and S. Humphries. 1951. New Haven, Yale University Press.

Darwin, C. 1873. The expression of the emotions in man and animals. New York, Appleton.

Descartes, R. 1649. Les passions de l'âme. Paris, Henry Le Gras.

Dewey, J. 1894. The theory of emotion. I. Emotional attitudes. Psych. Rev. 1:553–69.

Gardiner, H. M., R. C. Metcalf, and J. G. Beebe-Center. 1937. Feeling and emotion. New York, American Book Co.

McDougall, W. 1933. The energies of men. New York, Scribner.

REFERENCES FOR CHAPTER 6: THE DAWN OF SCIENCE: FROM JAMES TO DEWEY

Angier, R. P. 1927. The conflict theory of emotion. Am. J. Psychol. 39:390–401.

Bentley, M. 1924. The field of psychology. New York, Appleton.

Blatz, W. E. 1925. The cardiac, respiratory and electrical phenomena involved in the emotion of fear. J. Exp. Psychol. 8:109–32.

Dewey, J. 1894. The theory of emotion. I. Emotional attitudes. Psych. Rev. 1:553–69.

Dewey, J. 1895. The theory of emotion. II. The significance of emotions. Psych. Rev. 2:13–32.

Howard, D. T. 1928. A functional theory of the emotions. In: M. L. Reymert, ed. Feelings and emotions. Worcester, Mass., Clark University Press.

James, W., and C. G. Lange. 1884 and 1885. The emotions. Baltimore, Williams & Wilkins, 1922.

Paulhan, F. 1930. The laws of feeling. Trans. C. K. Ogden. New York, Harcourt, Brace.

Reymert, M. L., ed. 1928. Feelings and emotions. The Wittenberg symposium. Worcester, Mass., Clark University Press.

Reymert, M. L., ed. 1950. Feelings and emotions. The Mooseheart symposium. New York, McGraw-Hill.

Senden, M. v. 1932. Raum- und Gestaltauffassung bei operierten Blindgeborenen vor und nach der Operation. Leipzig, Barth.

REFERENCES FOR CHAPTER 7: EMOTION AND INSTINCT AS SEEN BY MCDOUGALL AND FREUD

Cannon, W. B. 1915. Bodily changes in pain, hunger, fear and rage. 2d ed., 1929. New York, Appleton-Century.

Freud, S. 1933. New introductory lectures on psychoanalysis. New York, Norton.

Freud, S. 1936. The problem of anxiety. New York, Norton.

Hartmann, H., E. Kris, and R. M. Loewenstein. 1949. Notes on the theory of aggression. In: A. Freud et al. The psychoanalytic study of the child. New York, International Universities Press.

McDougall, W. 1926. An introduction to social psychology. Rev. ed. Boston, Luce.

McDougall, W. 1928. Emotion and feeling distinguished. In: M. L. Reymert, ed. Feelings and emotions. Worcester, Mass., Clark University Press.

McDougall, W. 1933. The energies of men. New York, Scribners.

REFERENCES FOR CHAPTER 8: THE MODERN SCENE

Beebe-Center, J. G. 1951. Feeling and emotion. In: H. Helson, ed. Theoretical foundations of psychology. New York, Van Nostrand.

Bull, N. 1945. Towards a clarification of the concept of emotion. Psychosom. Med. 7:210–14.

Bull, N. 1951. The attitude theory of emotion. New York, Ass. Nerv. Ment. Dis. Monogr.

Darrow, C. W. 1935. Emotion as relative functional decortication: the role of conflict. Psych. Rev. 42:566–78.

Duffy, E. 1934. Emotion: an example of the need for reorientation in psychology. Psych. Rev. 41:184–98.

Duffy, E. 1951. The concept of energy mobilization. Psych. Rev. 58:30–40.

Dumas, G. 1932. Nouveau traité de psychologie. 4 vols. Paris, Alcan.

Dumas, G. 1948. La vie affective. Paris, Presses Universitaires.

Fenichel, O. 1945. The psychoanalytic theory of neurosis. New York, Norton.

Gardiner, H. N., R. C. Metcalf, and J. G. Beebe-Center. 1937. Feeling and emotion: a history of theories. New York, American Book.

Gemelli, A. 1949. Orienting concepts in the study of affective states. Part I. J. Nerv. Ment. Dis. 110:198–214.

Gemelli, A. 1949. Orienting concepts in the study of affective states. Part II. J. Nerv. Ment. Dis. 110:299–314.

Hebb, D. O. 1946. Emotion in man and animal: an analysis of the intuitive processes of recognition. Psych. Rev. 53:88–106.

Helson, H., ed. 1951. Theoretical foundations of psychology. New York, Van Nostrand.

Hodge, F. A. 1935. The emotions in a new role. Psych. Rev. 42:555–65.

Hull, C. L. 1943. Principles of behavior. New York, Appleton-Century.

Hunt, W. A. 1941. Recent developments in the field of emotion. Psych. Bull. 38:249–76.

Jacobson, E. 1952. Problems in the psychoanalytic theory of affects. Psychoanal. Quart. 21:459–60.

Leeper, R. W. 1948. A motivational theory of emotion to replace "emotion as disorganized response." Psych. Rev. 55:5–21.

Lindsley, D. B. 1951. Emotion. In: S. S. Stevens, ed. Handbook of experimental psychology. New York, Wiley.

Lund, F. H. 1939. Emotions: their psychological, physiological and educative implications. New York, Ronald.

Meyer, M. F. 1933. That whale among the fishes—the theory of emotion. Psych. Rev. 40:242–300.

Michotte, A. E. 1950. The emotions regarded as functional connections. In: M. L. Reymert, ed. Feelings and emotions. New York, McGraw-Hill.

Rapaport, D. 1942. Emotions and memory. Baltimore, Williams & Wilkins.

Rapaport, D. 1953. On the psychoanalytic theory of affects. Int. J. Psychoanal. 34:1–22.

Reymert, M. L., ed. 1928. Feelings and emotions. The Wittenberg symposium. Worcester, Mass., Clark University Press.

Reymert, M. L., ed. 1950. Feelings and emotions. The Mooseheart symposium. New York, McGraw-Hill.

Ruckmick, C. A. 1936. Psychology of feeling and emotion. New York, McGraw-Hill.

Sartre, J.-P. 1948. The emotions: outline of a theory. Trans. by Bernard Frechtman. New York, Philosophical Library.

Skinner, B. F. 1938. The behavior of organisms. New York, Appleton-Century.

Stevens, S. S., ed. 1951. Handbook of experimental psychology. New York, Wiley.

Tolman, E. C. 1932. Purposive behavior in animals and men. New York, Century.

Watson, J. B. 1919. Psychology from the standpoint of a behaviorist. 3d ed., 1929. Philadelphia, Lippincott.

Young, P. T. 1943. Emotion in man and animal. New York, Wiley.

Young, P. T. 1949. Emotion as disorganized response—a reply to Professor Leeper. Psych. Rev. 56:184–91.

REFERENCES FOR CHAPTER 9: PHENOMENOLOGICAL ANALYSIS OF EMOTION

Adler, A. 1929. The practice and theory of individual psychology. London, Routledge & Kegan Paul.

Allport, G. W. 1937. Personality: a psychological interpretation. New York, Holt.

Allport, G. W. 1954. The nature of prejudice. Cambridge, Mass., Addison-Wesley.

Arnold, M. B. 1954. A theory of human and animal learning. In: M. B. Arnold and J. A. Gasson, eds. The human person. New York, Ronald.

Bergson, H. 1911. Creative evolution. New York, Holt.

Blake, R. R., and G. V. Ramsey, eds. 1951. Perception: an approach to personality. New York, Ronald.

Cannon, W. B. 1915. Bodily changes in pain, hunger, fear and rage. 2d ed., 1929. New York, Appleton-Century.

Cantril, H., and W. A. Hunt. 1932. Emotional effects produced by the injection of adrenalin. Am. J. Psychol. 44:300–7.

Dewey, J. 1896. The reflex arc concept in psychology. Psych. Rev. 3:358–70.

Dumas, G. 1932. Nouveau traité de psychologie. 4 vols. Paris, Alcan.

Goldstein, K. 1948. Aftereffects of brain injuries in war: their evaluation and treatment. New York, Grune & Stratton.

Grinker, R. R., and J. P. Spiegel. 1945. Men under stress. Philadelphia, Blakiston.

Hebb, D. O. 1949. The organization of behavior. New York, Wiley.

Heider, F. 1958. The psychology of interpersonal relations. New York, Wiley.

Helson, H. 1947. Adaptation-level as a frame of reference for prediction of psychophysical data. Am. J. Psychol. 60:1–29.

Lashley, K. S. 1938. The mechanism of vision. XV. Preliminary studies of the rat's capacity for detail vision. J. Gen. Psychol. 18:123–93.

Lehmann, A. 1914. Hauptgesetze des menschlichen Gefühlslebens. Leipzig, O. R. Reisland.

Lewin, K. 1935. A dynamic theory of personality. New York, McGraw-Hill.

May, R. 1950. The meaning of anxiety. New York, Ronald.

Newman, E. B., F. T. Perkins, and R. H. Wheeler. 1930. Cannon's theory of emotion: a critique. Psych. Rev. 37:305–26.

Senden, M. v. 1932. Raum- und Gestaltauffassung bei operierten Blindgeborenen vor und nach der Operation. Leipzig, Barth.

Walter, W. G. 1953. The living brain. New York, Norton.

Wertheimer, M. 1945. Productive thinking. New York, Harper.

Young, P. T. 1943. Emotion in man and animal. New York, Wiley.

REFERENCES FOR CHAPTER 10: BASIC EMOTIONS

Arnold, M. B., and J. A. Gasson, eds. 1954. The human person: an approach to an integral theory of personality. New York, Ronald.

Bender, L. 1950. Anxiety in disturbed children. In: P. H. Hoch and J. Zubin, eds. Anxiety. New York, Grune & Stratton.

Bridges, K. M. B. 1931. The social and emotional development of the preschool child. London, Routledge & Kegan Paul.

Dennis, W. 1941. Infant development under conditions of restricted practice and minimum social stimulation. Genet. Psychol. Monogr. 23:143–89.

Dumas, G. 1932. Nouveau traité de psychologie. 4 vols. Paris, Alcan.

Féléky, A. M. 1914. The expression of emotion. Psych. Rev. 21:33–41.

Freud, S. 1915. Instincts and their vicissitudes. Collected papers, Vol. IV, 1925. London, Hogarth.

Greenacre, P. 1948. Infant reactions to restraint. In: C. Kluckhohn and H. A. Murray, eds. Personality in nature, society and culture. New York, Knopf.

Halstead, W. C. 1951. Brain and intelligence. In: L. A. Jeffress, ed. Cerebral mechanisms in behavior. New York, Wiley.

Hebb, D. O. 1946. Emotion in man and animal: an analysis of the intuitive processes of recognition. Psych. Rev. 53:88–106.

Heider, F. 1958. The psychology of interpersonal relations. New York, Wiley.

Landis, C. 1924. Studies of emotional reactions. II. General behavior and facial expression. J. Comp. Psychol. 4:447–501.

Landis, C., and W. A. Hunt. 1939. The startle pattern. New York, Farrar.

Langfeld, H. S. 1918. The judgment of emotion by the facial expression. J. Abn. Psychol. 13:172–84.

Maslow, A. H. 1954. Motivation and personality. New York, Harper.

Piaget, J. 1926. The language and thought of the child. New York, Harcourt, Brace.

Scheler, M. 1923. Wesen und Formen der Sympathie. Bonn, Cohen.

Shand, A. F. 1896. Character and the emotions. Mind, New Ser. 5:203–26.

Sherman, M. 1927. The differentiation of emotional responses in infants. I. Judgments of emotional responses from motion picture views and from actual observation. II. The ability of observers to judge the emotional characteristics of the crying of infants, and of the voice of an adult. J. Comp. Psychol. 7:265–84.

Spitz, R. A. 1946. Hospitalism: a follow-up report on investigation described in volume I, 1945. Psychoanal. Stud. Child 2:113–17.

Spitz, R. A., and K. M. Wolf. 1946. The smiling response. Genet. Psychol. Monogr. 34:57–125.

Sullivan, H. S. 1953. The interpersonal theory of psychiatry. Ed. by H. S. Perry and M. L. Gawel. New York, Norton.

Watson, J. B. 1919. Psychology from the standpoint of a behaviorist. 3d ed., 1929. Philadelphia, Lippincott.

Wolff, W. 1943. The expression of personality. New York, Harper.

Young, P. T. 1943. Emotion in man and animal. New York, Wiley.

REFERENCES FOR CHAPTER 11: EMOTION AND MOTIVATION

Allport, G. W. 1937. Personality: a psychological interpretation. New York, Holt.

Allport, G. W. 1953. The trend in motivational theory. Am. J. Orthopsychiat. 23:107–19.

Arnold, M. B., and J. A. Gasson, eds. 1954. The human person: an approach to an integral theory of personality. New York, Ronald.

Bruner, J. S., and D. Krech. 1950. Perception and personality, a symposium. Durham, N.C., Duke University Press.

Frankl, V. E. 1948. Ärztliche Seelsorge. Vienna, Deuticke.

Frankl, V. E. 1953. Angst und Zwang. Acta psychotherap. 1:111–20.

Freeman, G. L. 1948. Physiological psychology. New York, Van Nostrand.

Harlow, H. F. 1953. Motivation as a factor in the acquisition of new responses. In: Current theory and research in motivation: a symposium. Lincoln, University of Nebraska Press.

Harriman, P. L., ed. 1946. Encyclopedia of psychology. New York, Philosophical Library.

Harris, G. W. 1948. Neural control of the pituitary gland. Physiol. Rev. 28:139–79.

Hebb, D. O. 1949. The organization of behavior. New York, Wiley.

Kinsey, A. C. 1948. Sexual behavior in the human male. Philadelphia, Saunders.

Korzybski, A. 1933. Science and sanity. Lancaster, Pa., Science Press.

Krech, D. 1951. Cognition and motivation in psychological theory. In: W. Dennis, ed. Current trends in psychological theory. Pittsburgh, University of Pittsburgh Press.

Leeper, R. W. 1948. A motivational theory of emotion to replace "emotion as disorganized response." Psych. Rev. 55:5–21.

Linton, R. 1955. The tree of culture. New York, Knopf.

McClelland, D. C., J. W. Atkinson, R. Clark, and E. L. Lowell. 1953. The achievement motive. New York, Appleton-Century-Crofts.

Maslow, A. H. 1954. Motivation and personality. New York, Harper.

Thomas Aquinas. In decem libros ethicorum Aristotelis ad Nichomachum expositio. A. M. Pirotta, ed. 1934. Turin, Italy, Library Marietti.

Tinbergen, N. 1951. The study of instinct. Oxford, Oxford University Press.

Young, P. T. 1943. Emotion in man and animal. New York, Wiley.

Young, P. T. 1952. The role of hedonic processes in the organization of behavior. Psych. Rev. 59:249–62.

REFERENCES FOR CHAPTER 12: BASIC EMOTIONS IN PSYCHOLOGICAL THEORY

Allport, G. W. 1954. The nature of prejudice. Cambridge, Mass., Addison-Wesley.

Appel, M. H. 1942. Aggressive behavior of nursery school children and adult procedures in dealing with such children. J. Exp. Educ. 2:185–99.

Arnold, M. B., and J. A. Gasson, eds. 1954. The human person: an approach to an integral theory of personality. New York, Ronald.

Bergler, E. 1949. The basic neurosis. New York, Grune & Stratton.

Bettelheim, B. 1943. Individual and mass behavior in extreme situations. J. Abn. Soc. Psychol. 38:417–52.

Boggs, S. T. 1947. A comparative cultural study of aggression. Unpubl. Ph.D. thesis. Cambridge, Harvard University, Social Relations Library.

Bondy, C. 1943. Problems of internment camps. J. Abn. Soc. Psychol. 38:453–75.

Dollard, J., L. W. Doob, R. R. Sears, N. E. Miller, and O. H. Mowrer. 1939. Frustration and aggression. New Haven, Yale University Press.

Frenkel-Brunswik, E. 1951. Personality theory and perception. In: R. R. Blake and G. V. Ramsey, eds. Perception: an approach to personality. New York, Ronald.

Freud, S. 1926. The problem of anxiety. Trans. by H. A. Bunker. 1936. New York, Norton.

Freud, S. 1940. An outline of psychoanalysis. Trans. by J. Strachey. 1949. New York, Norton.

Goldstein, K. 1939. The organism. New York, American Book Co.

Goldstein, K. 1951. On emotions: considerations from the organismic point of view. J. Psychol. 31:37–49.

Guitton, J. 1951. Essay on human love. Trans. by M. Chaning-Pearce. London, Rockliff.

Jones, M. C. 1926. The development of early behavior patterns in young children. Ped. Sem. and J. Genet. Psychol. 33:537–85.

Maier, N. R. F. 1949. Frustration—the study of behavior without a goal. New York, McGraw-Hill.

Marquart, D. I. 1948. The pattern of punishment and its relation to abnormal fixation in adult human subjects. J. Gen. Psychol. 39:107–44.

Marquart, D. I., and P. L. Arnold. 1952. A study in the frustration of human adults. J. Gen. Psychol. 47:43–63.

Maslow, A. H. 1954. Motivation and personality. New York, Harper.

May, R. 1950. The meaning of anxiety. New York, Ronald.

May, R. E., E. Angel, and H. F. Ellenberger, eds. 1958. Existence: a new dimension in psychiatry and psychology. New York, Basic Books.

Miller, N. E. 1948. Theory and experiment relating psychoanalytic displacement to stimulus-response generalization. J. Abn. Soc. Psychol. 43:155–78.

Miller, N. E., R. R. Sears, O. H. Mowrer, L. W. Doob, and J. Dollard. 1941. The frustration-aggression hypothesis. Psych. Rev. 48:337–42.

Montagu, M. F. A. 1950. The origin and nature of social life and the biological basis of cooperation. In: P. A. Sorokin, ed. Exploration in altruistic love and behavior. Boston, Beacon Press.

Morlan, G. K. 1949. A note on the frustration-aggression theories of Dollard and his associates. Psych. Rev. 56:1–8.

Pastore, N. 1950. A neglected factor in the frustration-aggression hypothesis: a comment. J. Psychol. 29:271–79.

Reymert, M. L., ed. 1950. Feeling and emotion. The Mooseheart symposium. New York, McGraw-Hill.

Sargent, S. S. 1948. Reaction to frustration—a critique and a hypothesis. Psych. Rev. 55:108–14.

Sears, R. R. 1941. Non-aggressive reactions to frustration. Psych. Rev. 48:343–45.

Sorokin, P. A., ed. 1950. Explorations in altruistic love and behavior. Boston, Beacon Press.

Spitz, R. A., and K. M. Wolf. 1946. The smiling response. Genet. Psychol. Monogr. 34:57–125.

Stagner, R. 1944. Studies of aggressive social attitudes. I. Measurement and interrelation of selected attitudes. J. Soc. Psychol. 20:109–20.

Stagner, R. 1944. Studies of aggressive social attitudes. II. Changes from peace to war. J. Soc. Psychol. 20:121–28.

Stagner, R. 1944. Studies of aggressive social attitudes. III. The role of personal and family scores. J. Soc. Pyschol. 20:129–40.

Sullivan, H. S. 1948. The meaning of anxiety in psychiatry and life. Psychiatry 11:1–13.

Suttie, I. D. 1952. The origins of love and hate. New York, Julian Press.

Tillich, P. 1952. Anxiety, religion and medicine. Pastoral Psychol. 3:11–17.

Wolf, S., and H. G. Wolff. 1943. Human gastric function. New York, Oxford University Press.

Wolff, H. G. 1950. Life situations, emotions and bodily disease. In: M. L. Reymert, ed. Feelings and emotions. New York, McGraw-Hill.

INDEX

Abreaction, 258

Ache, 40-41

Action: anger, fear and, 275-76; Bull's theory of, 151; change or continuation by emotions of, 195-96; development of, 241; Dewey's system and, 116-17, 118-23, 124; emotion and, 177; emotional expression and, 211-12; emotional organization and, 155-57; functional autonomy of motives and, 222-23; homeostasis and, 221-22; impetus for, 253-54; inherent tendencies to, 241; initiation by motives of, 223-32; McDougall on emotion and, 127; motivational systems and, 247-48; needs and, 220-21; physiological appetites and, 242-43; physiological state and, 227-28; relation to appraisal of, 232-35; relation to emotion of, 177-82; sentiments and, 200; stimulus-response theories and, 218-19; *see also* Instinctive action

Action tendencies, at birth, 241; development of, 242-44

Active emotional states, Dumas' distinguishing of, 148

Activity: forces motivating, 217-23; in sleep and waking, 223; instincts and ordering of, 246; pleasure as result of, 237-39

Adolescence: love in, 215; sexual urge in, 243-44

Affect, 9; Bull's theory of, 151; psychoanalytic emotion theories and, 144-46

Affect charge, 136-37; Rapaport's theories about, 145-46

Affection, Wundt and Titchener on nature of, 22-24

Affectivity, Nafe's approach to psychology of, 36-43

Aggression: anger and, 250-66; contending emotion and, 253-54; displacement of, 259-63; Freudian theory and, 134-36, 139-41, 250-53; frustration and, 255-58; theories of, 250-66

"Aktualneurose," 267

Alechsieff, N., 24

Allport, G. W., 222-23, 237, 254, 256, 260-61

Anesthesia: sense experience in, 77; sensory feelings and, 109

Anger, 178, 249; aggression and, 250-66; Aristotle on, 94; bodily changes in, 178; Darwin on, 101-2; Freud on, 141; frustration and, 256-58

Angier, R. P., 124

Animals: appraisal in, 130, 234-35; constancy of perception of, 183n; emotion and instinct in, 244; emotional attitudes and habits in, 192; instinct in, 230-31; instinctive behavior in, 225; memory and imagination in, 234; motivation in, 234-35; recognition of emotion in, 208-9

Annual Review of Psychology, 10

Antithesis: Darwin's principle of, 103; Dewey and principle of, 114

Anxiety, 10; attitude of, 274-75; existentialism and, 272-73; fear of inadequacy in, 273-74; fear of the unknown in, 271-72; inability to react as factor in, 268-69; Freud on, 137-39, 141, 266-68,